READING MUSICAL INTERPRETATION

This book is dedicated to the memory of my father, a sensitive, deep-thinking man and a steadfast Bahá'í

Reading Musical Interpretation

Case Studies in Solo Piano Performance

JULIAN HELLABY
Coventry University, UK

ASHGATE

© Julian Hellaby 2009

All rights reserved. No part of this publication may be reproduced, stored in a retrieval system or transmitted in any form or by any means, electronic, mechanical, photocopying, recording or otherwise without the prior permission of the publisher.

Julian Hellaby has asserted his right under the Copyright, Designs and Patents Act, 1988, to be identified as the author of this work.

Published by
Ashgate Publishing Limited
Wey Court East
Union Road
Farnham
Surrey, GU9 7PT
England

Ashgate Publishing Company
Suite 420
101 Cherry Street
Burlington
VT 05401-4405
USA

www.ashgate.com

British Library Cataloguing in Publication Data
Hellaby, Julian
  Reading musical interpretation: case studies in solo piano performance
  1. Piano music – Interpretation (Phrasing, dynamics, etc.) – Case studies
  2. Music – Interpretation (Phrasing, dynamics, etc.)
  I. Title
  786.2'143

Library of Congress Cataloging-in-Publication Data
Hellaby, Julian, 1956–
  Reading musical interpretation: case studies in solo piano performance / Julian Hellaby.
     p. cm.
  Includes bibliographical references.
  ISBN 978-0-7546-6667-7 (hardcover : alk. paper)
  1. Piano music – Interpretation (Phrasing, dynamics, etc.) I. Title.

ML700.H44 2008
786.2'146–dc22

2008045781

ISBN 978-0-7546-6667-7

Bach musicological font developed by © Yo Tomita.

Printed and bound in Great Britain by
MPG Books Group, UK

Contents

List of Figures	*vii*
List of Tables	*ix*
List of Music Examples	*xi*
Preface	*xiii*

PART I   CONSTRUCTING A FRAMEWORK FOR LISTENING

1	Writing, Performing and Listening	3
2	Constructing a Framework	21

PART II   CASE STUDIES: APPLYING THE FRAMEWORK

3	Bach: Toccata in D major BWV 912	63
4	Messiaen: 'Première communion de la Vierge'	89
5	Brahms: *Variations and Fugue on a Theme by Handel* Op. 24	117
6	Conclusion	159

Appendix 1	*169*
Appendix 2	*171*
Bibliography	*173*
Discography	*187*
Index	*189*

List of Figures

2.1	Graphic depiction of (a) a literal or *Texttreue* performance and (b) a highly personalized performance	27
2.2	The interpretative tower	47
2.3	Pianist X's hypothetical performance of the third movement of a nineteenth-century piano sonata mapped onto the interpretative tower	49
2.4	Beethoven: Sonata in E major Op. 109, first movement; interpretation by Denis Matthews, indicating interpretative links to levels one and two in the interpretative tower	50
2.5	Mozart: Sonata in A major K 331, first movement; interpretation by Glenn Gould, indicating interpretative links to levels one and two in the interpretative tower	51
3.1	Bach: Toccata in D major BWV 912, bars 111–126 (instrumental recitative); interpretations by (a) Gould and (b) Richter mapped on to the interpretative tower	78
3.2	Bach: Toccata in D major BWV 912, bars 177–277 (gigue-fugue); Hewitt's interpretation mapped on to the interpretative tower	86
4.1	Messiaen: 'Première communion de la Vierge'; interpretations by (a) Loriod and (b) Hellaby, mapped on to the interpretative tower	115
5.1	Brahms: *Variations and Fugue on a Theme by Handel* Op. 24, Variation 5; interpretation by (a) Arrau (b) Kovacevich and (c) Hellaby, mapped on to the interpretative tower	131
5.2	Brahms: *Variations and Fugue on a Theme by Handel* Op. 24, Variation 7; 'general' interpretation mapped on to the interpretative tower	136
5.3	Brahms: *Variations and Fugue on a Theme by Handel* Op. 24, Variation 19; interpretations by (a) Osorio and (b) Hellaby, mapped on to the interpretative tower	143
5.4	Brahms: *Variations and Fugue on a Theme by Handel* Op. 24, Variation 20; interpretations by (a) Arrau and (b) Hellaby, mapped on to the interpretative tower	149
5.5	Brahms: *Variations and Fugue on a Theme by Handel* Op. 24, Variation 23; interpretations by (a) Petri and (b) Hellaby, mapped on to the interpretative tower	155

List of Tables

3.1 Notational differences between Bärenreiter (1999), Henle (1962), Kalmus (*c*. 1948), Könemann (1998), Peters (1956) and Wiener Urtext (2000) editions of Bach's Toccata in D major BWV 912, bar 111 to the end   66

4.1 Messiaen's metronome markings in 'Première communion de la Vierge' and average tempos adopted by Aimard, Hellaby, Hill and Loriod   103

4.2 Messiaen: 'Première communion de la Vierge'; observance of marked right-hand accents between bars 37 and 51 by Aimard, Hellaby, Hill and Loriod (accent number given at the top)   110

5.1 Brahms: *Variations and Fugue on a Theme by Handel*; Rink's condensation of expression and tonality in variations 1–25 (Rink 1999a: 87). By kind permission of Cambridge University Press   118

5.2 Brahms: *Variations and Fugue on a Theme by Handel* Op. 24; tempos adopted by Hellaby, Kovacevich and Petri in Variations 22 and 23   152

List of Music Examples

3.1	Bach: Toccata in D major BWV 912, bars 111–126, as interpreted by Gould	74
3.2	Bach: Toccata in D major BWV 912, bars 127–130; Richter's and Hewitt's articulation	80
3.3	Bach: Toccata in D major BWV 912, bars 253–256; Gould's articulation	81
3.4	Bach: Toccata in D major BWV 912, bars 131–134; (a) Richter's and (b) Hewitt's articulations of the counter-subject	81
3.5	Bach: Toccata in D major BWV 912, bars 151–155; Richter's articulation	82
3.6	Bach: Toccata in D major BWV 912, bars 164–165; Hewitt's articulation	82
3.7	Bach: Toccata in D major BWV 912, bars 164–167; Hewitt's articulation	82
4.1	Messiaen: 'Regard de l'Esprit de joie', bars 60–61; *dhenkî* rhythm	98
4.2	Messiaen: 'Première communion de la Vierge', bars 21–23	98
4.3	Messiaen: 'Première communion de la Vierge', bars 21–23; Hill's pedalling	99
4.4	Messiaen: 'Première communion de la Vierge', bars 21–23; Aimard's pedalling	99
4.5	Messiaen: 'Première communion de la Vierge' Bars 21–23; Loriod's placement	99
4.6	Messiaen: 'Première communion de la Vierge', bars 47–51	101
4.7	Messiaen: 'Première communion de la Vierge', bars 34–35	104
4.8	Messiaen: 'Première communion de la Vierge', bars 39–43	107
4.9	Messiaen: 'Première communion de la Vierge', bars 1–4	109
5.1	Brahms: *Variations and Fugue on a Theme by Handel* Op. 24, Variation 5, bars 1–2	125
5.2	Brahms: *Variations and Fugue on a Theme by Handel* Op. 24, Variation 7, bar 1, as played by Hellaby	135
5.3	Brahms: *Variations and Fugue on a Theme by Handel* Op. 24, Variation 19, bars 1 and 5	137
5.4	(a) Mozart: Sonata in A major K 331, Andante grazioso, bars 1–2 (transposed) and (b) Brahms: *Variations and Fugue on a Theme by Handel* Op. 24, Variation 19, bar 1	139

5.5	Brahms: *Variations and Fugue on a Theme by Handel* Op. 24, Variation 20, bars 1–8	144
5.6	Brahms: *Variations and Fugue on a Theme by Handel* Op. 24, Variation 20, bars 8^4–12^4, as phrased by Arrau	147
5.7	Brahms: *Variations and Fugue on a Theme by Handel* Op. 24, Variation 23, bars 1 and 5	151

Preface

Performance studies as an academic discipline is a continually developing field of research and one which as Nicholas Cook warns is 'vulnerable to the claim that the voices of performers have not really been heard, that theorists have as it were taken it upon themselves to speak for performers in a kind of ventriloquism' (Cook 2005: 6–7). Tension between theory and practice seems to have a long history: as far back as the late fourteenth century, Geoffrey Chaucer's Wife of Bath asserts that 'Experience, though noon auctoritee Were in this world, is right ynogh for me' (Chaucer (1965 [1387–1400]): 35) and unless more active performers become involved in the theoretical debates surrounding their practice, it is hard to envisage an easy resolution to the dichotomy.

Whilst not suggesting that this book provides any such resolution, I believe that an inside knowledge of performance informs what I have written. I am entering the academic field relatively late in my career, the earlier part of which was spent as an active performer, albeit in a mostly modest and unspectacular capacity. In the event my book has turned out to be as much about listening to performance as about performance itself, but the former was heavily dependent on my experience of the latter as well as on my many years of teaching, concert-going and CD gathering. I hope therefore that the voice of the performer can be detected in the pages of this book, especially as I have where possible drawn upon ideas from eminent performers both past and present and developed these alongside theories and ideas from the academic community. As with all research, it is in a spirit of ongoing discovery that I offer my thoughts.

The core idea underpinning the analytical theory that I am presenting in this publication came to me several years ago when I was out on an evening stroll. Although I believed then that the idea had potential for growth, I had no idea how long and difficult the passage from conception to completion was going to be. At every turn a new obstacle seemed to present itself and I doubt if I would have seen the project through to completion if it had not been for the help of many people.

In particular I would like to thank: Heidi Bishop and staff at Ashgate Publishing for their confidence in this project and their help and support; Peter Johnson, for his expert advice and guidance; Helen Coll and Ron Woodley, for their suggestions and meticulous proof-reading; Gill Evans, Coventry University music librarian, for procuring every book I asked for and for helping with inter-library loans and RILM searches; Madeline Hellaby, for her proof-reading; Coventry and Thames Valley Universities, for their financial assistance; Kevin Bazzana, Angela Hewitt and Peter Hill for their responses to my questions; Hazel Stalker, for her substantial help with the musical examples; Paul and Barbara

McGowan, for their translations; Mike Whitcroft, for his skills as recording engineer; staff at the British Library, for their unfailing co-operation; Linda Merrick and Sarah Whatley, for their invaluable moral support.

Julian Hellaby 2009

PART I
Constructing a Framework
For Listening

Chapter 1
Writing, Performing and Listening

Preamble

Although for Rida Johnson Young (1910) the 'sweet mystery of life' proved remarkably easy to solve ('''tis love, and love alone'), a solution to the perhaps rather lesser mystery of musical performance has proved harder to discover. Like all enduring and tantalizing mysteries, no single solution is ever likely to be identified but there have nonetheless in recent years been many attempts to demystify the art and act of performance. Its many and diverse elements have attracted a growing body of literature, particularly since music theory drew performance and perception into its discourse (Samson 1999: 53) in the latter years of the twentieth century.

Performance literature has approached its subject from many different angles. Some authors have written on performance from the perspective of work analyst, some from the perspective of musical authenticist or archaeologist, some from the perspective of empirical psychologist, some from an anatomical or spatial perspective, whilst others have taken a philosophical approach – and the list goes on. Many useful discoveries have been made in the field of performance studies especially with, in more recent years, the aid of 'artificial intelligence', but the individual perspectives adopted by the various writers have rarely overlapped to any great extent. Discrete islands of research have thus emerged between which only a few tentative connections have been made – by for example John Rink (2004) – in an attempt to achieve a more holistic approach.

Further to the diversity of perspectives listed above is the question of whether an author's research appears to be theorizing about performance or whether it is based on listening and responding to what a performer actually does. The subject of listening to musical performance in the Western art music tradition adds another layer of complexity to the area, and literature on this subject, though growing, is not yet particularly extensive. My book aims in some measure to redress this imbalance and, by proposing an analytical tool applicable to such performance, seeks to establish a means by which an appropriately informed listener may gain insights into the acoustic phenomenon of performance and, more particularly, interpretation.

The central concern of this book is the development of an analytical framework which enables a suitably informed listener to hear and analyse a performance of a particular work in terms of a number of identifiable constituent elements. These elements and the framework itself are explored in Chapter 2, but in this chapter I will discuss some established ideas about Western art music performance in order to determine the extent to which existing performance literature can account for how a performance may be heard. The discussion will identify ideas which point towards my analytical approach, but will also expose some theoretical gaps which the analytical framework developed in Chapter 2 aims to fill.

The areas under discussion, coming as they do from within the broad field of performance studies, inevitably interrelate and overlap, but, for the sake of convenience, I will group them into two main sections. The first section ('The Performance and the Work') deals chiefly with how the relationship between performance and musical work has been perceived, whilst the second section ('The Performer at Work') mainly explores the act of performance itself. Thus the chapter moves from examining writings which tend to focus on performance to those which tend to focus on the performer, with the relationship of these writings to the listening experience being of particular concern. A third section ('The Performance, the Performer and the Work') opens by reviewing a more recent idea which draws the two above perspectives into a conceptual whole. By proposing a particular relationship between performance, performer and work, the idea shares some common ground with the concepts underpinning the analytical framework presented in Chapter 2.

As stated, the framework is designed as a means by which a listener may achieve insights into particular performances of particular works of Western art music, and the question of how far existing literature takes the reader towards such insights is the focus of the following evaluation. Much of the cited literature does not directly address performance as a listening experience but has implications for the experience nonetheless, and it is these implications that will be my primary concern and from which I can draw some conclusions. The conclusions will provide the starting point for my own theoretical scheme and for the remainder of the book.

The Performance and the Work

Werktreue

Amongst scholars of music, claims Christopher Small, 'there is one matter on which there is virtually unanimous agreement ... that the essence of music and of whatever meanings it contains is to be found in those things called musical works – works, that is, of Western classical music' (Small 1998: 4). By 1998, Small's claim was already questionable, but it does reflect the overwhelming focus of twentieth-century musicological thought and forms a useful starting point for my discussion: can *Werktreue* performance – faithfulness to the musical work as originally conceived – offer any insights into the interaction between work, performance and listening?

Lydia Goehr has shown how what she regards as an essentially nineteenth-century notion of *Werktreue* accorded supremacy to the musical work concept.

This meant that '[p]erformances and their performers were respectively subservient to works and their composers' so that '[a] performance met the Werktreue ideal ... when it achieved complete transparency ... transparency allowed the work to shine through and be heard in and for itself' (Goehr 1992: 231–2). One of the consequences of such thinking is that if the *Werktreue* ideal is to be met then 'the public must first be assured of the merit of the [performer] who presents the work to it and of the conformity of that presentation to the composer's will' (Stravinsky 1998 [1942]: 132–3). Another consequence of which listeners should presumably also be aware is that:

> Once a performance does take place, one must realise that thereby, new elements are added to a complete work of art: the nature of the instrument ... properties of the hall ... the audience, the mood of the performer, technique, et cetera. Now if the composition is to be inviolate, kept as it was prior to the performance, it must not be compromised by these elements (which are all entirely foreign to it). (Schenker 2000 [1911–35]: 3)

These two consequences generate problems for the listener. Firstly, there is no reliable way of knowing that a performance conforms to a long-dead composer's wishes and, secondly, the elements which Schenker identifies as additional to the complete work of art are essential to performance and are perforce part of the listening experience. Furthermore, due to the non-material nature of a musical work, it is very difficult to define in any precise way what a musical work actually is, thus raising questions as to how a performance can be 'true' to something that lacks a clear substance or definition and how listeners can be sure that what they are hearing is in fact the unadorned work.

It is the rather ill-defined nature of *Werktreue* performance that underpins Alfred Brendel's remark that '*Werktreue* is at best marginal and suggestive; *Texttreue*, by comparison, is rather more concrete' (Brendel 1976: 26). The work as notated in a score provides one possible answer to the questions raised above in that the critical listener can follow a performance by following the score, and work-fidelity in performance has sometimes been thought of as synonymous with fidelity to the score. If all performances followed Sviatoslav Richter's belief that 'you've got how it has to be in front of you and you play exactly what's written' (Monsaingeon 2001 [1998]: 142), then it might be thought that the listener would have all the information needed for a full understanding of the performance of a particular work. However, this simplistic solution omits any reference to what Richard Taruskin calls the 'spiritual or metaphysical dimension' of the work-concept, leaving 'work-fidelity ... coextensive with text-fidelity' (Taruskin 1995: 12).

To the listener, rigid concepts of *Werktreue* or more particularly *Texttreue* are especially unhelpful because, although a score is an essential link with a work, the same piece may regularly be heard in different performances with varied phrasings, articulations, dynamics and tempos – perhaps reflecting the 'spiritual or metaphysical dimension' of which Taruskin writes – all of which seem to be more dependent on the performance than on the work, even as represented by the score. Maybe a more concrete and less philosophical notion of both work and text gained from score-based analysis is helpful for the listener in that an analytically informed performance does at least have some theoretical support, should a claim to work-fidelity be advanced.

The Analytical Approach

The question of how formal analysis may influence performance has been addressed by, amongst others, Erwin Stein (1962), Edward Cone (1968) Eugene Narmour (1988) and Wallace Berry (1989). As has been pointed out by Cook (1999a), the authors' arguments rely on the primacy of the theorist and the tool of theoretical analysis to direct the performance. Such a reliance is evident in Narmour's assertion that '[i]t is obvious that if formal relations are not properly analysed by the performer, as well as carefully delineated in the performance itself, then many negative consequences follow' (Narmour 1988: 319); and similarly from Berry: 'The awareness of deep structures can guide a performer's conduct through a piece, affording a rational perspective' (Berry 1989: 65).

For the listener – the analytically informed listener at least – the results of this 'one-way' system can be constricting because, if the listener's and the performer's analytical insights are at variance, the former may dismiss the performance as a misrepresentation of the work and therefore as 'wrong'. Just such a situation occurs in Narmour's evaluation of Julius Katchen's performance of the Brahms Intermezzo Op. 118/1. Because Narmour does not hear Katchen's performance of the opening bars as reflecting the author's motivic analysis of the passage, the performance 'lacks analytical insight and therefore perceptual consistency' (Narmour 1988: 319), which 'ramifies negatively throughout' (321).

Dogmatic viewpoints such as Narmour's have been questioned by, amongst others, John Rink who is 'dubious about the musical viability of 'one-to-one mappings' between rigorous analytical methodologies and performance' (Rink 2004: 40)[1] and as a result has developed a broader, more flexible approach which also eschews dogmatism. Drawing on various sonic and temporal parameters, Rink has produced post- and pre-performance graphic analyses of music by Brahms (1995, 1999a), Liszt (1999b) and Chopin (2002), which represent a serious attempt at synthesizing performance issues with work analysis, suggesting that it is helpful for a performer to appreciate the acoustic structure of a piece and the function of tension and release within this, rather than in purely theoretical terms. Although Rink's graphs may not capture 'the whole aesthetic (emotional/physical/

---

[1] Rink's 1990 review of Berry's book claims that 'analytical expertise should certainly be brought to bear on one's performance if this facilitates one's understanding of a piece, but … it is by no means the only way in which to penetrate the work; sometimes "informed intuition" is sufficient' (Rink 1990: 328). Later the author described the review as 'a personal manifesto and an agenda for future research' (Rink 2004: 40).

intellectual) complex that music ... can evoke' (Pierce 2007: 82), they can suggest some helpful insights to the potential performer when preparing the relevant work. They are however rather less helpful for the listener in that the insights will probably be inapplicable to performances in which Rink's perspective is not reflected, and may lead the listener to hear such acoustic structures[2] as alternative, even 'wrong', rather than on their own terms.

Nevertheless, whilst not necessarily agreeing with structural emphases projected by a performer (either intuitively or by design), the analytically aware listener can hear a link between performance and work, and identify at least some reasons why the performance sounds the way that it does. Such identification, however, provides limited insights into the complexities involved in the performance of a work and is still based on the *Werktreue* principle, suggesting that work analysis can, at best, only partially account for variant individual artistic choices such as are heard in different performances of the same work. So if *Werktreue/Texttreue* accounts of performance are inadequate, is it possible to remove the work concept altogether and does this take the listener any closer to an understanding of Western art performance?

The Performance-as-work

Perhaps due to the philosophical and practical problems surrounding the *Werktreue* principle, more recently its polar opposite has received some attention. The question as to whether the performer delivers a performance 'of' anything at all has been raised, implying that a musical work *only* exists in performance. Robert Martin suggests that '[p]erformances of musical works, rather than scores, are at the heart of the listener's world ... musical works, in the listener's world, simply do not exist ... musical works are fictions that allow us to speak more conveniently about performances' (Martin 1993: 121–3).[3] Christopher Small writes similarly: 'If a musical work exists in the relationships between the sounds as performers make them and as hearers hear them ... then it exists only in performance' (Small 1998: 113). A more radical account offered by 'contemporary performance theory' is cited by Nicholas Cook, who summarizes its conclusions thus: 'there is no

---

[2]   According to Jerrold Levinson (1997), in developing an acoustic structure, a performer can only operate through time on a moment-by-moment basis. The interpreter's 'moulding' of a musical phrase or passage is likely to be determined by a series of aurally perceived, interrelated 'sound bites', which build up the unfolding soundscape through a process that Levinson terms 'concatenationism'. Levinson concedes that large-scale form is a valid concern for performers and, if they have a good structural grasp of the music, this 'may produce a performance whose specific soundings enable listeners to synthesise the musical stream in a concatenationist manner more effectively' (Levinson 1997: 172).

[3]   In a footnote, Martin accepts that 'musical works in the world of the listener are types of which performances are tokens' (Martin 1993: 123).

ontological distinction between the different modes of a work's existence, its different instantiations, because there is no original' (Cook 2001: 7).

Whilst these ideas clearly have validity in the world of *extempore* music, notably jazz, or, perhaps, in some collective music which is preserved through oral (and aural) tradition, it is harder to reconcile such ideas to the performance of Western art music, where 'masterpieces' are traditionally prized. Since the notion that performance is heard as being 'of' a work is central to the analytical framework developed in Chapter 2, it is worth digressing slightly from my focus on listening to investigate the matter a little further.

If we are to dispense with the idea of an 'original', that a performance is not 'of' something, the teasing question arises as to what *is* being performed. Maybe the thinking outlined above is putting the ontological cart before the empirical horse, or as Aaron Ridley has it: 'putting misleading or redundant things first, not first things' (Ridley 2004: 115). In fact he seems keen to dispense with ontological thinking altogether:

> I have argued ... that performances can show us things about works; and that requires nothing more than the thought that (some) performances are interpretations *of* works – not, I surmise, a proposition ... that involves or presupposes (or should prompt) the slightest flicker of ontological reflection. (Ridley 2004: 125)

Christopher Small, despite his assertion that works only exist through performance, admits that the notation of musical ideas operates as a 'medium through which the act of composition takes place ... in silence, solitude and imagined time in the composer's study. The composition is complete before a sound is actually heard' (Small 1998: 114). Goehr dismisses the thought that the act of composition might in any sense be identified with the work, claiming that 'it has been regarded as a most unsatisfactory manoeuvre' (Goehr 1992: 19). Personally, I find it less easy to disregard; after all, a 'work' is surely the product of work.

The life of a work may start conceptually in the composer's musical imagination, thence to be transferred as closely as means permit onto an informative musical score, thus allowing it another existence through performance. Roger Scruton equates the conceptual form of being with the 'sound pattern intended by the composer' which 'defines the salient features of the musical work, and can be written down in the form of a score' (Scruton 1999 [1997]: 109), but Ludwig Wittgenstein deftly connects conception and score by suggesting that there is a 'law of projection' which 'projects the symphony into the language of musical notation' (Wittgenstein 2004 [1921]: 24).

Two potential problems suggest themselves in connection with the projection of work to score. The first concerns the notational tool itself, which is by no means free of lacunae. As Godlovitch asserts: 'notated works massively underdetermine whatever emerges in performance' (Godlovitch 1998: 82). Maybe this overstates the case, but it is true that however sophisticated the notational graphic system has become, and however much its intention is enhanced by performance indications, it will always leave open areas:

> no matter how scrupulously a piece of music may be notated, no matter how carefully it may be insured against every possible ambiguity through the indications of *tempo*, shading, phrasing, accentuation, and so on, it always contains hidden elements that defy definition, because verbal dialectic is powerless to define musical dialectic in its totality. (Stravinsky 1998 [1942]: 123)

The second potential problem with the idea of work-to-score projection is that musical texts themselves may sometimes be subject to changes by the composer himself, or to mistakes and additions by copyists, or to printing anomalies by early publishers. Cook uses Beethoven's Ninth Symphony as an illustration:

> There is no such thing as Beethoven's text, except as an interpretive construct; there is an autograph score, there are a few autograph parts and a larger number of non-autograph ones, and a variety of copyists' scores, but all of them contradict one another to a greater or lesser degree. And to see this as the kind of transient difficulty that can be put right by a proper critical edition is to miss the point: Herrnstein Smith would say that the *Urtext* editions of Beethoven's symphonies that are at last beginning to appear do not replace the earlier texts but just add new ones. (Cook 2001: 8)

There may, admittedly, be no such thing as a single text, but differences between the autograph score, autograph parts and early editions[4] have proven to be insufficient to obscure a common point of reference when discussing 'Beethoven's Ninth' or to undermine recognizability in performance. Cook also cites Chopin and Liszt as composers whose works 'often exist in a number of versions', pointing out that there are no 'clear criteria according to which it might be asserted that one version is definitive while others are not' (Cook 1999b: 25). The types of question that Cook raises are, as he implies, perhaps more properly concerned with editorship than work identity, although the two are necessarily interrelated. However, for the performer – and the listener – minor variants between scores merely offer fractionally more latitude than that permitted by a definitive source.

Notation may be an imperfect tool and its arrangement into a 'text' may sometimes leave loose ends but, in a Western art music setting, the score

---

[4]   These seem 'lesser' rather than 'greater' differences and it is hard to imagine what the references of the latter might be. Differences between the autograph manuscript and most printed editions in, for example, bars 301–304 and bar 312 of the Ninth Symphony's first movement can hardly be thought to constitute 'greater' contradictions within the work's overall conception. Even performances which reflect confusion over Beethoven's metronome markings still perceptibly relate to the same work.

10   *Reading Musical Interpretation*

nevertheless remains the performer's and often the critical listener's chief source of information with regard to any particular work. The 'work-as-score' is the point of primal contact for all those who wish to know a composition, the notation providing detailed support mechanisms both for performance and informed reception of performance. Despite its imprecisions, notation represents time, pitch and the basic sound 'matter' which the prospective executant can mould into an interpretation; as Brendel has it, notation indicates a 'foundation' upon which the performer's 'edifice' may be built (Brendel 1976: 28). Therefore we do give performances 'of' a work as represented through a score (the work-as-score), and the fact that the listener will know the work through its performance does not alter this because without a performance 'of' a score, the listener would not know the work at all. This is both firmly and amusingly illustrated by Ridley:

> When was the last time you came away from a performance of a piece of music – live or recorded – seriously wondering whether the performance had been of *it*? My guess is, never. Even if you were to hear the Bach-Busoni *Chaconne* as played by me, or by some comparably giftless pianist, it would still not occur to you to doubt that the victim of the musical murder you had witnessed was, indeed, the *Chaconne*. (Ridley 2004: 113)

Accommodating the Extremes

The listener can recognize differences in performances of the same work but can still recognize the same work in different performances, suggesting that neither unyielding concepts of *Werktreue* nor of performance-as-work offers the listener a satisfactory account. What is suggested by this is that the apparently irreconcilable polarity of *Werktreue* and performance-as-work can be helpfully narrowed and redesigned into a workable truce. Goehr points a way through the two extremes when firstly she differentiates between 'the perfect performance of music' and the 'perfect musical performance' (Goehr 2004 [1998]: 134), with the former tending towards a basis in *Werktreue* and the latter tending towards a focus on the act of performance. She then concludes that '[m]any performers ... aimed to be both great virtuoso and great *Werktreue* performers ... and they did this by aspiring to produce a perfect performance of music as they aspired also to produce a perfect musical performance' (170–71). This alliance also finds support from within the performing community, and a commitment to the interaction of both work and individual performance may be surmised from Claudio Arrau's comment that 'fidelity and loyalty to what the composer wanted is only the basis on which the artist builds his own vision, his own idea of the work' (Mach 1981: 4). The implications of this for the listener are that a work, by having a score as its symbolic equivalent, retains its essential identity in performance but that its specific soundings, including those heard as structural, are dependent on the performance, which is a variable factor.

A 'middle way', then, is beginning to suggest itself and a listener can perhaps appreciate that the delicate balance between work and performance is liable to generate tensions which yield variable acoustic results. However, theories about the work/performance partnership, contradictory or otherwise, have so far failed to offer much more than some broad generalities about the performance of a work and how it may or may not be understood by a listener. One reason for this is because they cannot account for the practice of performance.

The Performer at Work

Turning to the practice of performance as a primary focus, it is now worth investigating how far an understanding of such practice can lead to an enhanced appreciation of its acoustic outcomes and their relationship to a work. Prominent in the field of performance practice are the debates surrounding historically authentic performance.

Historical Authenticity

The epithet 'authentic performance' inevitably raises the spectre of the now quietened historical performance controversy which gathered momentum in the 1950s but perhaps climaxed in the 1980s and early 1990s, when period-instrument bands started moving into the Classical and early Romantic repertoire.[5] Although concepts of authenticity seem akin to the spirit of *Werktreue*, apologists were more concerned with *Praxistreue*: if sound and practice were correct, then a historical alignment with the composer was achieved and presumably his 'intentions' were also better realized. '[T]he implication was that performers should follow only the historical evidence, should withhold their own personalities, and not overlay what resulted with any present-day gloss' (Kenyon 1988: 6). 'I have nothing to say, I am only a player' claimed Gustav Leonhardt (quoted in Butt 2002: 45).

There have been recent critics (Kivy 1995; Ridley 2004) and supporters (Davies 2001) of period-instrument performance but, for the listener, the type of sound that was common in 1980s period-instrument performances of eighteenth-century music – featuring constrained, vibratoless tone, short and steeply contoured phrases, a limited dynamic range and generally fast tempos[6] – was symbolic of an ethos of subservience to a perception of style. In one way, this

---

[5] The historical performance movement was spearheaded by performer-scholars but, as Peter Walls has pointed out: 'it is hard to think of any other area in music in which ... "stakeholders" are so numerous or so varied. Performers, musicologists, instrument makers, music critics, journalists, concert promoters, record company producers and ... audiences ... all have an interest' (Walls 2003: 6).

[6] 1980s recordings by in particular Christopher Hogwood and the Academy of Ancient Music demonstrate these characteristics very clearly.

helped the listener to appreciate why the performances sounded the way that they did, but in questions of balance, dynamics and *rubato*, commitment to a more individual interpretative solution was still evident and its origins in the work being performed left unexplained. Even those areas which the listener could attribute to a performer's espousal of 'authentic' practice tended to appear across a range of eighteenth-century repertoire and could therefore be heard as a commitment to a way of doing things rather than as necessarily proper to a particular work.

However, what is now known as 'HIP' ('historically informed performance') has become acoustically less clichéd, and more recent approaches have tended to adopt much greater flexibility:

> Those elements of style which a composer found unnecessary to notate will always remain for us a foreign language, but eventually we may be able to converse freely with it as musicians, and so bring a greater range of expression to our interpretations, rather than merely pursuing some kind of unattainable 'authenticity'. (Lawson and Stowell 1999: 2)

Furthermore, the practice of HIP has moved well beyond an application only to eighteenth- and early nineteenth-century repertoire. Supported in some instances by prevenient recordings, historically informed thinking has, for example, been applied to performance of Brahms's violin sonatas (Milsom 2001), to Leif Ove Andsnes's recording of Grieg's piano music (2002) and to Colin Lawson's of simple-system English clarinet music (2005). As early as 1992 the New Queen's Hall Orchestra had launched itself with the aim of recreating early twentieth-century orchestral performance practices, its style being based on surviving recordings from the period.[7]

These developments broaden, possibly cloud, the field somewhat for the listener since the stylistic points of reference are now much looser, and a historically informed performance is less immediately obvious than it was two decades earlier. Nevertheless, a listener's familiarity with the debates surrounding HIP still provides clues which help to explain the sound properties of period performance as well as some of the other stylistic choices made by performers in the field. Such familiarity, however, supplies only a general set of reference points which are hard to apply with any certainty to particular performances of particular works, harder if no firm claims are made that the performance of a piece of eighteenth- or nineteenth-century music is historically informed.[8] Another probable reason why interpretative markers for listeners are so vague is because debates about historical performance have been concerned primarily with how players should play, leaving listeners largely to draw their own conclusions.

---

[7]   Two years later the orchestra's programme booklet disavowed a 'sole claim to the high ground in any debate over style' (Philip 2004: 223).

[8]   This issue is of particular relevance to the case study presented in Chapter 3, where performances of Bach's Toccata in D BWV 912 are analysed.

Personal Authenticity

Awareness of historical authenticity may offer the listener some stylistic insights into a performance but there is, however, another kind of authenticity to consider. In the play *Hamlet*, Polonius' comment to Laertes has gained proverbial status: '[t]his above all: to thine own self be true' (Shakespeare 1980 [1603]: 83), and the sentiment seems to underlie Peter Kivy's notion of 'personal authenticity' (Kivy 1995: 108) in performance. The idea that artists can be true to their own personal artistic visions seems to promise some more genuine insights into individual performances as heard by the listener.

Kivy recognizes this quality of personal authenticity when we are praising a performance for

> bearing the special stamp of personality that marks it out from all others as Horowitz's or Serkin's, Bernstein's or Toscanini's, Casals's or Janigro's: we are marking it out as the unique product of a unique individual, something with an individual style of its own – an 'original.' Because performances are works of art we can praise them for two qualities that they ... are particularly valued for having: the qualities of personal style and originality. Thus it appears to me that when we say a performance is personally authentic, that is shorthand for 'having personal style,' 'being original' or both. We are praising the effect by naming the cause. (Kivy 1995: 123)

This resonates surprisingly closely with Oscar Wilde's description, in *The Critic as Artist*, of Anton Rubinstein's playing of Beethoven:

> it is evident that personality is an absolute essential for any real interpretation. When Rubinstein plays to us the *Sonata Appassionata* of Beethoven, he gives us not merely Beethoven, but also himself, and so gives us Beethoven absolutely – Beethoven reinterpreted through a rich artistic nature, and made vivid and wonderful to us by a new and intense personality. (Wilde 1994 [1891]: 1131)

Both of these passages as well as Godlovitch's assertion that 'an individualistic performance ... displays the signature of a person' (Godlovitch 1998: 140) suggest that performance crucially involves performers' individual artistic personalities and choices, and cannot simply be explained by philosophical or theoretical maxims about what a performance should or should not achieve.

The idea of personal authenticity, and all that it implies, offers the listener a general explanation as to why performances of the same work can sound so different, in that the work has been 'processed' through the individuality of the artist. The idea sits comfortably alongside the analytical framework that I will develop in Chapter 2 but, as Kivy generally does not account for the more specific operation of personal authenticity within the constraints of a particular work, it is hard to apply it in any very concrete fashion.

The projection of a personal voice in performance, seemingly balancing the work as represented in the score with the artist's vision, or personal conception of the music, betokens a partnership which nicely matches 'the middle way' of which I wrote earlier. Recognition of this relationship perhaps takes the listener a little closer to an appreciation of the interpretative processes that become audibly fused into the single act of performance, but more has yet to be detailed concerning how the exercise of personal authenticity or an artistic vision may be perceived. It is therefore now appropriate to turn to an area of performance studies that relies on the listening experience as applied to performance: expression.

Expression

Brahms once said to his English pupil, Florence May: 'But you are playing without expression ... Now ... with expression' (quoted in May 1948 [1905]: 18). Musical expression is a feature of performance that can establish an artist's personal authenticity whilst at the same time can project an apparent lack of authenticity to an unsympathetic hearer. A performer's use (or non-use) of personal or culturally received expressive devices will often be the aspect that most clearly determines his or her musical identity and is most likely to provoke critical debate regarding the validity of the interpretation on offer.[9] It was surely a perceived lack of 'expression' in Steven Kovacevich's recording of Beethoven's *Hammerklavier* Sonata that prompted Nalen Anthoni to write in a review that '[Kovacevich] rather dilutes the "complex emotion and anguish" that he perceives ... for example ... *espressivo* and *molto espressivo* markings are underplayed' (Anthoni 2003: 56).

The study of this type of expression in performance has tended to fall within the orbit of music psychology and has been empirically investigated by Eric Clarke (2000 [1988], 1995), Janet Schmalfeldt (1985), Bruno Repp (1994), Neil Todd (1985, 1989, 1994) and many others. Despite differing approaches, their theories explore the truistic notion that expression is a performer's way of interacting with and responding interpretatively to musical stimuli, often structural. This expressive interaction has been viewed as deviation from 'neutral' regularity. As far back as 1938, psychologist Carl Seashore suggested that 'artistic expression ... consists in esthetic deviation from the regular – from ... even dynamics, metronomic time, rigid rhythms etc' (Seashore 1967 [1938]: 9). This is partially in accord with the definition given more recently by Desain and Honing, although by 1992 they felt compelled to focus exclusively on parameters set by the performance itself, rejecting any suggestion of reference to other external factors (such as a score). Their revised definition became: 'expression within a unit is defined as the deviation of its parts with respect to the norm set by the unit itself' (Desain and Honing

---

[9]   As Patrik Juslin explains: 'The shaping of the expressive code continues throughout life, along with accumulated experience ... In the professional career, the code is modulated by advice from music teachers, performance conventions and the use of metaphors' (Juslin 2002 [2001]: 323).

1992: 175). Soon after this, Todd (1994) developed a system of 'rhythmograms' to reflect *rubato* and dynamics in performance[10] whilst Clarke suggested a semiotic explanation (1995, 2002).

The shadow of theoretical work analysis is rarely far away from these theories, which often emphasize the overlap between analytical and expressive musical thinking. Symptomatic of this approach is the following from Clarke: 'an interpretation is not only an expressive coding, but also a structural coding … The structural component then acts as a framework around which the expressive markers are organised' (Clarke 2000 [1989]: 15), and from Ridley: 'The features in which musical expressiveness resides … are … the very same features as those addressed by musical analysis' (Ridley 2004: 156). Some of Nicholas Cook's recent research (2007) into the expressive use of tempo and timing in recorded performance widens the analytical scope by drawing in issues of acoustic ambience, performance practice and rhythmic characterization. However, concerns over 'the problem of coherence' (Cook, 2007: 185) in Chopin's Mazurka Op. 17/4 are addressed and, despite no mention of a score in Cook's discussion, these concerns, along with references to bar numbers and a table of 'sectional designations', point inevitably back to score-based information, from where it is only a very short return journey to work analysis. To borrow Anthony Storr's linguistic analogy, most of the above theories of expression in performance tend to focus on how the 'syntactical' elements of a composition, those concerning 'grammatical structure or literal meaning', may be expressed in performance rather than the prosodic, those concerning 'emotional significance' (Storr 1997 [1992]: 9).

The listener then can take deviation from regularity as an expressive projection of primarily structural concerns, 'regularity' being set either by the score or by a mean established by the performance itself. But is this the only way in which expression can be understood?

Alf Gabrielsson and Erik Lindström accept that not all expression is necessarily structurally derived, suggesting that '[p]erceived expression is dependent both on factors in the composed structure and factors in the performance' (Gabrielsson and Lindström (2002 [2001]: 223), and work by Patrik Juslin makes similar allowances. Whilst admitting that a 'function of expressive variations may be to clarify the structure of the piece to the listener' (Juslin 2002 [2001]: 312), he demonstrates how differences in phrasing can arise from 'ways of giving "expressive shape" to one and the same structure' (312). From within the pedagogical community, Alan Fraser further develops the notion of 'non-structural' expressivity, claiming:

> When a great pianist plays at his best I feel that she or he accesses direct human experience archetypes encoded in our genes and expresses them through the schematic of the composer's notes, which the composer arrived at through the

---

[10]   His research found that '[a]s is so often the case in the performance of much music of the Classic and Romantic period, points of maximum harmonic tension are reflected in the rhythmic expression' (Todd 1994: 52).

16 *Reading Musical Interpretation*

> same process of divination. Your conscious self must understand the nature of these emotional, experiential *facts* which exist implicit in the music and which wait to be expressed through it. (Fraser 2003: 367)

This type of expression seems more intuitively than analytically derived and will most likely be based on a performer's engagement with the more overtly expressive properties of a piece of music. For the listener, such an engagement can be of vital importance 'in determining the emotional expression of a piece of music' (Juslin 2002 [2001]: 310), regardless of structural concerns. An illustration of how emotional expression may be determined by performance comes from a perhaps surprising source: Eric Clarke admits that a certain way of ending Chopin's Prelude in E minor Op. 28/4 'produces a sense of resignation and hopelessness' (Clarke 1995: 36). Despite later condemning 'attempts to describe listeners' affective responses to music with a crude vocabulary of emotional states' (50), it seems that there are occasions when even the most sceptical author cannot avoid doing the same.

It is, however, use of a vocabulary of emotional states, as illustrated above, that can enable the listener to 'interpret' a performance, and it is one that has informed Juslin's research work in which he has studied the 'cues' by which performers communicate the emotions of tenderness, happiness, sadness, fear and anger. These 'expressive cues include tempo, sound level, timing, intonation, articulation, timbre, vibrato, tone attacks, tone decays and pauses' (Juslin 2002 [2001]: 316).[11] This might raise an eyebrow from, amongst others, Meyer (1956) and Kivy (1980, 2001) who differentiate between felt emotions – 'the garden variety' (Kivy 2001: 95) – and their transmuted identity as musical emotions. However, Juslin's notion concerning a performer's use of 'expressive cues' by which a listener may recognize emotions as 'sound properties' (Juslin, Friberg, Schoondervaldt and Karlsson 2004: 249) does not imply that a listener actually experiences the 'garden variety'. Nevertheless, Juslin and his colleagues allow that emotional language of the 'everyday' kind can be useful to the performer as a 'powerful [source] of expressive form' (Juslin *et al.* 2004: 250).

The implications of the above are significant in that the listener can now take virtually all acoustic parameters engaged by a performer as tokens of emotional expression. The expression may reflect a structural point in a work, but it may also reflect the perceived 'shape' of a melodic line, musical intensity, a mood, an atmosphere, a raw emotion, and no doubt much else besides.

The discussion of emotion in performance, given that such emotion is not the 'garden variety', perforce involves the use of metaphor, and Juslin *et al.* acknowledge the relevance of emotional metaphor to the teaching and performing communities because 'emotions experienced in a non musical context can help

---

[11] Peter Johnson believes that Juslin's experiments only serve to confirm that 'we share a set of codes for the verbal description of topics in the Western art music tradition' (personal communication 12 January 2007).

shape musically relevant emotions' (250). Generally, his research accepts time- and teacher-honoured devices such as phrasing, balance, dynamic manipulation, agogic accentuation and *rubato* as carriers of expression and the means by which an artist provokes an emotive response (whatever the precise nature of that response may be). His methods also acknowledge that the foregoing expressive means are recognized primarily through an individual's aural perception, even if they can in part be measured by metronomes and spectrograms as well as by 'cognitive feedback' software. In my forthcoming exposition, I shall likewise accept and acknowledge these time- and teacher-honoured devices, employing a related vocabulary as appropriate.

Work in the field of expression has not only identified its subject as an intrinsic property of performance but, with such a growing body of literature, has positively celebrated its emotive power. Although the cited research is conducted from the perspective of the listener, it operates within a designedly narrow field and does not seek to assimilate expression into an overview of how a musical interpretation may be understood in a more holistic sense. Indeed, Juslin *et al.*'s more recent research (2004) seems mainly to investigate expressive and emotional communication outside the context of Western art music's standard repertoire or, indeed, any clear musical setting. As has been already conceded, expression is a means by which performers may project their artistic identities, but it cannot operate in isolation and, in a Western art music context, it needs to have a recognizable link with a work if performance and score may be heard to interface.

The Performer, the Performance and the Work

Making Connections

The foregoing discussion has taken us some way towards a fuller understanding of the multi-faceted nature of performance and has provided some pointers as to why performances sound the way that they do: the performance may be heard as an interpretation of a work as accessed through a score; it may be heard to reflect structural features and a perception of style; it may be heard as a statement of 'personal authenticity' and as a means of conveying perceived emotions. However, the areas that have been reviewed tend to be a collection of discrete fields of study from which no fully developed theory has yet emerged which attempts to assimilate relevant aspects of these separate fields. Perhaps the closest so far is John Rink's interpretative 'refraction' model, which draws together the performance, the performer and the work into a conceptual alliance. The model shows in some detail how a work may have been processed through the individuality of the artist, suggesting that an interpretation is the result of a performer's artistic decision-making, based on certain performance-related factors within a work. The refraction model is specifically applied to Chopin's Prelude Op. 28/4, in which the author sees the factors of genre, performing history, notational idiosyncrasies, compositional style, structure as 'shape' and physicality feeding into the 'performer's artistic prerogatives', thence resulting in the 'performance conception' (Rink 2004: 47–8). This potentially provides a suitably informed listener with a set of reference points through which to receive an interpretation of the Chopin prelude, but the model is as yet 'in microcosm' (48) as the writer describes it and designedly does not primarily engage with the acoustic results of a performance. Its main concern is with a possible process of interpretation rather than with a finished product or how this may be understood by a listener, so, if the latter is to be achieved, a different approach is called for.

Towards an Analytical Theory

The conclusions of the foregoing discussion suggest that there is room for a theoretical framework by which the performance of a musical work may be analysed, not just in terms of one particular element but in terms of a multiplicity of interpretative components which are heard to cohere in the act of performance. Without such an overview, a number of questions remain unanswered: are there any identifiable factors by which an interpretative compound heard in the performance of a work may be elucidated? How might an interpretative scheme as reflected in the final 'product'[12] be understood? Why can some interpretations be heard to emphasize certain aspects of a work at the expense of others? Why do no two recordings of the same work seem to offer exactly the same interpretative solutions? Why do some types of music apparently promote greater similarity of interpretation than others? Do training and fashion play a part in the interpretative formations heard in performance? To propose some answers to these questions, a holistic examination of acoustically experienced interpretative outcomes and their relationship to a score is necessary.

In a passage concerned with the role of the interpreting 'self', Naomi Cumming suggests that it could be 'informative to give an account of an interpretive process in which the terms of description are fallible, incomplete, and subject to ongoing reinterpretation' (Cumming 2000: 70). Chapter 2 will attempt to develop just such an account. Based on the listening experience, the account uses tools that are undoubtedly 'subject to ongoing reinterpretation' but in a way that points creatively both to and from others that have greater certainty. The account is broad, adopting a holistic brief which incorporates appropriate elements of the areas discussed in this chapter as well as others. Its theoretical background includes some basic ideas drawn from the fields of aesthetics, hermeneutics, logical philosophy and semiotics which have a bearing on the listener's critical reception and understanding of performance. The account aims to develop a framework for analysing performance, from which answers to questions raised in the previous paragraph may emerge. As I am a pianist, my discussion will focus on pianists

---

[12] The term 'product' seems particularly appropriate when CD recordings are under discussion.

and piano literature but, it is hoped, may have wider applications too. Using CD recordings of piano music, the framework for analysis will then be tested in a series of case studies presented in Chapters 3, 4 and 5.

Chapter 2
Constructing a Framework

An Empirical Approach

If, as I suggested at the beginning of this book, acts of performance enshrine an essential mystery, then solutions to this mystery, as reflected by the ideas examined in Chapter 1, seem so far to have been at best partial and certainly diverse. Constituent elements of performance in the Western art music tradition, as represented by the various fields of research, have been perceived as many and varied, but if a listener witnesses a synthesis of these elements as they combine in the performance of a work then further light may be shed on our mystery if a conceptual overview which can absorb this multiplicity is developed. Although Rink's 'refraction' model draws many of these constituents together into the notion of a 'performance conception' (Rink 2004: 48), his ideas, as noted in Chapter 1, primarily address how a performer might achieve such a conception but do not draw a listener's reception of this into the theoretical framework.

It may therefore be appropriate for a theoretical endeavour which has performance at its heart to take the performance of a work as its focal point rather than as its final point. By viewing a work through the medium of performance as an acoustic experience, one can reintroduce the empirical element that has arguably been squeezed out of traditional music theory. Traditional music theory based round the study of works or more particularly scores has, during the twentieth century, tended to become ossified through 'entrenched ways of thought' and 'empirical resistance' (Cook 1999b: 41). The frequent result of this has been that 'a dominant discourse (… composed structure) … is mapped onto a marginalised one (… performance)' (Cook 1999b: 52), presumably in an attempt to explain performance through the analytical methods of established music theory. By reintroducing the empirical element and acknowledging the primacy of the acoustic experience, the performance discourse is no longer marginalized and gains its own independence. In a sense, an empirical approach aligns the construction of a musical theory with the scientific method of induction, which recognizes that 'our information derives from empirical observation' and that there is ultimately 'no solution by whose means particular explanatory theories could be conclusively shown to be true' (Howson and Urbach 1991 [1989]: 3–4). It may therefore be hoped that an empirical approach to performance studies can protect any subsequent discourse from the entrenchment lamented by Cook.

I have stated several times that my chief empirical concern is with performance as a listening experience, and it is from the perspective of the listener that my framework for performance analysis will be constructed. In this chapter I will present the theory behind my analytical framework and the framework itself in a series of nine steps. An analytical framework which depends on the centrality of the listening experience presupposes an analytical listener, and Step One discusses the necessary attributes of such a listener; Step Two explains how potential problems in the analyst–performer relationship may be philosophically accounted for; with the aid of further philosophical thoughts, Step Three identifies necessary common points of reference with which to negotiate between analysis and performance; Step Four describes how analysis can work when applied to a performance; Step Five suggests that certain components are necessary for the construction of a workable analytical framework; Step Six introduces the analytical components; Step Seven presents the framework itself; Step Eight demonstrates how the framework functions as an analytical tool; and Step Nine elaborates on the relationship between analysis and performance in the light of Steps One to Eight. In the remainder of the chapter, I will explain the precise methods I used in order to apply the analytical framework to the case studies in Chapters 3, 4 and 5.

Step One: The Analytical Listener

As a first step in formulating an empirical method of performance analysis, it is necessary to establish what criteria for appropriate analytical listening are likely to be necessary. Nicholas Cook defines two types of listening: 'musical listening … for purposes of direct aesthetic gratification' and 'musicological listening … whose purpose is the establishment of facts or the formulation of theories' (Cook 1992 [1990]: 152). Of the two, Cook regards the former as defining 'the real object of the listening process' (160), and it could be argued that the musicological listener begins and ends as a musical listener, but gains a deeper understanding and appreciation of the object of his or her listening after establishing facts and formulating theories. However, as I am developing an analytical theory, it is musicological listening that is of immediate concern in the present context. Cook's discussion of musicological listening does not involve performance, but has relevance to performance analysis nevertheless. He suggests that '[t]o hear a complex sound musicologically is to hear it in terms of the particular pitches that are played and the particular instruments that play them; it involves the co-ordination of what is heard with some scheme of representation that is adapted to the purpose in hand' (154). Nicola Dibben argues that 'listeners make associative links between musical elements that are present in any given piece, and at the same time make associations with similar or functionally equivalent elements or gestures in the wider repertoire of music with which they are familiar' (Dibben 2003: 196). If the words 'piece' and 'music' in the foregoing sentence are substituted by the word 'performance' – that is, if one shifts the conceptual location from work to performance – then Dibben's and Cook's concepts can form the basis for a theoretical discussion which embraces both work-as-score and performance as perceived by a musicologically informed listener.

The analytical listener, as with the analyst of musical works, needs to be musicologically informed in appropriate ways. Whereas traditional analysis seeks to gain insights into musical works solely through analysis of the score, performance analysis in the Western art tradition, by engaging primarily with sound, will seek to gain insights into the acoustic realization of works as variously heard in performance. To achieve this, the analyst needs to draw on all the various types of knowledge discussed in Chapter 1: knowledge of the work-as-score; knowledge of the relationship between score and performance; knowledge of the performance act itself and the processes that it involves; and in my own case knowledge of the physical aspects of playing the piano. By drawing on this knowledge bank, what Cook describes as 'pre-existing knowledge' (Cook 1992 [1990]: 154), the analyst can co-ordinate the work or works being performed with their respective scores (or 'texts') and also with acts of interpretation as manifested in performance – and all that these imply. By establishing 'associative links' between text and act and/or act and act, this knowledge may then be adapted to the analytical purpose in hand. An analytical listener must be an 'informed' listener and a workable framework for analysing musical interpretation, based on informed listening, may thus aid the analyst 'to 'parse' the acoustic environment [of performance] effortlessly' (Sloboda 1985: 155).

Step Two: Hermeneutics and the Relationship between the Analyst and Performance

There are two potential problems regarding the analyst/performance relationship arising from the above discussion. To address these, in Steps Two and Three, I turn to some ideas drawn from the fields of aesthetics, hermeneutics, logical philosophy and semiotics. Semiotics has been applied to performance studies by Naomi Cumming (2000) but the other areas have received scant attention, yet they can be shown to have a bearing on matters of performance and, in the present context, on the informed listener's reception of performance.

The first problematic area concerns the reception of an interpretation. A concern for performance analysis introduces the question of how the performer might be perceived to interpret the score. The acoustic phenomenon of performance provides audible evidence of interpretative outcomes with regard to a particular work and presents the informed listener with a set of signs through which an appreciation of the relationship between score and performance may be achieved. By placing the analyst in the position of a critical 'receiver', the act of listening involves further, or 'secondary', interpretation (of which more in Step Nine). The difference between the two is that the performer is responding to printed scores or 'texts' which have a semiotic relationship with a musical work, whereas the analyst is listening to (recorded) performances, 'acoustic texts comparable in extent and significance to … notated texts' (Cook 2003: 208), which have a semiotic relationship with a performer's exercise of artistic prerogatives, and which therefore have a 'once removed' relationship with the printed text. A word of caution is given by Luke Windsor about this chain of pre-analysis interpretations: 'the number of stages of interpretation through which information must pass before analysis should always be considered. This chain of interpretation must be taken into account when analysing data: each stage introduces uncertainty – which may be necessary but must be noted' (Windsor 2004: 199).

By placing the informed listener in the position of receiver, there is also the danger of ensnarement by what Monroe Beardsley and William Wimsatt designated 'The Intentional Fallacy' (1946). Ideas behind Beardsley and Wimsatt's thesis – of which more anon – closely relate to the hermeneutic stance later adopted by Hans-Georg Gadamer, whose ideas about the interpretation of texts or artworks in general can easily be extended to include the reception of a performance which, as Kivy (1995) argues, can itself be seen as a work of art. Gadamer protests against the idea that 'the knower's own situation can have only a negative value' or that '[h]istorical understanding ... is the action of subjectivity purged of all prejudices ... achieved in direct proportion to the knower's ability to set aside his own horizons' (Linge 1977 [1976]: xiv). In contradistinction to this view, Gadamer proposes that '[t]he creator of a work of art may intend the public of his own time, but the real being of his work is what it is able to say, and this being reaches fundamentally beyond any historical confinement' (Gadamer 1977 [1964]: 96). To an extent, this raises the status of the interpreter from one of subservience to that of creative agent and establishes a dialogical relationship between text or artwork and interpreter, and, by extension, between musical work, performer and informed listener. This relationship is reflected by Rod Coltman when he suggests that such dialogue can allow 'the subject matter to unfold according to its own consequences. What determines the course of this self-movement is the matter's own historical situatedness as it fuses with the historical horizon of the interlocutors' (Coltman 1998: 110). A relationship of 'dynamic fluidity' (Bowman 1998: 406) may helpfully be thought to exist between the interpreter and the interpreted.

The Intentional Fallacy, although predating Gadamer's hermeneutics, develops similar ideas, claiming that 'the intention of the author was neither available nor desirable as a standard for the interpretation and evaluation of a literary text' (Stern 2004: 109–110). Since 'we have come to think of the intentional fallacy not only in the context of literary artworks, but also in the context of visual or musical works of art' (110), then it is equally possible to think of it in the context of musical performance as well. In other words, the receiver needs to interpret a performance on its own terms rather than with regard to some notion of intentionality on the part of the originator so that 'reference is detached from the referrer to the symbol [i.e. the performance]; in a new sense the marks or gestures themselves are said to refer, and quite apart from any intentions' (Beardsley 2004: 191).

If one is to accept Gadamer's hermeneutics and Beardsley's thesis in all their particulars, it leaves the receiver of the artwork – in this case the performance analyst – in a position of interpretative freedom, but in a position wherein there is a danger that his or her interpretation fails to find points of contact with interpretations by other similarly free receivers. The decentralization of an author's or performer's supposed intentions, or *mens auctoris*, from any interpretative exegesis liberates the analyst – but not to the point of isolation and analytical anarchy. In reality pre-existing knowledge of works and performances is likely in itself to establish sufficient points of contact between members of a similarly informed community, even if these points of contact do not yield a single interpretation either of a work or performances of a work. William Tolhurst finds a satisfactory solution to the problem when he writes that the meaning of a text 'is best understood as the intention which a member of the intended audience would be most justified in attributing to the author based on the knowledge and attitudes which he possesses in virtue of being a member of the intended audience' (Tolhurst 1979: 11). Thus as performer and performance analyst, I can attribute justifiable 'meanings' (or interpretations) to the performance of a work, based on the knowledge and attitudes that I possess as a member of an intended audience. Since the 'intention' of both composer and performer are taken out of the argument, other than as they may be 'read' by the receiver, other possible uncertainties, noted above, brought about by a chain of interpretations also cease to be problematic, in that the analyst is hearing a performance and its relationship to a work-as-score on its own terms, rather than in terms of what the authors of each might have intended.

Step Three: Language, Semiotics and Common Points of Reference

Step Three addresses the second of the possibly problematic areas and relates to the practical means by which a performer's interpretative decisions may have been made and through which informed listeners are enabled to perceive such decisions according to their own 'self-understanding' (Gadamer 1977 [1964]: 102). I explained in Chapter 1 that, despite its lacunae, the score is normally the principal means by which performers may access a musical work and through which they may arrive at an interpretation, hence my use of the term 'work-as-score'. In Step One I also identified knowledge of the relationship between the performance and the work-as-score as necessary to performance analysis. If this relationship is going to be investigated effectively then the score, as a common point of reference between performer and analyst, needs also to form part of the analytical tool-kit.

Scores usually involve both notation and text, the latter often stipulating tempo, dynamics and articulation for performance. The implied relationship seems straightforward: the work as represented by the score issues a set of instructions to the performer which the performer then carries out. However, listening experiences indicate that the ways in which a score's instructions are carried out differ, sometimes considerably, from performer to performer, reflecting varying perceptions of how meanings are encoded in the instructions. It would therefore be worth investigating the broad implications of musical terminology and notation, and how these interact with both performing and informed listening.

Musical terms such as 'gigue style', 'Classical style', 'rhythmic accentuation', 'rubato' or 'dynamics', form a recognizable vocabulary for both the performer and the performance analyst, but the capacity of language to secure exact meanings has long been a subject for debate. As Richard Rorty explains: 'A respectable body of opinion within analytic philosophy holds that the existence of causal relations between language and non-language does not suffice to give a sense to the notion of "correspondence between language and reality"' (Rorty 1995: 3). Thus it is not surprising to read in the writings of Frege that '[t]he meaning of an expression cannot be identified with its semantic value' (Miller 2003: 271). Similarly, Saul Kripke writes of a 'designating expression' bearing a 'cluster of properties' (Kripke 1981 [1972]: 64) which approaches the semiotic notion that a 'code' 'associates a conventional label with a constellation of ... signs' (Klein 2005: 56).

The semiotician Charles Peirce regarded most words as symbols, 'which have become associated with their meanings by usage' (Peirce 1998 [1894]: 5). If a word is symbolic, so too is musical notation, although its referents are sounds rather than things. As discussed in Chapter 1, it may not be possible to ascribe an exact musical equivalence (or 'semantic value') to notation but, as with words, notational signs have become meaningful through usage. Given Wittgenstein's oft-quoted maxim that 'the meaning of a word is its use in the language' (Wittgenstein 1978 [1953]: 20), it could equally well be said that the meaning of a notational sign is its use in a score. It is this use that testifies to a sufficient commonality of understanding amongst the community of users for performance analysis not to be a meaningless pursuit.

By taking a performance on its own terms, as a free-standing artistic statement, and by acknowledging the constellation of signs attached to a score's notational and terminological codes, the performance analyst seeks to explain an interpretation by applying his or her own competence as an informed, unbiased listener. Codes such as '*andante*', a notational sign, or the name of a work or composer form part of a broad system of reference with which the analyst can negotiate between performance and score to interpret a performer's interpretation. As a performer myself, I am familiar with the sorts of concerns that interpretation of a score entails, so the reference system available to me as a performer, in particular of piano repertoire, can combine with other systems available through listening experiences and performance-related literature to support my analytical perceptions.[1]

---

[1]   Similarly, the notion of a 'subject-position', often applied to the study of film, 'accepts that different individuals can interpret a text in different ways, while insisting that the text itself imposes definite limits on their room to manoeuvre' (Johnston 1985: 245). Eric Clarke (2005) applies the notion to musical interpretation.

Step Four: Applying Analysis to a Performance

So how might an analyst's perceptions actually be applied to a performance? A useful starting point for Step Four is to show, in the broadest possible terms, how an analyst's perception of the score–performer dialogue might be represented. Two contrasting dialogues will serve as illustrations. Denis Matthews' 1946 recording of the first movement of Beethoven's Sonata in E major Op. 109[2] may be heard to follow the score's instructions very closely, suggesting that the performer has been in search of a *mens auctoris* and that a *Texttreue* approach has governed the exercise of his artistic choices. At the other extreme, the performance may depart radically from the printed text, as in Glenn Gould's recording of the first movement of Mozart's Sonata in A major K 331, so that the receiver may perceive a very strong personal statement about the work. Figure 2.1 suggests a way in which these two artistic approaches may be represented in graphic form.

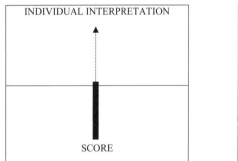 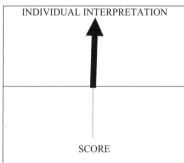

Dotted lines indicate weak emphasis; bold lines indicate strong emphasis

Figure 2.1   Graphic depiction of (a) a literal or *Texttreue* performance and (b) a highly personalized performance

Such diagrams as those in Figure 2.1 may tell us something in visual terms about the relationship between a performance and a score as perceived by an informed listener but both represent extreme interpretations. Neither the simple two-tier framework nor its flimsy theoretical basis can account for the rich diversity of interpretations which a single work can generate, most of which are likely to fall between the two extremes. To construct such an account, it is necessary to build a theoretical framework which provides informed listeners with many points of reference whereby they can evaluate perceived interpretative markers and draw some informed conclusions about the nature of a particular performance.

---

[2]   Full details of cited recordings are given in the Discography. Recording dates, as opposed to release or re-release dates, are referred to throughout the text.

The framework will draw on a broad span of score-based information, notational and terminological codes recognizable within the community of performers and analytical listeners which allow sense to be made of the listening experience; it will enable the justifiable attribution of interpretative profiles to performances in that the analyst, as a member of the intended audience, possesses the necessary knowledge and attitudes.

Another simple example will serve to illustrate the point. If the term '*allegro*' appears at the head of a score, neither performer nor performance analyst is likely to infer that the piece should be played slowly. '*Allegro*' as a performance direction carries well-established connotations, so it would be unwise for the analyst to ascribe a misunderstanding of the term if a performer's tempo choice in a piece marked '*allegro*' does not seem to match any conceptual consensus with regard to the term. It may be that the score's tempo direction is attached to siciliano-like music, which can therefore be associated with the pastoral style. So by drawing on this pastoral association, the analyst can ascribe an underlying, contextually based reason for a tempo choice, reflecting the artist's seeming projection of a pastoral character.

The above example of how the term '*allegro*' may be read by the analyst when negotiating between score and performance implies that there may be deeper reasons behind artistic choices heard at the audible or 'surface' level of a performance. One is reminded of the role of analysis as explained by Wittgenstein in relation to language: we 'see in the essence, not something that already lies open to view ... but something that lies *beneath* the surface. Something that lies within, which we see when we look into the thing, and which analysis digs out' (Wittgenstein 1978 [1953]: 43). By extension, a framework for performance analysis may be constructed in a manner which is able to reflect an interpretative rationale lying beneath the surface of a performance.

The idea of searching beneath the surface, a musical one in this case, suggests a parallel with Schenkerian score analysis. The framework for Schenkerian analysis relies on its ability to derive a hierarchically arranged *Hintergrund*, *Mittelgrund* and *Vordergrund* from a score. This does not imply that a composer was necessarily conscious of such a hierarchy, but Schenker's method has proven to be a useful and enduring tool for providing structural insights into musical works. Similarly, performance issues may be hierarchically arranged into a framework for analysis which, whilst not presupposing that performers are consciously aware of any specific hierarchy of concerns when preparing a performance, may nonetheless provide a useful frame of reference. It is thus possible to advance a system of analysis which is based on a layering of score-derived information in a perceived relationship to performance.

Step Five: The Need for Analytical Components

The next step in developing an analytical framework is to particularize and categorize score-derived information into a fuller conceptual hierarchy of performer engagement. Using terms and names associated with musical scores, a framework of reference points may be constructed which aid the analysis of performance outcomes. The whole mass of interpretative information provided by a composer through the medium of a score can be usefully grouped into several named categories. I have therefore identified nine broad categories of information relevant to performance and ordered them in a series that moves progressively from ideas to acoustic outcomes. These categories include score-derived information ranging from when and by whom a work was composed, through to details of phrasing, tempo, articulation and dynamic, either written in the score or suggested by musical syntax. Having described these categories in some detail, I will then structure them into a four-tier tower framework, an 'interpretative tower', in which those that seem closest to the work itself constitute the base level and those that supply the analyst with acoustic data – and could therefore be thought directly and actively to engage the performer – constitute the top level. Since a score provides information for both performer and analyst, and since I will be constructing a conceptual framework for analysing interpretations, I will call these categories *informants*.

In the light of my earlier discussions concerning hermeneutics and words, the informant categories will allow for latitude of understanding on the part of both executant and analyst, since their meaning can never be absolutely defined. Also, although I believe there to be a logical flow within the tower from one category to the next and from one level to the next, it is not the intention of the framework either to force all interpretations of a work into a single mould or to imply any rigid analytical or ontological statement about a musical work or its interpretation. Indeed, its strength lies in the fact that it can show how some performances can be heard to emphasize aspects (or informant categories) of a work at the expense of others or even leave some out altogether, reflecting how a single work can generate multiple 'readings'. As Goehr puts it: 'if one acknowledges that alternative expressions of a shared ground are possible, one may well allow the alternatives to coexist' (Goehr 2004 [1998]: 169).

Given Components

As stated, the notated score lies at the point of intersection between composer and performer and, for this reason, basic notation and performer reading skills will be taken for granted. The interpretative tower is for analysing interpretations, not reading skills. In the event of a performance seeming to be no more than a 'read-through' – what may be termed a 'nominal performance' (Friberg and Battel 2002: 200–201) or a 'sonic *Urtext*' (Kivy 2001: 16) – I will still treat this as an interpretative viewpoint, especially if it achieved commercial release as a CD recording.

30   *Reading Musical Interpretation*

As with reading skills, I shall also be treating technique as a given. Clearly, technique is the foundation on which an interpretation can be raised: '[technique] must come first' said Brahms to his English pupil Florence May (quoted in May 1948 [1905]: 10). The performers whose recordings I will be using will have laboured long and hard to refine their technical expertise in a variety of different ways[3] but, in my analyses, I am assuming that this expertise will be at more or less the same level and that the technique to carry out interpretative choices can be taken for granted. In his 'refraction' model, John Rink makes the same assumption. He includes 'the physical dimension' (Rink 2004: 47) but this refers to factors such as 'keeping the left hand light ... expressive use of the body' (47) rather than basic technical skill. Leopold Godowsky refers to the latter as 'mere mechanics' and compares it with 'technic', which has 'to do with the intellectual phase of the subject rather than the physical' (Cooke 1999 [1917]: 133–4). Similarly, Rachmaninov writes that the 'technical ability of the performer should be ... applied to all the artistic demands of the composition' (1999: 209). The concept of *applied technique* is useful in this connection and will be referred to again in the following discussion.

The following exposition of the nine informants draws on both the performing and listening experiences that I have acquired as part of the community of performers and analytical listeners, as well as on the plausible assumption that other performers listen critically to their own and others' performances. The areas discussed are therefore relevant to performance analysis through their relevance to performance. For the sake of clarity, these informants will initially be numbered but subsequently left simply as names, to reflect the intended fluidity of their interrelationship and inter-dependency.

Step Six: Introducing the Informants

Category 1 – Era (Style)

'Baroque', 'Classical' and 'Romantic' are names that have well-established implications or 'rules' (Meyer 1989: 17). They present a taxonomy of musical eras in relation to the historical process of growth and development which is familiar to the musical cognoscenti. They are clearly connotative[4] because, although the time period in which a work appeared is an objective fact about that work, these

---

[3]   According to Harald Jørgensen, the practice schedules of music students in higher education averages around 'an unwritten norm' of 'around 20–25 hours per week' (Jørgensen 2004: 90).

[4]   The philosopher John Stuart Mill saw names as either *connotative* or *non-connotative*. He defined the former as 'one which denotes a subject and implies an attribute' (Mill 1961 [1843]: 20).

descriptors – or just a date[5] – connote stylistic expectations and, in the broadest sense, can form a foundation for interpretation. Consequently, a primary category which, through its stylistic implications, may usefully be thought to inform a performance is that of *era (style)*.

The development of stylistic awareness and its relationship to era forms an important part of a performer's training, hence the many pedagogical publications and other studies which address the subject.[6] Whilst the exact nature and perspective of a performer's stylistic understanding is liable to differ from one interpretation to another, the analyst may reasonably anticipate that the era from which a piece of music originates will, in general terms, be heard to influence (if not necessarily dictate) most other interpretative features of a performance, despite varying acoustic results.

One possible reason for constrasting stylistic and interpretative outcomes is the historical location of a performance, and an example of how tempo can be heard to reflect a perception of era (style) may be used as illustration. In a 1995 recording of Beethoven's Piano Concerto No. 5, the Orchestre Révolutionnaire et Romantique under John Eliot Gardiner with soloist Robert Levin start the second movement, *Adagio un poco mosso*, at a flowing crotchet = *c.* 60, whereas Ferdinand Leitner and the Berlin Philharmonic Orchestra, in 1962, open at a more reflective crotchet = *c.* 48. Yet the soloist here is Wilhelm Kempff who was, in his own time, known for taking slow movements on the fast side of *adagio* or *andante* (Manildi 2000 [1993]: 5). This comparison supports Rosen's suggestion (2002: 99) that present-day practices in 'slow' movements can accommodate the stylistic aptness of relatively fast tempos within a late Classical setting. The inherent sound properties of the two recordings also reflect changing views of style in that the Eliot Gardiner performance uses period instruments and falls under the provenance of HIP, illustrating how the promotion of performance practice material over recent decades has infiltrated contemporary thought.[7]

However, as the Beethoven illustration suggests, it would be unwise to let early twenty-first-century tastes dictate a narrow view of era (style). Performers are surrounded by an evolving heritage of performing practices which may be heard to affect the projection of this informant. As Robert Philip reminds us: 'the qualities that make early twentieth-century recordings of "Old Music" endure and still be enjoyed seventy or eighty years later, have little to do with the extent to

---

[5]   Labels such as 'Baroque' or 'Classical' may seem unduly limiting, especially when dealing with 'transitional' figures such as Beethoven or Schubert.

[6]   Examples include books by James Thurmond (1991 [1982]) and David Milsom (2003), and publications edited by Denes Agay (1981) and Anthony Burton (2002a, b, c).

[7]   Such material includes *Urtext* editions and treatises on performance by, for example, Leopold Mozart, Quantz and Czerny. According to Lawson and Stowell, an over-estimation of the value of treatises has sometimes led performers to 'devise theories mistakenly, make inferences … too hastily and use performing conventions erroneously' (Lawson and Stowell 1999: 23).

32   *Reading Musical Interpretation*

which they approach any later notions of "correct" period performance' (Philip 2004: 211). Our current use of *rubato* in Bach is unlikely to resemble that of Violet Gordon Woodhouse, whose employment of the expressive device was, according to Philip, 'as much a nuance of her time as a historical adoption' (208). Yet both her understanding and ours relate to the same era. Another more work-specific example is provided by the contrasting styles adopted in the Beethoven concerto recordings discussed above, in which comparisons can be made not just between the respective tempos adopted but between the sound properties of the two recordings as well. Cone suggests that style may well be 'the ultimate morality of performance' (Cone 1968: 57), yet these two instances indicate a morality to which no absolutes can be ascribed but one that 'depends for its preservation on the approving taste or sense quality of later generations' (Gadamer 1977 [1964]: 100). All of which illustrates that a concept of era or style, and how an understanding of performance may be determined by this, adapts to changing tastes and circumstances.

This is not, however, to maroon the performance analyst (or the performer) by denying the era (style) concept any useful meaning, but rather to allow it a broad field of operation; to view it, perhaps, as 'a set of constraints that establishes a repertory of alternatives from which to choose' (Meyer 1989: 8). Thus whatever the tastes and circumstances of our time may be, it would be hard to disagree with the sentiments expressed in the early years of the last century by the ageing Joseph Joachim, which provide evidence that historically aware thinking is by no means new:

> a work by Bach or Tartini demands a different style of delivery from one by Mendelssohn or Spohr. The space of a century that divides the two first mentioned from that last two means in the historical development of our art, not only a great difference with regard to form, but an even greater with respect to musical expression. (Lawson and Stowell 1999: 1)[8]

Joachim links his views about era to pairings of composers, and the recordings of Beethoven and Bach, discussed above, as well as indicating contrasting understandings of era, also seemingly present the composer's musical thoughts in rather different ways. This takes us to the next informant category.

Category 2 – Authorship (Score)

The individuality of a composer's work determines the second but still fundamental category of authorship. As discussed in Chapter 1, the score is an important means by which a musician can interface with a work and 'know' a composer as an

---

[8]   '[E]in Werk von Bach oder Tartini erheischt eine andere Vortragsweise als eines von Mendelssohn oder Spohr. Der Zeitraum von rund hundert Jahren, der die beiden Autorenpaare voneinander trennt, bedeutet für die geschichtliche Entwicklung unserer Kunst nicht nur einen grossen Unterschied in formaler Hinsicht, sondern einen weit grösseren noch nach der Seite des musikalischen Ausdrucks hin' (Joachim 1905: 5).

authorial presence. Literary authors are recognized, through their texts, by turns of phrase, modes of expression, characteristic structures and syntax as well as by typical narrative themes. As Foucault writes: 'an author's name ... permits one to group together a certain number of texts, define them, differentiate them from and contrast them to others ... The text always contains a certain number of signs referring to the author' (Foucault 1998 [1969]: 369–71). Likewise a musical author is recognized by, amongst other traits, melodic or rhythmic patterns, characteristic harmonies, timbres or favoured structural methods. Meyer designates these as a composer's 'idiom', defining idiom as a subcategory of 'dialect' because stylistic features 'that a composer repeatedly selects from the larger repertory of the dialect define his or her individual idiom' (Meyer 1989: 24). No doubt for this reason, John Butt suggests that a composer can be inferred from his or her surviving music, resulting in 'an "implied composer" as it were' (Butt 2002: 77).

Regarding this informant's presence as a fundamental in the interpretative tower, authorship via the score, or *authorship (score)* as I shall call it, may be thought of primarily as an interpretative stimulant rather than a theoretical one, although, as Rink's work (cited in Chapter 1) has shown, the two can be complementary rather than mutually exclusive. The authorship (score) informant prompts questions relating to basic musical syntax, where no performance directions appear in the score, as well as to the implications of a composer's very detailed performance directions, and to everything in between. As will become apparent, of central importance in the context of the interpretative tower are the ways in which the informed listener may perceive authorial 'meaning' as variously presented and detected in a performance. How may the performance be heard to shape the manner and timing of the events that have been 'more or less stipulated by the composer' (Meyer 1967: 48)? A view of authorship may then be ascribed to the interpretation.

As with style, the role of performance in representing what a composer 'meant' by a score is partly determined by historical processes and is itself subject to varying perceptions on the part of the receiver. An example of this is furnished by Philip's comparison of recent recordings of Elgar's 'Nimrod' with the composer's own:

> Most modern performances of 'Nimrod' are much slower than Elgar's and therefore also substantially slower than the metronome marking ... The obvious explanation is that this music has become associated with funerals and ceremonies of remembrance. These sombre religious overtones cannot have been in Elgar's mind when he wrote it ... The lack of elegiac character in the variation is confirmed in his recording. But it is difficult for the modern conductor to escape the weight of this tradition. (Philip 2004: 145)

In other words, most modern performances of 'Nimrod' are heard to represent authorial design somewhat differently from the way in which it is presented by the author himself. Philip seeks a historical explanation, the implication being that such performances appear to 'leave the *mens auctoris* behind them' (Gadamer 1977 [1964]: 103).

Proper or 'singular' names, such as 'Elgar', have sometimes been thought of as *non-connotative* (denotative) because they 'are attached to the objects themselves, and are not dependent on the continuance of any attribute of the object' (Mill 1961 [1843]: 20). This, however, ignores the performance traditions that have developed around a composer's legacy, which have thereby become connotative musical attributes. Authorship (score) therefore embraces both denotative and connotative characteristics, and partially conforms to Kripke's idea of inheritance: 'When the name is "passed from link to link" the receiver of the name must, I think, intend when he learns it to use it with the same reference as the man from whom he heard it' (Kripke 1981 [1972]: 96). Learning the cluster of reference points surrounding a composer's name is certainly an important factor where connotation is concerned, but perhaps one should not forget the 'Chinese whispers' effect which Meyer (1956) designates as 'deviation'. So, in the present case, the referent is not just the name-bearer but the canon of evolving performance conventions (or 'deviations') too. This is, of course, truer if the name is an established one. Whilst most musicians are likely to have a fairly clear idea of what to expect from a score if the composer's name is Field, Franck or Fauré, even if not knowing a particular piece, they are far less likely to conceive, in advance of performance, a musical signature if the name is Farjeon, Farkas or Fock.

Authorship (score) presents a special case because a composer's name will paradoxically conjure up both broader and narrower expectations than any of the other informants. Expectations will be broader because a composer's *œuvre* will encompass many or all of the other informant categories to a greater or lesser extent. For example, the name 'Scriabin' is far more likely to generate an expectation of complex cross-rhythms (see 'characterizers', below) than is the name 'Mozart', but the first movement of Mozart's Sonata in F major K332 reveals that he, too, can compose cross-rhythms. On the other hand, expectations are narrowed because the composer's *œuvre* also represents a discrete body of work. Most informed listeners and performers will have an empirically based *a posteriori* conception of those authorial traits which are particular to one composer, but which are unlikely to be replicated in another. Haydn does not speak 'the language of his craft' (Stravinsky 1998 [1942]: 70) in the same way that Mozart does.

Category 3 – Genre

Musical labels corresponding to a sonic conception such as 'sonata', 'concerto' or 'symphonic poem' have a delimiting relationship to an *opus*, pressing an idea 'down … into the type belonging to a class' (Busoni 1965 [1907]: 87–8). Such designations are tokens of the type (or 'class') *genre*, which is the next informant in my categorial sequence. These reified concepts are the products of a creative authorial act at some point in time and so the genre informant, reliant as it is on the

Constructing a Framework 35

two fundamental categories discussed so far, establishes a new level in the tower framework. Its conceptual field is also broad.

Like most tokens, the above labels can themselves become types subject to further tokenizations. The word 'symphony' could suggest a Mozartian, a Brucknerian or a Webernian type, despite the strongly contrasted connotations. Even if the process were to be limited by adding the qualifier 'Romantic' or even 'Late Romantic', the roughly contemporary examples of Brahms's Fourth Symphony and Mahler's Second, *The Resurrection*, present widely different realizations of the now further qualified genre. Both Kripke's cluster theory, outlined earlier in this chapter, and Wittgenstein's notion that a 'word must have a family of meanings' (Wittgenstein 1978 [1953]: 36) seem of particular relevance in this context.

A generic title, such as 'sonata', in its Classical or post-Classical manifestations may not convey the specifics of performance delivery but will probably suggest to both performer and performance analyst an interpretative scenario that is unlikely to be the same as that suggested by, say, the title 'prelude'. The proportional and structural associations of 'sonata' are now so well established that, in performance, one may typically expect to hear a piece of significant duration, in which the performer pays heed to the main architectural cues, but in such a way as to bring the compositional elements into a cohesive whole. Once the genre is contextualized by the era (style) informant, and a descriptor such as 'Classical' or 'neo-Classical' is introduced, the very broad commonality of expectation is at once narrowed and a greater number – though by no means all – of the defining elements are identified. For example, the notion of a typical Classical sonata is likely to suggest a non-virtuoso piece, requiring a balancing of elements and textures to produce a reading of structural cohesion, poise and refinement, perhaps reflecting the 'logical coherence' (Rosen 1971: 57) of the style.

A title alone can therefore begin to raise performance expectations before any more detailed instructions are considered. Expectations will rely on connotations of, say, the name 'Mozart' allied to the genre 'sonata' and the era 'Classical'. Such anticipation can be further illustrated by the genre, 'variations', which also carries with it a set of acquired connotations. As the genre designation corresponds to a work that is going to reveal the creative potential latent in a (usually) short stretch of music, one may reasonably expect that a performer will sense the significance of the task to be undertaken. This response is likely to be reinforced if set against a backdrop of the 'weighty' and most frequently performed examples of the genre such as Bach's *Goldberg Variations*, Beethoven's *Eroica Variations* – described as 'marking an epoch in the history of the variation form ... in the position of the epic poem' (Tovey 1969 [1939]: 31) – the same composer's *Thirty Three Variations on a Waltz by Diabelli*,[9] Brahms's *Variations and Fugue on a Theme by Handel* and, a little more recently, Rachmaninov's *Variations on a Theme of Corelli*.

---

[9]   As Alfred Brendel has pointed out, most of Beethoven's sets of variations are little known and 'do not conform to the concept of Beethoven the Olympian' and that many retain 'the casualness and spontaneity of an improvisation' (1976: 17). He does, however,

If a major set of variations carries 'serious' credentials, then to combine this with a fugue, as does Brahms in his Handel set, may considerably reinforce the respectful attitude likely to be detected in a performance. This attitude can be found in the words of Denis Matthews when he refers to 'Brahms's conscientious attitude to variations' and the fugue's 'solid musical thought with no flamboyance or easy effect' (Matthews 1972: 11–13). The fugue also traditionally presents particular interpretative and technical problems for a performer, involving clarity of part-playing, translucence of texture and an 'academic' frame of mind.[10] Heinrich Christoph Koch cites fugal writing as an example of the *learned style* and in his *Musikalisches Lexicon* (2001 [1802]) records a series of characteristics which define the *strict* style, concluding with the observation that 'the strict style is best suited for church music ... the fugue is the principal product of this style' (Ratner 1980: 23). Although Koch is allowing the fugue an independent existence, his association of the genre with church music reinforces the idea of sobriety and correctness. A title such as *Variations and Fugue on a Theme by Handel*, even to one who is ignorant of the work, could therefore imply a certain frame of mind and manner of approach, even if the title does not convey interpretative detail.

Category 4 – Topic

A fourth category is the *topic*, a musical type often associated with a particular function (such as a dance, a march or a fanfare) and recognizable by certain related characteristics. A pioneer in investigating the role of topics in the Classical context[11] was Leonard Ratner, although his investigations have subsequently been expanded by Robert Hatten (1994), Robert Samuels (1995) and Raymond Monelle (2000) to embrace topical function in nineteenth- and early twentieth-century music, and by Esti Sheinberg (2000), who applies topic theory to the music of Shostakovich.

With reference to such musical types as those listed above, Ratner seeks to identify how these operate in a Classical art music setting, and to investigate how they work as expressive devices within this context. There is a parallel here with one of the implications of Aristotle's *allotrios* or 'alien name', which is that of borrowing. As Paul Ricoeur summarizes: 'The displaced meaning comes from

---

concede that this is not true of the 'masterpieces' such as the *Diabelli* and *Eroica* sets. These are also the most well known and frequently played, hence their relevance to the current discussion.

[10] This is not to deny that there are examples of 'good-humoured' fugues from the Baroque (for example the concluding movement of Bach's French Suite in G major BWV 816) but, as with the lighter sets of variations, they tend not to be featured in (piano) recital programmes with any regularity.

[11] Raymond Monelle argues that the most characteristic topics of Ratner's theory 'break the bounds of the eighteenth century and affect much recent, not to speak of older, music' (Monelle 2000: 30).

somewhere else; it is always possible to specify the metaphor's place of origin or of borrowing' (Ricoeur 2000 [1975]: 19).[12] Ratner illustrates this musical displacement as follows:

> From its contact with worship, poetry, drama, entertainment, dance, ceremony, the military, the hunt and the life of the lower classes, music in the early 18th century developed a thesaurus of *characteristic figures*, which formed a rich legacy for classic composers. Some of these figures were associated with various feelings and affections; others had a picturesque flavour. They are designated here as *topics* – subjects for musical discourse. (Ratner 1980: 9)

Ratner divides his topics into 'types', which are 'fully worked out pieces' (mainly dances) and 'styles' which he identifies as 'figures and progressions within a piece' (9). Robert Hatten (1994) broadly adopts the same paradigm from which to develop his semiotic hermeneutics in Beethoven, but Raymond Monelle extends topicality to include the Wagnerian leitmotif (Monelle 2000: 41). Michael Klein, who views topics as intertextual constructs,[13] simultaneously condenses and broadens their scope by describing the topic as simply 'a code of communication' (Klein 2005: 58). Although this presents a concise definition, in practice the topic can now embrace anything from *Sturm und Drang* to a tarantella–horse hybrid (56), so that what 'begins by pointing to meaning ... ends by scattering meaning' (62).

Ratner, Hatten, Monelle and, to a large extent, Klein discuss topic from the perspective of the work, rather than from that of the performer or informed listener. However, if topics offer composers the means for a musical discourse, then their presence in a composition may be amenable to projection and further elaboration in performance. Thus to ensure that the topic informant in my interpretative framework points to rather than scatters meaning for the analyst, I will build it around Ratner's 'types', leaving 'styles' to be subsumed by other informant categories, as appropriate. This locates topic, as a fully worked-out piece or episode, on the same hierarchical level within the tower as genre. The delimitation of topical reference also provides, as with genre, some general clues as to an anticipated manner of performance.

Advice concerning an appropriate manner of performance features in one of Ratner's sources for his list of topics. In Part Four of Daniel Gottlob Türk's *Klavierschule*, the author enumerates 'Various Dances and Other Smaller Compositions' (Türk 1982 [1789]: 393) and, as his book is a treatise on playing

---

[12]   Roger Scruton's view (1999 [1997]) that all musical language deals in metaphor, that musical lines, high sounds or low sounds and the like do not actually occupy physical space, concerns a different species of trope which could be thought of as conceptual metaphor or 'metaphor as model' (Spitzer 2004: 92). In the case of topics, the metaphorical aspect has more in common with 'poetics ... metaphor as figure' (92).

[13]   Klein (2005) describes topics as intertextual because of their consistent, transhistorical presence in multiple texts, through which they acquire a code status.

rather than composing or musical form, it is significant that Türk provides instructions as to how these topics should be played. For example the musette should be played in 'a very beguiling and legato manner' whereas the sarabande 'requires ... a rather slow tempo in addition to heavy execution'. Lack of conformity to what Türk perceived to be the correct topical manner of execution no doubt led to his censorious comment that: 'In some regions the minuet is played much too fast when it is not used for the dance' (395–6). Such comments can join other era-related reference points whereby the analyst may assess topicality in performance.

As the above passage implies, topicality, be it compositional or performative, will on many occasions be signalled by a name – often that of a dance – at the head of the score. This is regularly the case with the German Baroque suite in particular, a genre that consistently interfaces with topics. In other settings the topic is not specified anywhere in the score but is implicit in the writing. The implications may correspond to one of a range of 'schemata' which are 'congruent ... with prevalent stylistic ... constraints, are memorable, tend to remain stable over time, and are therefore replicated with particular frequency' (Meyer 1989: 51). For example, the siciliano topic is not specified anywhere in the text of the second movement of Haydn's Sonata in F major HobXVI/23, yet its presence can be felt throughout. Instances of topicality can be detected either by reading through the score and experiencing the result internally or by playing and listening to the music, thence connecting the data to an *a posteriori* knowledge of the relevant schema. In many instances the notational appearance is in itself sufficient for an experienced musician to deduce a topic.

Category 5 – Topical Mode

Closely allied to topical matters are performance qualifiers which appeal to the imagination (*maestoso*, *dolce*) or the emotions (*espressivo*, *agitato*) but do not specifically instruct concerning tempo or articulation (although are obviously intimately connected, as are topics). Their scope is wide, ranging from very generalized directions such as the *quasi Recitativo* at the opening of Liszt's first Hungarian Rhapsody to the relatively specific *quasi Tromboni* found in Busoni's arrangement of Bach's Chaconne BWV 1004. They are symbols of the inner life or 'field of tension' (Brendel 1976: 40) of a composition and are therefore, in the context of the interpretative tower, also dependent on the previous four informants. Directed to the performer as a means by which to mould the eventual soundscape of the music, they may also be projected in performance and heard by the analyst as evidence of yet further musical discourse. They may be perceived as aids in the formation of an artistic structure, pointing away from a 'sonic *Urtext*' literalism. By supplying a *topical mode*, the composer is issuing an instruction to the performer for a *modus operandi* which can convey to the listener the expressive (in its broadest sense) qualities implicit in the music. So these topical modes form a fifth informant category and, with their further shift towards performer agency, move into a third hierarchical level.

Gottlob Frege required a word or expression to have an extra property in addition to its sense, or *sinn*. This he called '*Färbung*' ('colour' or 'tone') and described it, according to Michael Dummett, as 'the association with a word or expression of ... mental images ... tone [is] a feature of meaning that [is] in principle, subjective' (Dummett 1981 [1973]: 85). Dummett develops a robust criticism of Frege's thinking but the concept is useful in the present context. Topical modes do suggest images of which the musical community has a more-or-less agreed understanding but, because they depend more on an interpreter's perception and 'reading' of these images than on easily measurable commodities, the 'tone' of the word becomes even more important in this category than semantic precision. Here, topical mode implies a 'tone', the exact understanding and interpretation of which will almost certainly differ from one member of the musical community to another.

The tone may also be deduced from the music alone because topical modes may be hidden. To borrow Storr's linguistic analogy (1997 [1992]) once more, the development of 'prosody' from 'syntax' is especially likely to be observed in performances of pre-Classical music. A particular relationship with the first informant, era (style), arises here because instrumental scores written prior to approximately the middle of the eighteenth century rarely carry topical mode instructions. However, it is perfectly possible to regard an artist's interpretation of a passage as, for example, *doloroso* without having to link this to an explicit indication in the score. For Liszt, the second theme of Chopin's Scherzo No. 1 Op. 20 invited a 'very *cantabile*' delivery (Zimdars 1996: 119) and, presumably wishing this to be heard in performance, he had no hesitation in communicating the idea to his pupil, Luisa Cognetti, despite no written authorial sanction.

Earlier, I explained how the title *Variations and Fugue on a Theme by Handel* can trigger performance expectations. Having moved further into the list of informants, we can now, perhaps, appreciate why a designation such as 'Chopin's *Grande Polonaise Brillante*' carries so much initial performance information.[14] Its references touch all five of the informants so far described. The references to authorship and era are clear, but there are also references to topic (and by implication the genre of dance-based rondo type) and topical mode. *Polonaise*, a metre-and-manner-carrying topic, is allied to *brillante* and *grande*, which, as performance qualifiers, are topical modes. It is therefore reasonable to expect that the piece will be executed predominantly or exclusively in triple metre, in a typically defined rhythm; it is unlikely to be very long (genre allied to authorship) but will make technical demands, almost certainly of the more obviously 'showy' kind. Some flamboyance in performing manner is implied by the term '*brillante*'.

---

[14] Exceptionally the title can have the opposite effect and, indeed, be misleading. The title *Six Dances*, by the little-known Turkish-Armenian composer Komitas, does nothing to prepare the prospective performer or listener for the orientally flavoured quasi-improvisations which follow.

As suggested above, the informant categories are now moving from those that could be regarded as more-or-less objective 'facts' into areas in which the imagination would seem to be more obviously and directly engaged. The philosopher Schopenhauer sees imagination as extending the intellectual horizon 'both in quality and quantity ... beyond the objects which actually present themselves' (Schopenhauer 2004 [1819]: 110) and Roger Scruton develops this thought by suggesting that 'imaginative perception ... involves voluntary interpretation' (Cook 1992 [1990]: 19). The faculty of voluntary interpretation closely connects with responses to topical modes, and the remaining informants likewise tend to rely on this faculty. The next informant, however, still has a clear link with apparent syntactical elements within a work, although performances may be heard to translate these elements into sound in imaginative ways.

Category 6 – Characterizer

The next category is determined by distinctive musical features such as rhythmic, melodic or harmonic devices which give a stretch of music its unique character. I will therefore use the term *characterizer* for this informant. The musical phrase, the sequence, the false relation, the unexpected harmonic twist, the cross-rhythm and all manner of rhythmic devices are examples of this category. All are highly contextual in that they are dependent on timing and placement within a work. For this reason, the informant is one of the broadest and least subject to precise definition, covering most areas not included in other categories. Yet characterizers can play a vital role in determining the aurally discernible, or 'surface', features of a performance.

It could be argued that, in many cases, no particular gesture need be made to highlight a characterizer for its effect to be apparent in performance. For example, the hemiolas in bars 41–42 and 55 in Brahms's Intermezzo Op. 119/3 would almost certainly be heard whether the pianist consciously recognizes the compositional technique or not. However, the performance analyst may discern an apparent knowledge and appreciation of the relevant technique on the part of a performer if obvious measures to highlight it are taken. In the case of the Brahms Intermezzo, Moura Lympany, in her 1974 recording, makes a subtle adjustment of tempo in bars 41–42, thus underlining the hemiolas, whereas Stephen Kovacevich's 1968 account makes no such concessions. Admittedly, Lympany's task is facilitated by her overall tempo which is somewhat faster than Kovacevich's and allows her more room for the successful application of a minute *ritardando*.

A certain amount of analytical thought, such as that discussed in Chapter 1, is required for the identification of a characterizer. Where large-scale formal analysis as reflected in performance is related to the genre informant, characterizers concern microstructural features and how a performer may or may not be heard to bring these out.

Constructing a Framework 41

Category 7 – Tempo

The *tempo* category is one through which the performer's active engagement with an informant may be acoustically identified, so this informant belongs to a fourth (and final) hierarchical level. Along with the next two informants, this one functions as a 'terminus' in my conceptual progress from work to performance and needs no further categorial agency for the transmission of a performer's interpretation to a listener.

Gabrielsson and Lindström write that '[a]mong factors affecting emotional expression in music, tempo is usually considered the most important' (Gabrielsson and Lindström 2002 [2001]: 235). Stephen Davies goes further and suggests that a misplaced tempo can undermine a work's integrity. He cites as an example the admittedly exaggerated case of a 'performance' which adopts a tempo of 'crotchet = five years' and decides that this is 'failing to instance the work ... a non-performance' (Davies 2001: 59). Whether the informant is viewed philosophically or practically, it is a crucial aspect of musical information and a defining feature of any performance, including its emotional effect. The range of tempo instructions at a composer's disposal can therefore cohere as a seventh informant category, *tempo*.

A tempo heading, such as '*allegro*', as with the other informants, lacks a fixed semantic referent and has been defined in a number of subtly varying ways.[15] This could be why composers began to qualify the term to convey more accurately not only their desired tempo but also a manner and style of performance. Tempo descriptors thus frequently conjoin with topical modes to suggest both pace and character (*allegro vivace, andante espressivo*). In Mozart's keyboard sonatas, *allegro* first movements are variously qualified as *allegro assai* (K 280), *allegro con spirito* (K 309, 311), *allegro maestoso* (K 310), *molto allegro* (K 457), but plain *allegro* remains the norm. The opening movements to Beethoven's piano sonatas show many more nuances of tempo, and amongst other instructions are *allegro vivace* (Op. 2/2, 31/1), *allegro con brio* (Op. 2/3, 22), *allegro molto e con brio* (Op. 4, 10/1), *allegro assai* (Op. 57), *vivace ma non troppo* (Op. 109) and *allegro con brio ed appassionato* (Op. 111). For the first movement of the relatively slight E minor sonata Op. 90, the performer is instructed to play *Mit Lebhaftigkeit und durchaus mit Empfindung und Ausdruck*.[16]

In spite of this growing detail of tempo and topical mode connoted by the opening heading, performers can be heard to produce, according to musical understanding and (applied) technique, significantly different responses to the

---

[15] See Chapter 3.

[16] The desire for greater control over the performance life of his music is probably what led Beethoven to welcome the metronome. The *Wiener Vaterländische Blätter* of 13 October 1813 announced that 'Herr Beethoven looks upon this invention as a welcome means ... to secure the performance of his compositions ... in the tempos intended for them, which he regrets is so frequently lacking' (Rosenblum 1991 [1988]: 323).

42   *Reading Musical Interpretation*

information provided. Because it is not possible to be prescriptive as to an exact meaning, the terms under consideration are guides, yielding concepts which occupy a theoretical middle ground but whose field of operation can be quite broad. Davies believes that a work's tempo presents 'a range of possibilities to the performer. The tempo of a given work might lie within the range of 70–90 crotchets per minute, for instance' (2001: 59).[17]

This concept can be illustrated by examining performances of the opening to Beethoven's *Waldstein* Sonata Op. 53. As with its earlier C major companion, Beethoven asks for *allegro con brio* (tempo plus topical mode). *Brio* has been variously defined as 'spirit, vigour and force' (Stainer and Barrett 1898), 'vigour' (ABRSM 1958) and 'vigour, spirit, fire' (Kennedy 1991 [1980]), to mention a few. Despite the various historical positionings of these definitions, all are roughly in agreement, so one could reasonably expect that different interpretations would share some common ground. A comparison of three recordings, all made within a few years of each other during the 1950s, produces some interesting results. Claudio Arrau takes the music at crotchet = *c.* 119 in a near-*legato* reading, lightly pedalled. The performance suggests that the pianist wishes to underplay *con brio* elements in favour of bringing out the rising melodic contours of the music. Even the *acciaccatura* is slightly prolonged and softened to make the music sound more lyrical. Wilhelm Kempff adopts crotchet = *c.* 132, producing an altogether more detached account. With its lightly percussive approach and lack of pedal, rhythm predominates over melody. Solomon, at crotchet = *c.* 146, is more percussive still and his fast tempo seems linked to his perception of the music's dynamic contour in that the *crescendo* marked in the score at bar 9 starts a bar early and reaches its peak by bar 9, whereas the peak indicated by Beethoven is at bar 11. Nevertheless, by any criterion, the opening is played with force, fire and vigour. All three performers are responding to the same performance information, so their respective tempos helpfully illustrate the breadth of field that I mentioned above, in this case as it relates to *allegro con brio*.

The *Waldstein* Sonata's first movement establishes a reasonably clear tempo field, but a tempo field is harder to establish in earlier music where authorial guidelines are absent as, for example, in the first movement of Bach's Brandenburg Concerto No. 3 BWV 1048. In instances such as this, tradition and musical instinct may be appropriate guides but they can be supplemented by other aids as well. These include genre, harmonic rhythm, musical syntax, time signature and specified or unspecified topic. In connection with the latter, relevant treatises may be of help. Concerning the march, for example, Türk instructs: 'A march must be played in a tempo that is moderate enough to allow for two steps in each measure (4/4 measure); in alla breve only one step falls on each measure' (Türk

---

[17]   Ranges of tempo latitude may exceed those suggested by Davies. For example, Peter Johnson (2002) cites performances by the Flonzaley Quartet (1927) and the Busch Quartet (1934) of the *Lento assai* movement from Beethoven's String Quartet in F major Op. 135. The former open the movement at quaver = 58, the latter at quaver = 32.

1982 [1789]: 396) and from Quantz: 'A *tambourin* is played like a bourrée or rigaudon, only a little faster' (Quantz 2001 [1752]: 291). Perhaps the final word can be left to C.P.E. Bach, who gives this advice: 'the pace of a composition is based on its general content as well as on the fastest notes and passages contained in it' (Bach 1949 [1753]: 151). Nevertheless, it is safe to expect a broader tempo field in much pre-Classical music than in music from later eras.

Category 8 – Duration Manipulator

Closely associated with the tempo category is the *duration manipulator* informant. A performer may have made a choice concerning tempo but most performances demonstrate that this pace will not be accorded metronomic adherence throughout an entire stretch of music, especially from the Classical period onwards when contrasting affects are often juxtaposed within the same movement. This was recognized by Türk, who advises on instances where tempo can be expressively modified. In his *Klavierschüle* (1789), he identifies points at which appropriate manipulation might occur:

> Sometimes, when gentle feelings are interrupted by a lively passage, the latter can be played somewhat more rapidly … A tenderly moving passage between two lively and fiery thoughts … can be executed in a somewhat hesitating manner; but in this case, the tempo is not taken gradually slower, but *immediately* a little slower (however, only a *little*). Compositions in which two characters of opposite types are represented, especially provide a suitable opportunity for a gradual slowing of the tempo. (Türk 1982 [1789]: 360–61)

Fifty years later, Beethoven's pupil and Liszt's teacher, Karl Czerny, writes in a similar vein, advising that

> we must consider it as a rule, always to play each piece of music … in the time prescribed by the Author, and first fixed upon by the Player [*sic*]. But without injury to this maxim, there occurs in almost every line some notes or passages, where a small and often imperceptible relaxation of the movement is necessary, to embellish the expression and increase the interest. To introduce these occasional deviations from the strict keeping of the time in a tasteful and intelligible manner, is the great art of a good player. (Czerny 1839: 31)

Commentaries such as these indicate that affective changes were expected even though a score contains no instructions other than a general tempo heading. Durational changes start to receive more regular definition in the sonatas of Beethoven where a few localized instructions begin to appear: both *rallentando* and *ritardando* occur in the sonatas Op. 2/2 (first movement) and Op. 2/3 (last movement). Whilst such changes 'can be used to indicate the group structure of the music' (Clarke 2000 [1988]: 17), another, less structure-led function is their application as *rubato*, those '[c]hanges of tempo during the course of continuous music' (Hudson 1994: 4). It is this concept that occupies a focal position within the duration manipulator informant.

Directions for *rubato* do occasionally appear in scores, sometimes as a general indication of the work's overall manner of delivery (*languido e rubato* at the start of Chopin's Nocturne in G minor Op. 15/3), and sometimes more locally (*poco rubato* in bar 26^{3-4} of the Nocturne in E♭ Op. 9/2). Interestingly, in the E♭ nocturne, many pianists can be heard to apply *rubato* to the right-hand filigree of places such as bars 13–16 where no suggestion of tempo modification appears in the text, indicating that intuition, our 'educated discriminatory capacity' (Cumming 2000: 55) may, in practice, be a stronger influence than a written instruction. A number of factors may be read into a performer's use of *rubato* in a case such as this: a desire to give each note its full expressive value, not necessarily achieved in a Romantic context through metronomic adherence; engagement with the musical discourse which suggests a modification of the basic pulse to achieve expressive contouring; highlighting of a perceived structural point; promotion of technical clarity; acknowledgement of an inherited tradition. Maybe it is factors such as these which 'embellish the expression and increase the interest' and which in performance can reflect 'the great art of a good player'.

Czerny's ideas concerning *rubato* (implied if not named) as a freely expressive device, as opposed to the 'robbed time' expounded by pedagogues such as Türk and Tosi,[18] is more in accord with later 'romantic' practices in which 'performers … felt they had a right, if not a duty, to apply all manner of rhythmic flexibilities' (Hudson 1994: 300). Hudson's observation may help to account for Paderewski's response to the earlier theory of stealing and restoring time: 'We duly acknowledge the high moral motives of this theory, but we humbly confess that our ethics do not reach such a high level … The value of notes diminished in one period through an accelerando cannot always be returned in another by a ritardando. What is lost is lost' (Schonberg 1987 [1963]: 292).

Hudson notes that later twentieth-century performers have tended to 'reject excessive personal interpretation in favour of fidelity to the musical score' from which he surmises that 'new concepts of time and rhythm' have led to 'a far greater adherence to strict tempo' (Hudson 1994: 356). This more disciplined approach is reflected by Alan Fraser, who even suggests that a basic 'rubato strategy' can be systematically acquired 'to lend integrity to … spontaneity' thus 'enhanc[ing] expression by following rather than contravening the basic rules of declamation' (Fraser 2003: 323). The duration manipulator informant needs, therefore,

---

[18] Pier Francesco Tosi was the first writer to use the term '*rubato*', in his singing treatise *Opinioni de' cantori antichi e moderni* (1987 [1723]). *Rubato*, though not named as such, is referred to in treatises from the sixteenth and seventeenth centuries, indicating that the practice was already widespread by Tosi's time. David Epstein (1995) suggests that Tosi's requirement for accompaniments to be kept in time was a reaction to the excessive use of *rubato* by singers in early Italian opera.

to accommodate the way that performers may be heard to adopt expressive modifications to notated timings, reflecting their position within what Philip dubs 'the rhythmic environment of their time' (2004: 132).

Category 9 – Sonic Moderator

Terms such as '*forte*', '*piano*', '*staccato*' and '*legato*' and those related to pedalling are now so entrenched in the language of piano technique that they have come to connote sonic ideals to which performers can aspire and which informed listeners can recognize. They reflect the means by which an individual can experience the 'intimate relation between physical effort and expression' (Rosen 2002: 20). Symptomatically, comments like 'hasn't he got a magnificent *fortissimo*?' or 'doesn't her *staccato* dance?' use not only dynamic and articulative descriptors, but also imply personal possession, as if one pianist's *fortissimo* or *staccato* were not interchangeable with another's. This last category, *sonic moderator*, therefore intimates an especially individual quality.

This individual quality may be derived from the fact that a player's dynamic and articulative capacity is rooted in technique. Because technique is so intimately connected with physique, it is perhaps not surprising that each performer's engagement with this informant is, to some extent at least, anatomically predetermined. Hand structure, finger length, muscular strength and limb co-ordination all play their part in how a particular sound is produced and it is probably these physical properties, intrinsic to each pianist, that enable the informed listener to differentiate one player from another. Christopher Wynn Parry describes these physical individualities as 'antecedent factors' which include 'differences in basic anatomy and in how pianists engage physically with the instruments' (Wynn Parry 2004: 51). Rosen also stresses the importance of anatomical considerations: 'Not only the individual shape of the hand counts but even the whole corporal shape … Glenn Gould sat close to the floor while Artur Rubinstein was almost standing up … Shura Cherkassky decided on the piano he wanted in five minutes, but spent twenty minutes trying out different stools' (Rosen 2002: 3). The respective sound qualities associated with Rubinstein, Arrau, Kempff or Richter were defining features of their performing styles and were certainly not interchangeable. Kempff's most powerful *fortissimo* in Beethoven's *Appassionata* was no match for Richter's, and Arrau's intense melodic projection in Chopin could not be confused with the simple lucidity of Rubinstein. This category probably involves the notion of applied technique, discussed earlier, more than any other and is also one to which I, as a pianist, can bring my inside knowledge of the physical aspects of piano playing and their related sonic outcomes.

Questions of technique, applied technique in particular, have prompted many responses from pianists themselves. For example, Arrau is quoted as follows: 'The idea is to become one with the instrument. Not to have the piano as a dead thing in front of you to be *attacked*. Of course, sometimes you need power, and you must make the instrument produce it. But one must not brutalise the piano' (Horowitz

1999 [1982]: 100). For John Browning, '[i]t isn't Horowitz's technique; it is his sound. Schnabel had a certain kind of sound; Horowitz has a certain kind of sound. Technique isn't a matter of how quickly you can play scales; it's the ability to produce many different sounds. *That* constitutes the highest ideal of technique' (Mach 1981: 40). Vladimir Horowitz himself seems to agree: 'You see that piano over in the corner? That instrument is capable of sounds which are loud and soft; but in between there are many, many degrees of sounds which may be played. To be able to produce many varieties of sound, now that is what I call technique' (Mach 1981: 117). And Alicia de Larrocha thinks similarly: 'Beyond the mere mechanics, you have the real meaning of technique. It is sound, interpretation, tone and musical line' (Mach 1981: 61).

The varieties of sound the above pianists describe usually occur in Western art performance in response to some form of score-based information. Composers have provided specifications for dynamics and articulation in varying degrees for the last three hundred years or more, typically supplying growing levels of such performance direction from the second half of the eighteenth century on. This trend is designedly reflected in the forthcoming case studies but, when negotiating between score and performance, the analyst may need to bear in mind that 'it has always been the performer's responsibility to introduce those subtle, largely unnotatable dynamic inflections, whatever the style or period' (Lawson and Stowell 1999: 53).

Step Seven: The Analytical Framework

All the categories discussed in Step Six describe species of information relevant to performance through which the analyst may read an interpretation. The analyst can thus relate what Thom describes as the 'datum of a piece of interpretation' to the 'datum-as-interpreted' (Thom 1993: 93). As such, the term 'informant' has been used as a general designation for the individually specified categories. However, not all informants will yield either the same type or amount of information. As has been suggested, some will appear as objective 'facts' with which a practitioner can be thought to engage ideally whilst others seem to supply a great deal of acoustic data with which the performer can be heard to engage executively. Levinson sees this range of performance data as a 'continuum of concerns' which travels from the 'reconstructive' to the 'realizational' (Levinson 1993: 35). A conceptual framework may now be constructed which particularizes this continuum into a hierarchy of informants, demonstrating which of them are fundamental and which are supported by these fundamentals but become progressively of greater practical relevance in the formation of an interpretative synthesis as heard by the informed listener. This hierarchical framework is shown in the diagram at Figure 2.2. To reflect the essentially interactive nature of this hierarchy, I shall cease to number the informants but will retain the notion of four hierarchical levels.

Having introduced the tower framework, a brief description of how this may helpfully be thought to interface with a performer's interpretation is now due. The performance is likely to demonstrate awareness of era and related stylistic issues as well as of a particular composer's 'signature'. Both are fundamental concerns and thus form level one of the interpretative tower, which additionally supports and infiltrates all upper levels. Genre and topic at level two are dependent upon a composer having written them in the first place, their nature also being determined by the era in which they were composed, although topic, according to my adopted delimitation, may not always be a presence. These informants provide a basis for performance analysis, yielding signposts for an emerging interpretation. At level three, topical mode is reliant upon the setting of genre and topic for perceptions of mood, manner, affect and effect. Characterizers, as compositional techniques, also require the setting of genre or topic for their specific operation. As they may help to shape the next interpretative stratum, they share the same hierarchical level with topical mode.

executive

Tempo **level four**	Duration manipulator	Sonic moderator
Topical mode **level three**	Characterizer	
Genre **level two**	Topic	
Era (style) **level one**	Authorship (score)	

ideal

Tempo, duration manipulator and sonic moderator form level four.
Topical mode and characterizer form level three.
Genre and topic form level two.
Era (style) and authorship (score) form level one.

Figure 2.2   The interpretative tower

At the top of the structure, level four, come those informants that engage most directly with a performer's acoustic formations: tempo, duration manipulator and sonic moderator, where the personal choice and physical involvement of the performer are most obviously reflected. Since these informants interact with the production of the actual sound, its rate of motion through time and localized tempo fluctuations, all the lower layers of the structure feed into this uppermost one, and it is at this level that the relationship with those beneath becomes aurally manifest. In other words, the top-layer informants generate the 'surface' properties of a performance.

In performance, an interrelationship and dynamic flow between the various informants is perceived, yet the visual nature of the tower framework inevitably imposes a certain fixity. Although interpretation does not occur in a series of discrete and orderly steps, all analytical methods need a measure of stability to support their effective operation. In this sense, my method shares common ground with existing systems of musical work analysis, all of which identify stable features within works, thus enabling analytical practicability.

Step Eight: The Interpretative Tower in Operation

The next step shows how the visual nature of the interpretative tower framework enables a visual representation of a performance. By translating a soundscape into a 'picture', by converting the diachronic into the synchronic, it is possible to see at a glance what takes a little longer to digest and appreciate when propounded by words alone. Also, where interpretations are being compared and contrasted, the visual representations, by offering immediate access, render the comparisons more easily assimilable. The visual representations are generated by and therefore essentially linked to a musical performance, and it may be that they are an appropriate alternative to less succinct verbal descriptions. As will be demonstrated, they also integrate the analytical findings with the interpretative tower framework in a summative way.

An example of how a visual representation of a performance may be shown in graphic form, according to the tower framework, will illustrate the analytical system. Pianist X's hypothetical performance of the third movement of a nineteenth-century piano sonata shows strongly marked rhythmic properties (duration manipulator) and some idiosyncratic dynamics, not all marked in the score (sonic moderator), plus carefully chosen speeds (tempo). These can be traced back to the characterizer (say, an early second beat in a waltz) and a topical mode (for example, *grazioso*) which also seem to connect with some of the dynamic nuancing. These characteristics are supported at the level below by the waltz (topic) and its place as a contrasting movement within a four-movement work (genre). Tempo reduction, highlighting a trio section, also links to structural concerns associated with genre. Most of these features, especially those related to tempo, can be traced back to authorship (score), but also to some influences related to era (style). On reconstruction of these findings in the graph (Figure 2.3), it may be observed that X's performance connects to authorship (score) more strongly than to era (style), but significantly marked duration manipulation and, to a lesser extent, sonic moderation reveal the freer exercise of X's artistic choices. Degrees of informant emphasis observed within the performance are reflected by the relative boldness of the arrows.

An important point to emerge from this example concerns the performer's apparent emphasis of certain constituent parts within the work, by which the performance can be said to derive its special character. X's hypothetical reading apportions the greatest emphasis to tempo and duration manipulator, suggesting a concern with aspects of the work's surface properties, although the analysis as a whole does not imply anything extreme. Other performances could show strong allegiance to the score, suggesting a near-*Texttreue* account, whilst others may temper the 'plain' information in the score with historically derived notions of style. Yet others may take the score as a starting point only, thence to depart from it in radical, possibly 'intuitive' ways.

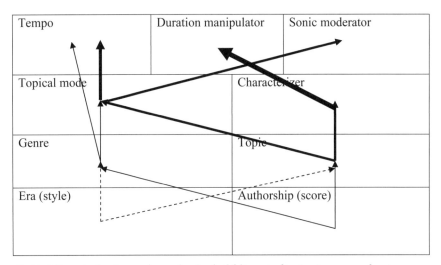

Dotted lines indicate weak emphasis; bold lines indicate strong emphasis.

Figure 2.3   Pianist X's hypothetical performance of the third movement of a nineteenth-century piano sonata mapped onto the interpretative tower

For further illustration, it would be worth returning to the two contrasting styles of performance mentioned earlier in this chapter, now examining them in the context of the tower. In Denis Matthews' recording of the first movement of Beethoven's Sonata in E major Op. 109, the acoustic outcomes seem to have a very strong connection to authorship. This occurs within the context of a British, mid-twentieth-century notion of 'tasteful' stylistic practice, a practice which, according to Schonberg, stems from J.B. Cramer and allies it 'more closely ... to the classical school than to the others' (Schonberg 1987 [1963]: 455). The analysis accordingly shows bold lines stemming from authorship (score) and upwards through genre, thence weakening as the 'executive' end of the axis is approached since the upper-level features seem very largely governed by an artistic commitment to the 'ideal' end (Figure 2.4).

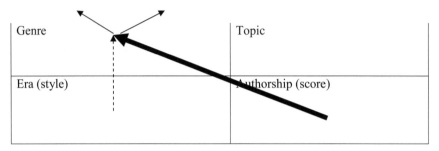

Dotted lines indicate weak emphasis; bold lines indicate strong emphasis.

Figure 2.4   Beethoven: Sonata in E major Op. 109, first movement; interpretation by Denis Matthews, indicating interpretative links to levels one and two in the interpretative tower

In marked contrast to this, the controversial Gould recording of the first movement of Mozart's Sonata in A major K 331 appears to pay heed to authorship (score) only in so far as it is recognizably a performance of Mozart's notation, but in almost no other way, thus demonstrating only very weak links to authorship (score). Links to era (style) seem even more obscure, in that no established convention of performance practice relating to the Classical period, or any other era, is detectable, although Gould himself invoked the compositional methods of Webern (Bazzana 1997: 49–50). Gould's performance appears to be responding largely to a notion of the variation genre and, in developing a personal acoustic structure, an idiosyncratic, quasi twentieth-century style emerges, hence the downward arrow to era (style) in the graph (Figure 2.5). His reading of the genre informant bypasses any suggestion of a pastoral topic in Mozart's score, and produces some strongly marked upper-level features which display freedom and independence (Figure 2.5).

The interpretative tower, then, is an analytical tool by which to trace, through heard evidence, interpretative formations as witnessed in individual performances. It is my belief that the analytical findings and means of structuring these will connect with the experiences of other informed listener–performers, a belief supported by Jonathan Culler's suggestion that 'one's notion of how to read and of what is involved in interpretation are acquired in commerce with others' (Klein 2005: 55).

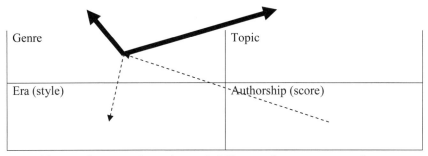

Dotted lines indicate weak emphasis; bold lines indicate strong emphasis.

Figure 2.5   Mozart: Sonata in A major K 331, first movement; interpretation by Glenn Gould, indicating interpretative links to levels one and two in the interpretative tower

Step Nine: Primary and Secondary Interpretation

Having illustrated ways in which the analytical function of the interpretative tower operates, in Step Nine I return to the issue of primary and secondary interpretation, which demands further explanation. Performance analysis involves a three-way negotiation on the part of the listening analyst between knowledge of the relevant score, the acoustic evidence of the performance and the analyst's own reading of this evidence. The analyst's reading of the evidence can be thought of as a 'secondary' interpretative act, epiphenomenal to the 'primary' interpretative act of the performer. It is now possible and appropriate to explain the specific operation of the analyst's role as secondary interpreter within the context of the interpretative tower and thus further define the delicate balance of relationships existing between all parties involved in my analytical system.

Jean-Jacques Nattiez describes the creative urges that precede a composer's production of a score as 'poietic' (from the Greek meaning 'to make') and he claims that 'the esthesic[19] [perceptual] process begins at the instant the performer *interprets* the work (Nattiez 1990 [1987]: 72). Nattiez further accounts for this by suggesting that what I am calling the primary interpretative act, that of the performer, is an extension of the composer's poietic process as well as an esthesic process, both being triggered by the performer's contact with the score (the work's 'trace'). By formalizing this scheme a little more, it is possible to regard the primary interpretative act, through which the work is projected into the performance, as esthesic in relation to the score but poietic in relation to the performance. The acoustic trace made by a performance (the recording) then becomes the analyst's

---

[19]   Nattiez borrows the term 'esthesic' from Paul Valéry (1944) who preferred it to 'aesthetic' 'on sound etymological grounds: the άισθησις was indeed the faculty of perception' (Nattiez 1990 [1987]: 12).

perceptual focus and so the relationship of the latter to the former is esthesic. In parallel with the performer's esthesic/poietic mediation between score and recording, the analyst's esthesic relationship with the recording becomes poietic in relation to the graphic construct as mapped onto the tower framework. Thus the secondary interpretative act is the means by which the recording projects into the graph, or analysis trace. However, the poietic/esthesic duality of the score-to-recording and recording-to-analytical graph processes implies projections both forwards and backwards. One is reminded again of Wittgenstein's law of projection

> by means of which the musician can obtain the symphony from the score, and which makes it possible to derive the symphony from the groove on the gramophone record, and ... to derive the score again. That is what constitutes the inner similarity between these things which seem to be constructed in such entirely different ways. (Wittgenstein 2004 [1921]: 24)

So the performer's primary interpretative act and the analyst's secondary interpretative act project outwards and inwards from and to a common point of reference, the work's trace, or score, thus making meaningful dialogue between the two interpretative acts possible. As listening analyst, I am therefore able in my forthcoming case studies to navigate between the work's trace and the performance trace, and the projection of the latter to and from the former, thereby enabling construction of my own analysis trace.

The acoustic evidence of a recording, level four in the interpretative tower, provides the measurable commodities or objective 'facts' about an interpretation. If when and by whom a work was composed are the objective 'facts' about a work, then this pair of facts represents the polarities of the poietic/esthesic dialogue between the work and the performer. By engaging with the objective facts of a performance – what the performer is actually heard to do – the analyst's poietic/esthesic trialogue can support statements about the performance as a whole, tracing it back to the objective facts about the work. This treats the performance as a free-standing artistic statement, apart from the intentions of the composer or the performing artist other than as perceived by the analyst, thereby avoiding entrapment by the Intentional Fallacy, outlined earlier in this chapter.

More personally, as secondary interpreter, my 'hermeneutical engagement is thoroughly conditioned and mediated by ... historical circumstances' (Coltman 1998: 11) and, as such, I cannot make definitive assertions, based on my own perceptions, about how performances are heard by the wider listening community. Nevertheless, by using recordings as evidence of performers' musical ideas, by drawing on my own performing experience, relevant performance literature and critical reviews, all of which partly depend on those common points of reference of which I wrote in Step Three, I can make supportable statements about how an informed listener in the early twenty-first century may respond to pianists' primary acts of interpretation.

Method

Recordings as Documents for Analysis

There has been a growing trend in recent years to use recorded performances as viable documents for academic research (Bowen 1999; Cook 2007; Johnson 1999, 2002, 2004; Philip 1992, 2004; Rink 1995), probably because they turn what are essentially prospective events into retrospective objects, artworks even, thus in a sense 'fixing' a performance and enabling close scrutiny. This fixity also correlates to some extent with the fixity inherent in graphic depictions, thus further supporting the rationale given under Step Seven above when justifying the use of graphs. In line with this evolving tradition, my own research uses commercial recordings (studio and live) and recordings of my own performances as documents for analysis, through which the efficacy of my interpretative framework may be gauged. The use of personal, live and studio recordings raises some issues which now need to be addressed.

In the case of my own recordings I am uniquely aware of the formative processes that occurred prior to arriving at my final interpretation whereas with the other artists' recordings no such insight is available. An evaluation of one's own recording inevitably involves an analytical bifurcation: on the one hand, the internal means by which an interpretation was formed are intimately known; on the other, the aural experience of the recording, heard objectively, can reveal discrepancies between intention and realization and may also highlight features which were not conscious to the interpreting mind. However, in the context of the interpretative tower, performance analysis via the recording is a more appropriate means of accessing an interpretation than self-analysis because listening to a finished product, a document for all to hear, brings the analytical points of reference for my own and other artists' recordings into some alignment. Useful analysis is necessarily undertaken after the event and, whilst analysis of documents is still not a revealer of objective truths, there is at least some stability. With regard to political analysis, Andrew Heywood suggests that: 'scientific objectivity in the sense of absolute impartiality or neutrality … must always remain an unachievable goal … however rigorous our research methods may be' (Heywood 1997: 17). In an attempt to achieve a measure of 'impartiality or neutrality', my analysis will draw mainly on the audible results of my recordings and observe how these work in the context of the interpretative tower. I will only refer to my intentions where relevant, but will otherwise aim to avoid attributing intention where none can be heard.

It should be mentioned in passing that my recordings are not commercial ones and, as such, lack the technological aids and production techniques of the other CDs. One item was recorded onto a minidisc at a live recital and the other two were recorded privately, in a living-room acoustic, on a Grotrian-Steinweg piano that may give the Brahms performance a period feel. In the latter cases, a small amount of editing took place mainly to remove the most obvious errors. Although the production standard would be unsuitable for commercial release, it is fully adequate to meet the needs of this book.

A live recording, if it has not been unduly tampered with after the event, documents a one-off artistic happening. It represents the artistic will of the performer under a certain set of circumstances, even though these circumstances are liable both to enhance mental alertness and reduce the fine motor control that is achievable in a studio setting. The live performing state is described by Salmon and Meyer: 'To some extent the sensations that are experienced while performing are affected by the degree of autonomic nervous system (ANS) activity. Activation of the ANS results in a preparatory state of alertness in which sensory acuity is enhanced. Performers ... experience a state that psychologists call *hypervigilance*, a heightened state of alertness and perception' (Salmon and Meyer 1992: 58). On the other hand, Andrew Steptoe concedes that, for the 'musician playing in public' a preoccupation with 'task-orientated thoughts ... tend[s] to [increase] the risk of errors in performance' (Steptoe 2002 [2001]: 298–9). Nevertheless, the interpretative impulses underlying both a studio and a live performance given by the same artist at roughly the same time period are likely, at the very least, to be similar. Arrau's studio (1970) and live (1971) recordings of Liszt's Sonata in B minor, for example, are recognizably from the same artist, demonstrating no significant interpretative differences. The former sounds like a very slightly tidier, if less headlong, version of the latter.

It is well known that a studio performance can be as much the result of the production team as of the individual artist/s. Davies believes it to be 'appropriate [that] the musicians are given the latitude to redress errors that occur' (Davies 2001: 193), and it is arguably due to the widespread practice of editing that the listener can be reasonably sure that what is being heard represents an interpretation which matches the performers' (and producers') artistic vision. After a detailed editing session, '[w]hat emerges at the end is a true picture of the musicians' interpretation on the day, but with all the imperfections removed, and the best available option chosen for each part of the work' (Philip 2004: 57). Susan Tomes goes a stage further and suggests that the carefully edited recording is preferable, as a lasting document, to a live one. 'Our record of [Schubert's] E flat Trio will have an accuracy and freshness it doesn't have in concerts, and as a recorded performance will be more enduring as a result' (Tomes 2004: 158–9).

I am assuming in my analyses that both recording styles represent equally valid, if not necessarily equivalent, artistic documents for the listening public. If it seems that a feature on a live recording may be the product of human error whilst in a state of hypervigilance, I will take this into account. However, as I am analysing interpretations rather than technical shortfalls, it is unlikely that this will be a significant consideration.

Constructing a Framework

Gathering the Evidence

Informed listening, as outlined earlier, is crucial to my analytical method, and all the recordings used for analysis were listened to many times over. Whilst listening I took careful notes concerning the surface features of the performances, typically those relating to tempo, timing, *rubato*, articulation, pedalling, dynamic range and nuances. Of these parameters, measurement of tempo demands a special word.

Where the measurement of human timing is concerned, exact metronome readings are hard to establish, and I have employed two methods in my research. Most frequently, I have used the tapping method[20] which produces average metronome readings for a particular passage as well as more localized details of tempo fluctuation. In all cases where I have sought to establish an average, the readings have omitted any terminal *ritenuto* since this would inevitably distort the outcomes downwards. Neither technological nor human error can be eliminated from these readings (Johnson 1999: 95) but they have proven to be more dependable than those suggested by a conventional metronome. Where the pulse had to be measured in too small a unit for tapping to be reliable (as in one Messiaen passage), I timed the passage in question, divided this by the number of pulse units and converted this into a metronome reading, again ensuring that there were no significant fluctuations of tempo within the measured passage. In all instances, I have taken the precaution of inserting *circa* in front of the readings because even tapping to the same stretch of music can produce marginally different results. Where I felt uncomfortable with an initial result, I tested the same passage three times and adopted the middle reading as being indicative of a mean. Where very large amounts of *rubato* are employed by an artist, which are bound to have an impact on the average speed for a passage, the reading carries an '*r*' as well as a '*c*'. Despite efforts to make the metronome figures as accurate as possible, there will almost certainly still be an element of approximation. This is highly unlikely to undermine the validity of any of the following discussion, since none of the arguments relies on metronomic exactitude. There will also be instances where the analytical details will be offset by my overall aural impression of a passage and considered in this context.

Presenting the Evidence; Verbal versus Graphic

In the forthcoming case studies, the data gained from the analysis of various recorded performances is presented in both *précis* and graphic formats, with the former preceding the latter. The *précis* takes the tower's fundamental level of era (style) and authorship (score) as a starting point and then arranges the remaining levels to indicate how the various informants interact with each other and feed into the superior levels. This reconstructive approach presents an interpretation moving

---

[20] A suitable computer programme enables an operator to tap to an appropriate time unit of a piece of music. The results are recorded and thus available for analysis.

developmentally from the ideal to the executive and, due to the conventions of written scripts, is most clearly explained by taking the reader down the page, as would be necessary when describing the construction of a building from foundations to summit, even though visually the physical structure is seen the other way up. Similarly, graphic presentation of the analytical data, which is not subject to written conventions, can, due to its its visual nature, be most advantageously presented rising upwards from level one to level four of the interpretative tower, as shown earlier in this chapter.

Use of Reviews

At strategic points in the forthcoming case studies, I introduce samples of critical reviews that were written in response to the recordings used in the studies. I am thus confirming the artistic value and status of the recordings as perceived by a respected organ of the evaluative listening community. More significantly perhaps, my analyses may suggest reasons for the critic's opinions which are 'not philosophically self-conscious' but 'give a fair representation of what might be a "popular" way of listening at least by a musically educated and alert listener' (Cumming 2000: 23). My own non-judgemental analytical deductions can therefore sometimes be set alongside the critic's judgements and, should shared ground be observed, some commonality between my structured analytical reception of the performance trace and the more intuitive responses of the critic may be inferred. In all cases, critiques are taken from issues of *The Gramophone*, the longest-standing of the magazines involved in reviewing classical recordings.

Use of Language

Until very recently, academic writing has largely avoided the use of pictorial or emotive language as opposed to analytical, treating the former with suspicion. Storr attributes this to the association of philosophical thought with neutral or objective language (Storr 1997 [1992]: 38). However, in publications that directly address emotional issues in music, a related vocabulary is perforce adopted. Thus we find Juslin (2002a [2001], 2002b, 2004) charting musical properties to emotions such as tenderness, happiness, sadness, fear and anger, the assumption being that the reader understands the emotions and related musical properties without the need for initial analytical explanation.

In the teaching and performing communities such language, including the use of metaphor (such as 'singing' tone or 'line'), has long been common parlance, thus pictorial and emotional language are perfectly coherent within teaching and performing circles. As Cumming writes: 'An important point to note ... is that, within a limited musical community such as that defined by the readership of ... magazines, references to subjective qualities as belonging to sounds ... are perfectly intelligible' (Cumming 2000: 23). The metaphorical and emotional language that sometimes appears in my analyses is directed at communities on whose comprehension I believe I can reliably depend.

However, to forestall any possible confusion, a special word is in order concerning my use of the term 'romantic' (lower-case 'r') as applied to performance (mainly in Chapter 5). Where I employ this adjective, I am not referring to performance practice as it was actually carried out in the Romantic period (upper-case 'R'); rather, I am referring to a manner of playing in which emphasis on tonal beauty, melodic line and expressive *rubato* are characteristics. In a sense, this notion of 'romantic' playing has much in common with a traditional notion of 'expressive' playing in which, as identified in Chapter 1, phrasing, balance, dynamic manipulation, agogic accentuation and *rubato* potentially play a significant role. These characteristics are documented in the twentieth century through recordings, and are exemplified by performers whose roots were either in the late nineteenth century (such as Paderewski) or who connected with it through temperament (such as Moiseiwitsch). Whether this is in fact how a Romantic pianist such as Chopin or Liszt actually played is here irrelevant; the description 'romantic' for this manner has acquired a particular significance through usage so that when Harold Schonberg claims that 'there is absolutely nothing "romantic" about [de Pachmann's] interpretations' (Schonberg 1987 [1963]: 336), the informed reader understands the connotations of such a statement. In other words, 'romantic/expressive' playing has become a 'historical construct' in 'the language game of a particular discourse of art music' (Johnson 2005: 199). For this reason, I will discontinue the use of inverted commas when discussing a romantic style of piano playing.

Interpretative Attribution and the Use of Names

Earlier I described the surface-level features of a performance, those concerning tempo, duration and touch, as the measurable commodities or objective 'facts' about a performance. As such, it is possible to personalize surface-level analytical data by describing a named pianist's specific tempo or dynamic, and this practice is regularly adopted throughout the forthcoming case studies. However, when using such data as evidence for drawing conclusions about an interpretation as a whole, especially with regard to the lower-level informants, it is the analyst's understanding of the evidence that is paramount. In line with my earlier discussion of the Intentional Fallacy, the conclusions that are presented are not ascribing specific artistic choices or intentions to a pianist but are the results of an informed listener's reception of the recorded performances. So, in this regard, when an artist's name is used during the case studies, it is for identification purposes only, to differentiate one performance from another.

58   *Reading Musical Interpretation*

Use of Models

Finally, it will be observed that in a number of instances, based on score-derived information, I construct possible interpretations of some passages in advance of analysing the recordings of them. Whilst I believe these interpretations to be viable, I am aware that they reflect only a limited, designedly *Texttreue* view and are therefore not intended to be definitive. What they do supply is a conceptual, interpretative model against which other interpretations, including those witnessed in my own recordings, may be assessed in terms of sound. Wittgenstein sums up the role of models when he states: 'we avoid emptiness in our assertions only by presenting the model as what it is, as an object of comparison – as, so to speak, a measuring-rod; not as a preconceived idea to which reality *must* correspond' (Wittgenstein 1978 [1953]: 51). Thus the *Texttreue* models are for comparative purposes only.

Summary

In conclusion, this chapter posits an analyst equipped with the necessary musicological credentials to be an informed listener who, as an informed listener, can perceive a poietic/esthesic relationship between performance and work. In response to this perceived relationship and two-stage to-and-fro projection between the traces left by the work and the performance, the analyst can engage in a secondary act of interpretation. This secondary act expands the two-stage projection to a three-stage to-and-fro projection which includes the analyst's own informed understanding of the primary act and the work-performer relationship manifested therein. The analyst's understanding can then be expressed graphically as a third trace, using the hierarchical framework of the interpretative tower. The framework is layered according to the manner in which a performance may be perceived to signify a progressive shift from ideal (or conceptually underpinning) factors to executive (or performer-controlled) factors acoustically experienced in the performance itself.

Much of the remainder of this book will be devoted to case studies which analyse performances of contrasting works, and which test the tower framework's efficacy. It must be stressed that such analysis is not intended to show whether a performance is 'right' or 'wrong' although, given that an analyst has both a historical and a subjective place – a 'horizon', to use Gadamer's term – any consideration of differing performances will apodictically entail elements of personal evaluation. Nevertheless the intention is, as Peter Johnson says, to seek 'the *informed* [my italics] evaluation of what a particular performance has to offer' (Johnson 1999: 61), an intention reinforced by my use of the term 'informant'.

To test the efficacy and scope of the interpretative tower, the three works to be investigated in performance come from different eras and display varying levels of authorial performance instruction in their respective scores. The works are Bach's

Toccata in D major BWV 912 (Chapter 3), Messiaen's 'Première communion de la Vierge' from *Vingt regards sur l'Enfant-Jésus* (Chapter 4) and Brahms's *Variations and Fugue on a Theme by Handel* Op. 24 (Chapter 5). Of these, only the Messiaen is short enough for the whole piece to be considered. In Chapters 3 and 5, I have selected passages of strongly contrasted or characterful material to test the tower's efficacy. As discussed earlier, my findings are consistently presented in both *précis* and graphic formats, but the methodology that I employ is adapted according to the nature of the work and task in hand. Reasons for these adaptations will be given in the relevant chapters.

As a pianist I am familiar with all three of the works named above, having performed them on a number of occasions, and so my observations are based on an intimate knowledge of the scores, their potential for interpretation and their related soundscapes. My reception and analysis of the recordings (including my own) of the works is supported by this 'inside' knowledge as well as by my knowledge of the physical aspects of playing the pieces. The latter is especially pertinent when discussing passages where interpretations seem embedded in the physical task of keyboard negotiation, as may sometimes be observed in the Messiaen and Brahms case studies. Nevertheless, my analysis traces only reflect interpretative outcomes and do not imply any judgement of artistic merit or a preference for one recording over another.

A CD of my recordings of the complete works is attached to this book, the track listings of which are shown in Appendix 1 and are referenced in the text as necessary. Where reference is made to a passage that occurs after the beginning of a track, the time position within the track is given. For example, if the passage in question occurs one minute and forty seconds after the beginning of track 2, this is shown in the text as (CD, track 2, 1'40").

PART II
Case Studies:
Applying the Framework

Chapter 3
Bach: Toccata in D major BWV 912

Some Background Issues

The philosopher Stephen Davies distinguishes between what he calls 'thin' works and 'thick' works, with the former exhibiting comparatively few 'determinative properties'. He suggests that, where thin specimens are concerned, 'most of the qualities of performance are aspects of the performer's interpretation, not of the work as such' (Davies 2001: 20). Whilst Davies' definition derives from 'works' such as those represented by a jazz musician's lead-sheet, it is possible to detect elements of 'thinness' in Bach's works too. The scarcity of tempo, dynamic and other performance instructions in his scores points to a broad interpretative field, one likely result of which is recordings that demonstrate very diverse performance profiles. Recordings of a comparatively thin work thus provide data for studying ways in which 'thinness' may be reflected in a performer's acoustic trace. This collection of data supplies evidence by which the analyst can investigate which 'artistic prerogatives' (Rink 2004: 47) have been exercised and whether their audible results corroborate the expectation of artistic diversity noted above.

The comparative thinness of a typical Bach work means that, at the interpretative tower's fundamental level, the authorship (score) informant might appear as a relatively remote presence in terms of performer engagement, and the analyst can anticipate that this informant has conceded some ground to era (style) as an interpretative determinant. In this connection, a possible influence is HIP and some examination of the interpretative evidence for signs of such influence is therefore appropriate, especially in view of the particular connection between HIP and the era (style) informant.

Era-related information, as mentioned in Chapter 2, exists in the form of treatises and contemporary accounts, and may be reflected in a performer's interpretation.[1] One such treatise is Carl Philipp Emanuel Bach's *Versuch über die wahre Art, das Clavier zu spielen* (1753 and 1762), and, although written after J.S. Bach's death, its author states that '[i]n ... keyboard playing I have never had any other teacher but my father' (Badura-Skoda 1995 [1990]: 248–9). Thus the

---

[1] There is even a species of 'recording' by mechanical instruments, which can provide evidence of tempo and ornamentation practices. A number of barrel organs built in the last decades of the eighteenth century include some Corelli, Vivaldi and Handel in their repertoires. Certain interesting features have been observed such as fast tempos, strictness of pulse, ornaments beginning on the main note as well as the auxiliary, and absence of double-dotting in the French overture style (Badura-Skoda 1995 [1990]).

treatise has often been considered helpful in shedding light on earlier practices concerning, in particular, embellishment and ornamentation (Schulenberg 1993 [1992]: 18), as well as articulation (Butt 1999 [1990]). Douglas Lee (1988) and David Schulenberg also regard C.P.E. Bach as a composer who especially advanced the earlier eighteenth-century free fantasy genre and so his views on the execution of this style of music are also of interest.

Recordings do not, however, supply incontrovertible evidence that recording artists have or have not consulted C.P.E. Bach's or any other era-related writings when preparing an interpretation. It may therefore be wise for the analyst to avoid becoming too enmeshed in performance practice issues, especially as eighteenth-century performance documents have limited value in promoting a work-specific 'authenticity'. Of necessity, such documents deal in principles and not specific works, so '[w]hile history tends to offer alternatives, performances have no option but to commit to a single solution' (Walls 2003: 26). Full consideration of aspects of Baroque performance practices, as detailed in Bach's essay and other writings, is beyond the scope of this study but reference will be made to these putative practices where the recorded evidence seems to invite comparison.

In this chapter interpretations of J.S. Bach's Toccata in D major BWV 912 will be investigated through analysis of recordings made on the piano by pianists whose names have often been associated with Bach performance. It is tempting to examine a performance on the harpsichord, but as I am confining my investigations to piano performance, it is pianists' interpretations of Bach that are necessarily the focus. Another justification for this delimitation is that it renders the analytical results more directly comparable both with each other and with performances of piano music that are considered in Chapters 4 and 5.

This forestalls any consideration of the sonic dimension of performance practice as it relates to the comparative sounds of the piano and the harpsichord. The much-aired controversy over the suitability of Bach's keyboard music for piano performance peaked in the 1970s when, as Robert Philip confirms, 'it was fashionable for the proponents of authenticity to deride the very idea of Bach played on the piano' (Philip 2004: 215). Some years later Paul Badura-Skoda, in opposition to this, claimed: 'Another reason why ... the modern grand piano is a legitimate instrument with a future in performances of Bach is the fact that his music often contains accents implied by the inner structure which have to be "suggested" rather than played on the harpsichord. These can be brought out even more on modern pianos than on fortepianos or clavichords' (Badura-Skoda 1995 [1990]: 174). This supports Richard Troeger's belief that '[t]oday's piano usually makes its best effect in Bach's music when played on its own terms, with its own resources' (Troeger 2003: 38). The piano's dynamic sensibility is, no doubt, one of the reasons why pianists have consistently been drawn to interpreting Bach on an essentially anachronistic instrument. It is therefore significant that, amongst keyboard players who have developed a close identity with his music in the latter part of the twentieth century, pianists have featured prominently: Tureck, Gould, Richter and Hewitt – to the last three of whose recordings I now turn.

The Recordings and the Work

Recording Artists

The following case studies are based on recordings made by Glenn Gould (1976), Sviatoslav Richter (1992), Angela Hewitt (2002) and a live recorded performance of my own (2003: CD, tracks 14–17).

Of these artists, Glenn Gould and Angela Hewitt are probably the two most closely associated with Bach performance, and I introduce their recordings by sampling the positive critical reception that they were accorded in *The Gramophone* magazine. The reviewer Nicholas Rast finds that Gould's performances of the toccatas show 'the relationship between the harmonic and contrapuntal material with beautiful clarity'. Rast also comments on the pianist's handling of the music's 'effortless flow', which demonstrates how 'Gould's scrupulous precision logically directs the melodic material towards its harmonic goals', his 'unique artistry' discovering 'musically and intellectually satisfying solutions' (Rast 1994: 80). As for Angela Hewitt's recording, Bryce Morrison commends her 'unfaltering sense of balance and perspective', continuing that 'few pianists have worn their enviable expertise in Bach more lightly … her performances could hardly be more stylish or impeccable' (Morrison 2002: 80). The recording by Richter, issued in 2002, received no *Gramophone* review, but an artist of his legendary status needs no justification for inclusion in this performance analysis. His teacher Heinrich Neuhaus certainly held Richter's Bach playing in high esteem, claiming that: 'The best performance of Bach I ever heard, or rather the one I found most convincing and closest to my own conception was by Sviatoslav Richter' (Neuhaus 1983 [1973]: 138).

Sources and the Work

A precise date of composition for BWV 912 is unavailable, but the seven keyboard toccatas all appeared some time between 1705 and 1714, and represent 'an early synthesis of the Italian and French styles (in conjunction with … North German examples …) as well as of strict and free forms' (Jones 1997: 140). All autograph manuscripts have been lost. Perhaps symptomatically, the compositions were subject to several revisions and complete early versions of two of them (including BWV 912) have survived. There are six main sources for the Toccata in D, but editor Tamás Zászkaliczky (1998) believes that these sources, although displaying a number of individual variants and internal 'corrections', nonetheless all stem from a common origin. Zászkaliczky's tabulation of the sources, which I shall adopt, letters them from A to F, with A (Mus.ms.Bach P 289), B (Mus.ms.Bach P 286), C (Go.S.309) and E (Ms II 4093) dating from after 1750, D (Mus.ms.Bach P 301), from the first part of the nineteenth century, and F (Ms.8), from between 1730 and 1740. The latter is notated by Johann Mempell but it omits the concluding section from bar 128 onwards. Sources A, B and D are in the Staatsbibliothek zu Berlin, source C in the Bach-Archiv, Leipzig, source E in the Bibliotèque Royale

66   *Reading Musical Interpretation*

Bruxelles and source F in the Musikbibliotech der Stadt Leipzig. In addition to these sources, Christian Eisert (2000) identifies two more: one copied by Scholz, which appears mainly to be a mix of A and E above, dating from before 1798, and another (MN 104), which may be a copy of D above, dating from before 1835. Scholz's copy is in the Göttingen Bach-Institut and MN104 is in the Salzburg Archiv des Domchores. Both Zászkaliczky and Eisert believe A to be the most reliable source.

Despite these uncertain beginnings, there is considerable textual accord amongst most current editions of the score. Bärenreiter (1999), Edition Peters (1956), G. Henle Verlag (1962), Kalmus (*c*. 1948), Könemann Music Budapest (1998) and Wiener Urtext Edition (2000) show only relatively insignificant differences (see Table 3.1), mainly in the free-style passages. Kalmus includes a number of clearly identified editorial performance suggestions[2] which are not shown in the table. In the following case studies, I will comment on a performer's textual divergence only if it appears to be unsupported by any of the editions, bearing in mind that not all were in print prior to the various recording dates. For example, only Henle, Kalmus and Peters were available to Gould and Richter. Gould's most likely source was Kalmus, since two heavily annotated copies of this edition were among his effects after his death, but Kevin Bazzana cautions that 'apparently a fair number of scores came and went during [Gould's] lifetime, so what happened to survive among his effects when he died may not be a complete record of the scores he studied' (personal communication 09 August 2005). In preparing her recording, Angela Hewitt used the Bärenreiter and Henle editions (personal communication 21 June 2005), whereas my chief source was the Könemann Music Budapest edition.

Table 3.1   Notational differences between Bärenreiter (1999), Henle (1962), Kalmus (*c*. 1948), Könemann (1998), Peters (1956) and Wiener Urtext (2000) editions of Bach's Toccata in D major BWV 912, bar 111 to the end

Edition	Bärenreiter	Henle	Kalmus	Könemann	Peters	Wiener Urtext
Bar 112	Beat 4^2: left hand has a♮	Beat 4^2: left hand has a♯	Beat 4^2: left hand has a♮	Beat 4^2: left hand has a♯	Beat 4^2: left hand has optional a♯	Beat 4^2: left hand has a♮
Bar 116	Alto voice f♯'s tied	Alto voice f♯'s not tied	Alto voice f♯'s not tied	Alto voice f♯'s tied	Alto voice f♯'s not tied	Alto voice f♯'s not tied
Bar 116	Beat 4: right-hand g' has trill	Beat 4: right-hand g' has trill	Beat 4: right-hand g' has pralltriller	Beat 4: right-hand g' has trill	Beat 4: right-hand g' has trill	Beat 4: right-hand g' has trill

---

[2]   The editor is Hans Bischoff.

Bach: Toccata in D major BWV 912

Edition	Bärenreiter	Henle	Kalmus	Könemann	Peters	Wiener Urtext
Bar 117	Beat 2: right-hand f♯′ has trill	Beat 2: right-hand f♯′ has pralltriller	Beat 2: right-hand f♯′ has trill; inverted mordent suggested in footnote	Beat 2: right-hand f♯′ has pralltriller	Beat 2: right-hand f♯′ has pralltriller	Beat 2: right-hand f♯′ has trill
Bar 117	Beats 2²–3: e′ and c♯′, but not (tenor) f♯, tied	Beats 2²–3: e′, c♯′ and (tenor) f♯ not tied	Beats 2²–3: e′, c♯′ and (tenor) f♯, not tied	Beats 2²–3: e′, c♯′ and (tenor) f♯ all tied	Beats 2²–3: e′, c♯′ and (tenor) f♯ not tied	Beats 2²–3: e′, c♯′ and (tenor) f♯ not tied
Bar 120	Beats 1–2: right-hand a♯′ has trill	Beats 1–2: right-hand a♯′ has trill	Beats 1–2: no trill	Beats 1–2: right-hand a♯′ has trill	Beats 1–2: no trill	Beats 1–2: right-hand a♯′ has trill
Bar 120	Beat 2: c♯′ below right-hand f♯′/e′	Beat 2: no c♯′ below right-hand f♯′/e′	Beat 2: no c♯′ below right-hand f♯′/e′	Beat 2: no c♯′ below right-hand f♯′/e′	Beat 2: no c♯′ below right-hand f♯′/e′	Beat 2: c♯′ below right-hand f♯′/e′
Bar 121	Beat 2: chord has *arpeggiando*	Beat 2: chord has *arpeggiando*	Beat 2: chord has no *arpeggiando*	Beat 2: chord has *arpeggiando*	Beat 2: chord has *arpeggiando*	Beat 2: chord has *arpeggiando*
Bar 124:	No tempo change marked	No tempo change marked	Marked *adagio*	No tempo change marked	No tempo change marked	No tempo change marked
Bar 125	Beat 1: no f♯′ in left-hand chord	Beat 1: no f♯′ in left-hand chord	Beat 1: no f♯′ in left-hand chord	Beat 1: no f♯′ in left-hand chord	Beat 1: f♯′ in left-hand chord	Beat 1: no f♯′ in left-hand chord
Bar 158 and 160	Last semiquaver has c♯″	Last semiquaver has c♮″	Last semiquaver has c♮″	Last semiquaver has c♮″	Last semiquaver has optional c♯″	Last semiquaver has suggested optional c♯″
Bars 201–204	No middle voice	No middle voice	Optional middle voice	No middle voice	No middle voice	No middle voice
Bar 276	Beat 3: right-hand f♯′ has pralltriller	Beat 3: no pralltriller	Beat 3: no pralltriller	Beat 3: no pralltriller	Beat 3: no pralltriller	Beat 3: no pralltriller
Bar 276	Beat 4: left-hand e has trill	Beat 4: left-hand e has trill	Beat 4: left-hand e has trill	Beat 4: left-hand e has trill	Beat 4: left-hand e has pralltriller	Beat 4: left-hand e has trill
Bar 277	Beat 4: right-hand d″ has mordent	Beat 4: right-hand d″ has mordent	Beat 4: right-hand d″ has mordent	Beat 4: right-hand d″ has mordent	Beat 4: no mordent	Beat 4: right-hand d″ has mordent

68 *Reading Musical Interpretation*

The complete work is too long to be considered in its totality so my approach will be selective. BWV 912 is typical of its genre, being characteristically episodic. It alternates between improvisatory passages (*stylus phantasticus*) and stricter contrapuntal or fugal sections, thus exemplifying the North German multipartite toccata (Crist 1997: 81).[3] Taking advantage of this multipartite structure, I shall examine recordings of a 'free' section and then a 'strict' one to ascertain how the four performances reflect the interpretative fields of these seemingly opposing elements.

The Instrumental Recitative

Con Discrezione

All sources for the Toccata in D's later version, other than E, apply the words '*con discrezione*' to the passage running between bars 111 and 126. The directive is not included in surviving sources for the work's early version, but it is interesting to note that, despite the absence of an autograph manuscript, the authorial origin of *con discrezione* in the later version receives tentative support from Schulenberg (1999: 119). He also suggests that Bach's later use of the term may have been a reminder to a generation that was starting to forget the practices of its predecessors (119). Of rather more significance to the performance analyst, however, is the fact that all recent editions of the score include this performance directive. As the four recordings under consideration are of the toccata's later version, it is reasonable to assume that the performances will reflect a response to *con discrezione* in one way or another. Thus I can safely project to and from performance and score where this is concerned.

So what might *con discrezione* imply? Johann Mattheson, Bach's compatriot and contemporary, writes: 'one is ... also in the habit of writing the words ... *con discrezione*, in order to observe that one need not be restricted to the beat at all, but might sometimes play slowly, sometimes fast' (Mattheson 1981 [1739]: 219). *Con discrezione* seems, therefore to invoke a free-style, *stylus phantasticus* or *fantasia*-like performance. Troeger notes that the term, as applied to the 'free-style section' of bars 111–126 of the Toccata in D, contains 'suggestions of vocal recitative' which entail 'considerable freedom in timing, as is of course appropriate to recitative' (Troeger 2003: 56–7). These ideas echo advice given by C.P.E. Bach, who writes of accompanied recitatives but extends his recommendations, by analogy, to the keyboard: 'metric signature is in many ... cases more a convention of notation than a binding factor in performance. It is a distinct merit of the fantasia that ... it can accomplish the aims of the recitative at the keyboard with complete, unmeasured freedom' (Bach 1949 [1753]: 153). It would seem, then,

---

[3]   Troeger compares the overall scheme of this toccata to the arrangement of a *dispositio* in classical rhetoric.

that *con discrezione* can be taken as an invitation to the performer to treat metre and notated rhythmic proportion in a very free manner, thus partially liberating him or her from the constraints of the score. The analogy with recitative points to an improvisatory manner of playing, which is appropriate if, as Jones suggests, the 'free fantasy interludes' in this toccata reflect the type of piece that the young Bach may have improvised (Jones 1997: 136).

In Chapter 2, I introduced the topical mode, suggesting that this informant especially engages the imagination, and a performance instruction that appears to call for a rhythmically free, quasi-improvisatory manner may be thought to engage the performer's imaginative faculties. Cumming, after Peirce, believes that a state of consciousness, such as imagination, 'can be distinguished only by considering the object at which [it is] directed' (Cumming 2000: 58), and she illustrates the idea by suggesting that 'an attitude of imagination' may be directed towards 'affective qualities in sound' (58). *Con discrezione* directs the imagination to the affective qualities of sonic duration so I will accord *con discrezione* the informant status of a very broad topical mode.[4] Due to its highly non-prescriptive nature, the term suggests an interpretative field which can accommodate personal choices, especially in the durational area, to a greater degree than do the interpretative fields surrounding most other kinds of notated music. The forthcoming analysis investigates the interpretative fields established by the four selected recordings of the passage with which the *con discrezione* injunction – unique in Bach – is associated.

The Instrumental Recitative: Richter

Throughout Richter's performance, recorded live and probably unedited, since several inaccuracies have remained on the disc, the interpretation seems designed to minimize any sense of personal idiosyncrasy. This matches Richter's belief that

> performing music doesn't mean contaminating the piece with your own personality ... The interpreter is really an executant, carrying out the composer's intentions to the letter. He doesn't add anything that isn't already in the work ... I was always certain that, for each work, it was in this way and no other that it had to be played ... because I looked closely at the score. (Monsaingeon 2001 [1998]: 143–53)

Richter's performance certainly implies a 'literalist' interpretation and the response to the broad topical mode *con discrezione* evident in his recording suggests, as far as the nature of this music will permit, an advocacy of the *Texttreue* principle.

At the outset of the passage in question (half way through bar 111), Richter retains the tempo of quaver = *c.* 80 which he adopted for the preceding fugal

---

[4]   The topic informant, according to the delimitation of my definition in Chapter 2, is not relevant in this context.

section. In fact, the pause over the quaver F♯ minor chord at bar 111³ lasts for almost exactly a dotted crotchet, so that the opening notes of the next section sound in time, as if a continuation of the same musical impulse. At bar 115, he does provide a significant increase of tempo, rising to quaver = *c.* 96, but then plays the hemidemisemiquaver flourishes in tempo, the first of which, in bar 116, arrives on its second beat only fractionally ahead of time. A slight *ritenuto* closes this section before he commences the *presto* at a constant crotchet = *c.* 100. The semiquaver rest that opens bar 122 is prolonged, and the pause over the E minor chord is not observed but is placed over the demisemiquaver rest that follows. He concludes the section at crotchet = *c.* 76 and holds this (if not quite precisely in bar 124³⁻⁴) until almost the end of the episode. A very slight *ritenuto* is discernible before Richter connects this passage to the concluding gigue-fugue.

When described like this, it seems as though a reasonable amount of interpretative engagement has occurred. Given that the tempo changes are very likely to be deliberate, the other interpretative features which emerge from the above account are belied by the aural experience, which processes most of these as no more than minor traits, perhaps generated in the heat of a live performance. Expressive *rubato* is limited to a *poco ritenuto* before the paused semiquaver chords in bars 112, 113, 114 and at the ends of bars 117 and 126. Otherwise the effect is of regularity, as far as such rhythmically unstable music will allow. This regularity is reinforced by a general lack of dynamic nuance other than the suggestion of a graded *crescendo* from the opening ***mp/mf*** to the *f* arrived at and retained from bar 120.

The 'colouring' of musical units in a free-style passage is tempting for a pianist, given the fragmentary nature of Bach's compositional gestures, so one should consider whether Richter's tendency to avoid such colouring may be in order to project a structural overview. Between bars 112 and 122, the music is tonally unstable, but the more active bass line from bar 123⁴ to the end of the section affirms D major and could be perceived as a release of the tension accumulated during the more tonally remote antecedent passages. For the analyst, this overview can project a feeling of musical strength rather than of improvisation.

The recorded evidence suggests that stylistic issues such as those cited by Mattheson and C.P.E. Bach are of little relevance to Richter's recording. Bach's 'unmeasured freedom' would need to be reflected by some significant duration manipulation, supported by freedom of tempo and possibly dynamics if the analyst is to read any extraordinary degree of performative licence. As described above, none of these surface properties is conveyed with any particular emphasis, the impression being given of an extension – initially, at any rate – of the preceding fugal writing and a rather 'levelled-out' musical landscape. Thus, the characterizer of (implied) rhythmic lassitude appears to be minimized and the topical mode *con discrezione* to be exerting only a very limited influence. Where genre is concerned, Richter's performance presents the episode as a segment of the toccata's musical continuum rather than as a discrete entity within a multipartite structure, further supporting a disciplined view of *con discrezione*. Given that Richter is heard to play 'literally', as far as the nature of the passage will allow, authorship (score) assumes precedence over era (style) in the performance as a whole – and this conclusion appears to concur with Richter's views, quoted above, regarding the primacy of the score.

In Richter's recording, the score seems to be used as a point of adherence rather than of departure, perhaps as a means to capture the composer's authorial presence in performance. Thus his interpretative tower might appear to be no more than a stump but, in reality, even his 'non-interventionist' approach represents a subjective view (a subjective decision to appear objective, an unconscious 'double bluff' perhaps), so the upper layers of the tower remain intact, if not strongly projected.

The Instrumental Recitative: Hewitt

Turning now to Hewitt's recording of the same passage, a generally brisker approach is evident throughout, but one which projects a sense of recitative in a more obvious manner. However, her initial tempo for the passage is not very different from the preceding measures, showing only a slight drop from quaver = *c*. 101 to a variable quaver = *c*. 98. This is increased to crotchet = *c*. 130 at bar 118[2], thus acknowledging the marked *presto*; then, after an initial pause on the b'''[5] the tempo is decreased to quaver = *c*. 150 at bar 122[3]. She holds this tempo almost until the end when a *poco ritenuto* is introduced at bar 126[4] to launch the ensuing fugue. In common with Richter, she increases the tempo at bar 115 but adds several further personal touches. Slight pauses are employed over the right-hand g♮' of bar 113, the right-hand c♯'' in 115 and the first triplet note, b'', in the right hand of 122, as noted above. An *arpeggiando*[6] is applied to the chords at bars 116[3] and 117[3], whilst extra notes are added to the written-out tremolo[7] in bar 114, and the harmonically resolving d♯' in bar 120 acquires a mordent. An *accelerando* shapes the hemidemisemiquaver runs of bars 116 and 117, thus freeing the music from its barring. Generally, Hewitt's tempos are both strongly contrasted but flexible, and generate what may be identified as an improvisatory character more obviously than do Richter's.

Like Richter, Hewitt also interprets the passage as moving from a softer to a stronger dynamic but her range is noticeably larger. Starting quietly she moves to a clear *forte* by bar 117[4], nearly three bars earlier than Richter and, like him, retains the dynamic until the final bar of the section, actually performing a slight *crescendo*

---

[5]   The pitch system adopted here indicates middle C as c', the octave above as c'' and so on. The octaves below are shown descending as c C C, and so on.

[6]   An *arpeggiando* affects not only the duration of a chord but also its sonic properties, so this feature engages both the duration manipulator and sonic moderator informants.

[7]   Hewitt appears to agree with Troeger that, when playing a tremolo, 'the player need not feel obliged to follow the precise number of repercussions notated' (Troeger 2003: 182).

through the last two beats of bar 126. Where she differs is in her employment of localized dynamic colouring. For example, there is an increase in dynamic level during the left-hand tremolo of bar 114 which leads through to the g♯ of the next bar and is followed by a *diminuendo* at 115[4]. Both her *crescendo* and *diminuendo* highlight the g♯ as a dynamic focal point. She also combines a *crescendo* in bars 116 and 117 with the *accelerando* described above.

The top-layer informants heard in Hewitt's recording provide evidence of considerable engagement with the topical mode *con discrezione* and its companion characterizer of rhythmic freedom. The two-second pause between the end of the central fugal passage (bar 111) and the recitative gives the latter a semi-independent role whose primary function is to contrast rather than to bind, thereby helping to project a view of genre. Through apparent respect for both the information in the score and the Baroque fantasy style, an equal regard for both of the interpretative tower's fundamentals, era and authorship, may be detected in the performance.

This balanced presentation of era (style) and authorship (score) is reflected in a number of personal touches in Hewitt's recording which do not, however, suggest complete unmeasured freedom. The impression is that it would ill-serve the music to take this freedom to such an extreme that all idea of musical syntax is lost, implying that: 'the relationship between the note values must be approximately preserved, even in recitative ... it would be incorrect to play quavers faster than semiquavers' (Badura-Skoda 1995 [1990]: 18).[8] Hewitt's reading certainly preserves a sense of proportion, despite the liberties she takes. These, however, all connect to an apparently balanced perception of the interpretative tower's fundamental level, so that the personal touches introduced higher up may be heard to have a logic that is developed from the more 'factual' information in the score. It is probably these qualities that prompted Bryce Morrison to write '[Hewitt] shows us that it is possible to be personal and characterful without resorting to self-serving and distorting idiosyncrasy' (Morrison 2002: 80).

The Instrumental Recitative: Hellaby (CD, track 16)

On the evidence of the live recording, my own view of this passage probably has more in common with Hewitt than with Richter, but is brisker still than hers. There is no real pause between the end of the central *fugato*, just a 'comma', and although there is a small drop in tempo (down to quaver = *c.* 116 from quaver = *c.* 120), the generally faster tempos tend to disguise this. However, the rhythm remains flexible and there are fluctuations in tempo at similar points to those found in Richter's and Hewitt's recordings, although there is only a very slight increase of pace at bar 115, probably due to an already faster speed. My *presto* is close to Hewitt's, moving at crotchet = *c.* 128, and the triplet semiquavers at bars 122–123

---

[8]   One must assume that Badura-Skoda is referring to passages that are moving at roughly the same tempo, because the quavers of a *presto* may well move faster than the semiquavers of an *adagio*.

match her tempo almost exactly (quaver = *c.* 150). Where I differ is that the tempo returns to quaver = *c.* 116 during bars 124–126, although, in common with both Richter and Hewitt, I include a *ritenuto* at the end of 126 to launch the concluding gigue-fugue. This recurrence of quaver = *c.* 116 suggests a basic 'tempo' for the section which, on the one hand, provides a degree of stability but, on the other, works against the concept of 'unmeasured freedom'. It should also be added that this feature was not intended and was one that I noticed only on listening to the recording. Measuring the pulse revealed, perhaps, an intuitive planning. Nevertheless, there are a number of personal touches, with a *poco ritenuto* shaping bar 112^{3-4} and at equivalent points in the following two bars. Elsewhere, a slight *ritenuto* is applied to bar 117^{3-4} and 123^4. An *arpeggiando* is added to the chords between 123^4 and 125^1 and, most notably, to the chord at 121^2, which ascends and descends. *Pralltriller* are added to the inner parts in the last bar of the section but all marked pauses are observed. In instances such as these, realization is clearly born of intent.

As with both Richter and Hewitt, my recording shows a general dynamic increase from bar 111 which opens *mp* and reaches *f* by 117^4. But, dynamically, the recording still shares more common ground with Hewitt's, featuring localized colourings within the broader context. For example, there is a *crescendo* to the g♯ at the start of 115 as well as dynamic dips in bars 120^4 and 122^1, with a *crescendo* applied to the ensuing semiquaver triplet run. The dynamic then remains *f* to the end.

In sum, my recording shows overall affinities with Hewitt's, although it differs in details. The surface informants reflect assimilation of both topical mode and characterizer, but within similar boundaries to those heard in Hewitt's recording. The performance presents the *con discrezione* episode as contrasting with those surrounding it, but this is partly offset by tempos which evolve from the preceding section. A character of fantasy is nonetheless realized in which interpretative individuality may be heard, even if the effect sounds more planned than Hewitt's. Again, a balance between authorship (score) and its counterpart, era (style), is apparent.

The Instrumental Recitative: Gould

By far the greatest interpretative freedom is found, unsurprisingly, in Glenn Gould's recording. Moving seamlessly from one section to the next, his tempo, in common with Hewitt's, drops downwards only slightly from the quaver = *c.* 82 of the preceding fugal section to quaver = *c.* 78. But at slower overall speeds, the differential is more noticeable. Generally speaking, he avoids a settled pulse at any point, so that the characterizer is strongly projected, but his fastest tempo appears in the semiquaver triplets at bar 122^3 rather than at the *presto* of bar 118. Extra notes, in-fills and pauses are added throughout, resulting in the version, transcribed from the recording, shown in Example 3.1.

Example 3.1 Bach: Toccata in D major BWV 912, bars 111–126, as interpreted by Gould

In Chapter 1, I suggested that the existence of a work's conflicting textual sources can offer an interpreter a range of choices, not available in a definitive text. Whilst the editions cited above may have achieved some degree of textual consensus, as analyst I cannot assume that Gould's departures from this consensus are only the result of personal idiosyncrasy when the possibility exists that his recording reflects influences from the toccata's disparate sources. The ornament at bar 116^4, present in modern editions, is missing in source D and in Gould's recording, and the *presto* instruction at bar 118, also found in modern editions, is absent in sources B, C, D and F, and is not reflected in Gould's performance. There are a few signs, then, that Gould may have drawn from a range of alternative sources, including the Kalmus edition in his possession,[9] but all remaining 'deviations' – and there are a significant number – appear to be unauthorized by any source.

Concomitant with Gould's free treatment of the text is his application of dynamics which, as may be observed in Example 3.1, displays considerable variety, more than is apparent in the other three recordings. Perhaps the most unexpected touch is the *diminuendo* from 126^{3-4} to prepare for the concluding gigue-fugue. Here, Hewitt inserts an anticipatory *crescendo* and Richter simply remains loud.

Nevertheless, his levels of duration manipulation and sonic moderation, in addition to the tempo changes, signify a vigorous engagement with characterizer and topical mode which, in turn, link to a notion of the toccata genre as primarily fantasy. This further links to a free view of authorship (changes to the text, not in any of the sources) but also to a particular, if personal, perception of era and related stylistic practices.

When examined through the agency of the tower, the surface-level features of Gould's recording might sometimes appear arbitrary. For example, in bars 111^3–114, the analyst can follow the links from genre (toccata/recitative) to topical mode (*con discrezione*) and characterizer, and thence to duration manipulator (extra pauses and the application of *rubato*). It is harder, though, to detect any such linkage for the articulation as manifested in his sonic moderation, in particular the absence of the slurs in bars 111^3–114 and substitution of these by semi-*staccato* articulation in bar 114.[10] Also, the *marcato* touch used for the last three semiquavers of bar 112, not employed elsewhere, seems equally idiosyncratic.

---

[9]   In bars 201 and 203 of the toccata's concluding section, Gould plays a middle voice, a third above the given bass part, an addition that appears as a suggestion in the Kalmus (*c.* 1948) edition he used. The editor, Hans Bischoff, casts serious doubt on its authenticity, but includes it, apparently in deference to the Peters Edition. Bischoff is presumably referring to the edition by Czerny, Griepenkerl and Roitzsch, which is published by Peters and includes the middle voice.

[10]   In this connection, John Butt's opinion that Bach's 'articulation marks are closely related to the *Decoratio* – i.e. the ornamental rather then the structural level of the composition' (Butt 1999 [1990]: 164) may be cited. It could be thought, therefore, that Gould is concerned with surface ornamental features rather than with structural principles. Despite this, the marks

76 *Reading Musical Interpretation*

Gould's very personal approach is still liable to arouse controversy since it may seem inconsistent with traditional notions of Bach performance, especially as it is known that the composer 'was famous for notating things that were normally left up to performers' (Schulenberg 1999: 114). However, it is hard to deny that Gould plays with plenty of unmeasured freedom, and it could be argued that the emphasis on topical mode, evident in his recording, truly manifests the spirit of *con discrezione*. In reality, very little evidence exists as to exactly how Bach might have played this passage himself (and certainly not on the piano), so, in the present conceptual context, it is more appropriate to analyse Gould's interpretation on its own terms rather than in relation to some elusive 'authentic' model, especially as, in common with Richter, he was not associated with the historical performance movement.

Arranged alphabetically according to artist, analytical data concerning the four performances can be shown thus:

Gould
> Level 1: **authorship (score)** and **era (style)** taken as 'points of departure' and interpreted freely, with numerous adaptations of/additions to the score →
> Level 2: **genre** – passage connected to surrounding material, but free and impulsive manner reflects the instrumental recitative *par excellence*; (**topic** not relevant) →
> Level 3: *con discrezione*, very freely expressive manner (**topical mode**) and very flexible rhythm (**characterizer**) supporting all three of →
> Level 4: **tempo** drops a little from the preceding fugue then fluctuates throughout with one major increase; pauses added (but rarely observed according to the sources), *accelerando* and *ritenuto* ever-present, *arpeggiandos* added or removed (**duration manipulator**); broad dynamic range, fluctuating overall with localized nuances, *arpeggiandos* added (doubling with duration manipulation), articulations sometimes idiosyncratic and loosely connected to lower levels (**sonic moderator**).

Hellaby
> Level 1: equal weight given to **authorship (score)** and **era (style)**, the latter prompting minor adaptations/additions to the score →
> Level 2: **genre** – free but logically ordered style with some regard for the passage's semi-independence, reflecting the instrumental recitative but suggesting a basic 'tempo' for the passage; (**topic** not relevant) →
> Level 3: *con discrezione*, flexible, expressive manner (**topical mode**) and rhythmic flexibility within a discernible tempo overview (**characterizer**) supporting all three of →

---

accord with Schulenberg's assertion that each 'authentic slur in Bach's keyboard music … can be understood as having the primary role of articulating a motive that arises as the embellishment of … a chord' (Schulenberg 1999: 120).

Level 4: **tempo** drops a little from the preceding fugue then includes two changes, one directed by the score (authorially?); pauses observed, *accelerando, ritenuto, arpeggiandos* added (**duration manipulator**); some dynamic range, localized nuances, general *crescendo* apparent, *arpeggiandos* added (doubling with duration manipulation) (**sonic moderator**).

Hewitt
Level 1: equal weight given to **authorship (score)** and **era (style)**, the latter prompting minor additions to the score →
Level 2: **genre** – free but logically ordered style, defining the passage as a semi-independent unit and reflecting the instrumental recitative but preserving tempo proportion; (**topic** not relevant) →
Level 3: *con discrezione*, freely expressive manner (**topical mode**) and rhythmic flexibility (**characterizer**) supporting all three of →
Level 4: **tempo** drops a little from the preceding fugue then includes three changes, one directed by the score (authorially?); pauses observed or added, *accelerando, ritenuto, arpeggiandos* added (**duration manipulator**); broad dynamic range, localized nuances, general *crescendo* apparent, *arpeggiandos* added (doubling with duration manipulation) (**sonic moderator**).

Richter
Level 1: **authorship (score)** seemingly favoured over **era (style)** due to quasi-literal score realization →
Level 2: **genre** seen as largely 'fixed' by the score, with no special attempt to define a free style or semi-independent unit; (**topic** not relevant) →
Level 3: neutral manner (**topical mode**); rhythmic instability minimized (**characterizer**), reflected by →
Level 4: **tempo** relates to the preceding fugue but includes three changes, one directed by the score (authorially?); *ritenuto* and pauses minimized (**duration manipulator**); dynamic 'colour' largely absent but slight general *crescendo* apparent reflecting a genre-derived overview of the passage (**sonic moderator**).

The two most contrasting performances, by Gould and Richter, are shown graphically in Figure 3.1.

Given that the recitative passage can be thought to imply an improvisatory style of performance, it is perhaps not surprising that, as anticipated, the pianists' recordings provide analytical evidence that they have exercised their artistic prerogatives in significantly divergent ways. The recordings also provide the analyst with clues concerning the interpretative horizon from which each artist is operating. In this instance, as the graphs show, the greatest opposition is between Gould's and Richter's horizons.

(a) Artist: Gould

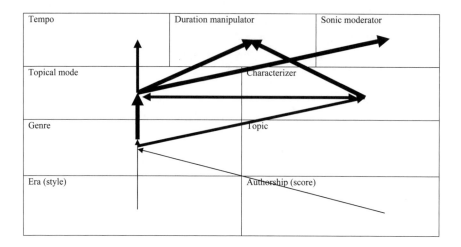

(b) Artist: Richter

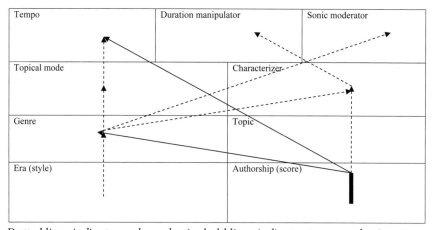

Dotted lines indicate weak emphasis; bold lines indicate strong emphasis.

Figure 3.1   Bach: Toccata in D major BWV 912, bars 111–126 (instrumental recitative); interpretations by (a) Gould and (b) Richter mapped on to the interpretative tower

Turning now to the concluding section of the toccata, the gigue-fugue, a rather different profile of performer response may be anticipated, due to the more regularized musical context in which the pianist is operating.

The Gigue-fugue

Mattheson's descriptions of different gigue types suggests that the gigue which concludes BWV 912 is either the 'common or English' variety or the canarie,[11] rather than the 'Italian' type, which is 'used for fiddling', or the loure, which is 'slow and punctuated' (Mattheson 1981 [1739]: 457). Meredith Little and Natalie Jenne (2001 [1991]) designate the gigue type in BWV 912 as simply 'giga 1', or more precisely 'giga 1-like', due to the absence of any label on the score. A similar gigue type is found in the fifth French Suite BWV 816 and the Fugue in F from the *Well-tempered Clavier* Book 2, the latter of which is, again, not labelled. Little and Jenne point out that textures in this type are 'normally contrapuntal, imitative and sometimes fugal' (Little and Jenne 2001[1991]: 154) and that the chief characteristics of 'giga 1' are 'joyous affect created by long phrases, few internal cadences and a rapid tempo' (160).

Gould, Hewitt, Richter and I seem to agree with this description, producing clearly voiced and dance-like performances from which the analyst may read the topical mode *vivace*. Because of these similarities, my analysis will follow a different plan, initially arranging the findings according to the interpretative tower's top-level informants, rather than on an artist-by-artist basis.

Tempo

It is worth, firstly, identifying a few factors which could have a bearing on the tempo informant. The gigue is commonly thought to be a lively dance both by composers (Troeger 2003: 233) and performers, and the use of a 6/16 time-signature for the gigue-fugue in BWV 912 lends further support to the notion, given the assertion by Bach's pupil, Kirnberger – as well as by the former's near-contemporary, Borin – that a 6/16 time signature implies a fast tempo (Houle 2000 [1987]: 37–49). Remembering C.P.E. Bach's injunction that the overall pace of a work should be determined by its fastest notes (Bach 1949 [1753]: 151), another factor in determining a suitable tempo is the demisemiquaver irruption that runs from bar 264^2 to bar 275. Too hasty an initial speed would render this unplayable without a slowing of the pace, which would probably be inappropriate, given the continued 'jigging' figurations in the left hand.

In seeming concurrence with the above, Gould, Hewitt, and I (CD, track 17) adopt a brisk but not headlong tempo, taking the music at dotted quaver = *c.* 122,

---

[11]   Quantz believes that the gigue and the canarie share the same tempo (Quantz 2001 [1752]: 291).

with Richter maybe fractionally slower at c. 119. This near tempo match between the recordings creates a similarity of effect (and affect) which is almost undisturbed by duration manipulation.

Duration Manipulator

Richter applies no *rubato* at all until the final two bars, where the music changes time-signature and Gould introduces a little, one bar ahead of this, subsequently applying a *ritenuto* in the last bar. Hewitt employs a tiny amount of *rubato* immediately prior to bars 238 and 253 (the latter to highlight a counter-subject entry) and at the end, but the tempo is otherwise held constant throughout. My recording includes a hint of *rubato*, apparently in anticipation of the left-hand subject entry in the second half of bar 163, and a *ritenuto* in the last bar, but otherwise the tempo is generally regular, despite an (unintentional) *accelerando* between bars 227 and 237.[12]

Sonic Moderator

All performers' articulations seem in accord with the dance topic (gigue), despite the differences described below. Richter, Hewitt and I employ similar articulations for the fugue subject (see Example 3.2),[13] but Gould plays the entire subject *staccato*.

Example 3.2   Bach: Toccata in D major BWV 912, bars 127–130; Richter's and Hewitt's articulation

Badura-Skoda claims that this fugue, along with the gigue from the fifth French Suite, is an example of the 'staccato gigue' (Badura-Skoda 1995 [1990]: 112), but as the statement is not substantiated, it remains a personal opinion – and one with which Gould's choice of articulation initially complies. But, although in the fugal exposition Gould presents both subject and counter-subject *staccato*, as early as the third entry his articulation of the counter-subject has changed. Here (bar 139–142),

---

[12] Distortions in perception of time are not uncommon in a live setting: 'Performers frequently note that their perception of time is affected during performance ... time appears to speed up, so that events seem to take but a brief percentage of their true duration' (Salmon and Meyer 1992: 60–1).

[13] This articulation for what Little and Jenne call 'tap level' (as opposed to bar or pulse level) notes accords with that indicated by Corelli and Rameau for other 'giga 1' types (Little and Jenne 2001 [1991]: 158).

the two upper parts now couple quaver to semiquaver, although the trochee at bar 139^2 remains fully *staccato* as does the left-hand enunciation of the trochees in bar 143. Similar inconsistencies can be observed throughout. For example, the simultaneous (tonic) entries of both subject and counter-subject at bar 180 are modified: the latter is now presented with the quaver slurred to its semiquaver complement, as played in bar 140, whilst the former uses the articulation adopted by Richter and Hewitt, shown in Example 3.2 above. For the prominent bass entry of the counter-subject at bar 253, Gould employs yet another mix of articulations, shown in Example 3.3. As Bazzana observes, Gould 'was not fanatical about maintaining consistent phrasing for a fugue subject' (Bazzana 1997: 226).

Example 3.3   Bach: Toccata in D major BWV 912, bars 253–256; Gould's articulation

In contrast to this, both Richter and Hewitt are fairly consistent. Both agree on the articulation of the subject, as shown in Example 3.2, but differ a little with regard to the counter-subject. For the latter, Hewitt phrases on a bar-by-bar basis, whilst Richter phrases beat-by-beat, as do I (see Example 3.4). Richter mostly retains this presentation of the trochees but there are exceptions. For example, in bars 151–159, he very slightly separates some of the lower-pitched quavers from their complementary semiquavers, as shown in Example 3.5, and extends this idea further in bars 190–191, 234 and 236–237, during which all notes of longer duration are slightly detached from their shorter counterparts. Despite this, there is no fundamental change in the idea of arsis–thesis, even if the surface details of execution differ. In my recording, the counter-subject's articulation remains consistent throughout.

Example 3.4   Bach: Toccata in D major BWV 912, bars 131–134; (a) Richter's and (b) Hewitt's articulations of the counter-subject

Example 3.5   Bach: Toccata in D major BWV 912, bars 151–155; Richter's articulation

Hewitt is a little more inconsistent in her choices. For example, in bar 164, at the dominant entry of the fugue subject, she changes the articulation of Example 3.2 to that shown in Example 3.6, and closely matches this with a re-articulation of the counter-subject, thereby avoiding any impression of arbitrariness (Example 3.7). She uses her original articulation of the subject for another dominant entry at bar 197, then, apart from one all-*staccato* passage in bar 211, mostly retains this and her revised enunciation of the counter-subject to the end.

Example 3.6   Bach: Toccata in D major BWV 912, bars 164–165; Hewitt's articulation

Example 3.7   Bach: Toccata in D major BWV 912, bars 164–167; Hewitt's articulation

The question of dynamics prompts thoughts concerning 'authentic' performance practice and, in this connection, one aspect that audibly unites all four performances is an observance of the 'hierarchy of the bar' (Lawson and Stowell, 1999, 56). Eighteenth-century writers shed some light on this hierarchy, with Quantz advising that 'the principal notes always must be emphasized more than the passing' (Quantz 2001 [1752]: 123), and John Holden stating: 'notes that come on the beat are notes to which we give a "superior regard" ... notation places these "good" notes after bar lines and on odd-numbered beats of the measure' (Houle 2000 [1987]: 78).[14] In line with this, slightly greater emphasis on the downbeats than on the second

---

[14]   According to Houle, Kirnberger 'allowed no stress on the first notes of beats in 6/16' (Houle 2000 [1987]: 48), but Houle's assertion seems to be based on Kirnberger's identification of 6/16 as a 'light' metre which, when played on the violin, should 'be played with just the point of the bow' (Kirnberger 1982 [1776]: 388).

beats of the bar can be heard in all four recordings, and the articulations outlined above ensure a still weaker emphasis on the 'passing' notes. It would, nevertheless, be unwise to conclude that the performers have necessarily consulted eighteenth-century treatises and it is again safer to assume that the implications of the music as sound are a strong enough guide to promote the pianist's articulative similarities. In any case, it is arguable that similar sonic implications prompted the pedagogical advice of Quantz and Holden in the first place.

With regard to the broader area of dynamics, it is interesting to note that none of the performances matches Kirnberger's instruction regarding the execution of a very similar gigue, the Fugue in F major BWV 880: 'if this fugue is to be performed correctly on the keyboard, the notes must be played lightly and without the least pressure' (Kirnberger 1982 [1776]: 388). His exhortation did not of course concern performance on a modern piano, but none of the four recordings obviously reflects Kirnberger's advice – especially Richter's, where the dynamic levels sound mainly loud or fairly loud.[15] It could be argued that, mechanical changes aside, uniformity of dynamic is a property of the harpsichord, the instrument for which the piece was presumably intended. This is not, however, an inherent property of the piano and experience has led the informed listener to expect varied dynamics. Probably due to such pre-set acoustic expectations on the part of the listener, a generally un-nuanced performance on the piano produces a far more relentless effect than an un-nuanced rendition on the harpsichord, where touch-related volume control is not a relevant concern. Troeger points out that '[t]rying to emulate the harpsichord [on the piano] by leaving out natural dynamic gradations produces a motoric effect that … has nothing to do with eighteenth-century musical perceptions' (Troeger 2003: 40). This could help to explain why Richter's dynamic levels attract attention and can be heard as one of the defining features of his interpretation.

Dynamic variety is a notable feature of both Gould's and Hewitt's versions, as it is to some extent in my own, and can be heard to contribute to the character of the interpretations. Hewitt uses dynamics mainly in three ways: to bring out a voice entry, as is traditional in fugal playing on the piano and hence can be linked to genre (bars 201 and 253);[16] to enhance intensification through repetition (*crescendo* in bars 224–227, 230–231[1] and 232–233[1]); and to reflect her perceived character of a passage (the *subito p* at bar 220).

Gould's treatment of dynamics, despite some conventional terracing, sounds rather less traditional, illustrating perhaps that 'his views on where and to what degree the performer may properly assert himself set him apart from many of his

---

[15]   The most noticeable drops in dynamic level occur when the texture is reduced from three parts to two at bar 184[2], then to a single voice at bar 219, so the effect is partially inbuilt.

[16]   Both of these instances concern projection of a counter-subject entry, significantly, in the lowest part of the texture. Bass entries tend to need more performance 'help' to project their role to the listener than do those in the treble, which are more readily discernible. Richter also strongly projects the second of these two entries.

84 *Reading Musical Interpretation*

contemporaries among performers ... music critics and philosophers' (Bazzana 1997: 40). Sometimes he brings out individual parts which, although attracting interest in their own right, are rarely at prominent subject or counter-subject entry points. For example, the bass entry of the fugue subject at bar 164 is not especially projected, although its *staccato* articulation makes it audible, whereas the bass line, which starts on the upbeat to bar 190 and is related to the counter-subject, is given prominence, thus drawing the listener's attention to the polyphonic contribution of this fragment. Even more intriguing is the prominent role allotted to the bass line of 251, two bars ahead of a counter-subject entry, which tends to attract the listener's attention away from any structural significance that this entry might otherwise be given, seemingly reflecting an idiosyncratic view of genre. These could also be instances of what Bazzana describes as 'the exaggeration of lower parts in many Gould performances' which suggests 'that strong "counter-signals" are needed to break conventional listening habits' (149). Also, textual invitations to *crescendo* such as those highlighted in Hewitt's recording receive a very different treatment in the hands of Gould. Where the former applies a *crescendo* in bars 224–227, Gould opts for a *diminuendo*, and her localized nuances, commencing at bar 230, contrast with the uniform *mp* of his performance between bars 228 and 233.

My own use of dynamics also highlights entries (bars 197 and 253), emphasizes repetitions through the application of a *crescendo* (bars 212^6–216), and can be taken to reflect the character of the passage as I perceive it (*p/mp* at 161^2 and 219^4). However, two further uses may be identified where dynamic drops correspond to a change of register at bar 248, and to a change from major to minor at bar 201.[17]

The Importance of Topic

Earlier, I noted a degree of similarity amongst performances of the gigue-fugue, and the detailed evidence of the four recordings demonstrates a much greater accord between the interpretations of this section than between those of the preceding recitative passage. This is very likely due to the prominence of the topic category, clearly detectable in all four recordings. Because the gigue, with its inherent dance feel,[18] is such a readily identifiable musical type and one which is regularly included in Baroque dance collections, especially as a lively concluding movement, its role as an informant is hard to avoid.

The presence of the gigue topic in BWV 912, as noted earlier, can exert a strong influence on the tempo informant, and this influence is further highlighted when

---

[17] The general dynamic level on the recording is higher than was my intention. This could be accounted for in part by a resonant acoustic and a less-than-top-quality microphone, which tends to compress dynamic extremes.

[18] The gigue has no firmly established choreographic link, although Little and Jenne suggest: 'It seems likely that gigas ... were originally a spin-off from the jigs of English country dance fame but by the late seventeenth century gigas have a life quite apart from dance steps' (Little and Jenne 2001 [1991]: 157).

performances of the gigue section of this toccata, for which no specific tempo designation is given, are compared with those of a preceding, apparently fast, section running from bar 10[4] to bar 67. Modern editions and four out of the six manuscript sources actually label this passage '*allegro*', for which a roughly contemporary definition can be found in Walther's *Musicalisches Lexicon*: 'happy, merry, quite lively or awake; very often also quick or fleeting; but sometimes also a moderate but happy, lively measure' (Badura-Skoda 1995 [1990]: 79).[19] The notation's appearance as well as the music's syntax also strongly suggest a lively pace. Both Richter and, especially, Hewitt adopt a brisk tempo with the former on crotchet = *c.* 91 and the latter on crotchet = *c.* 100, although, at crotchet = *c.* 118, my recording goes considerably faster (CD, track 15). Gould at crotchet = *c.* 81 sounds decidedly more tentative. Significantly, then, there is much more agreement amongst the four performers regarding the motion of a gigue than there is regarding the direct tempo instruction '*allegro*', even though neither topic nor tempo designations are supplied for the former. This comparison reinforces the primacy of the topic category over the tempo category within the context of BWV 912 .

To conclude, the influence of the gigue topic, especially in its fugal arrangement, also seems to yield relatively close matches between the remaining informants heard in four otherwise very different interpretations. There is a large measure of similarity regarding era (Baroque dance style), authorship (almost no textual additions or changes) genre (part-playing in a fugue), topical mode (*vivace*), characterizer (observance of the hierarchy of the bar), tempo and duration manipulator (general absence of *rubato*). Even sonic moderation has recognizable points of contact: a tendency to use detached articulation to a greater or lesser extent (but always in keeping with the dance topic) and to adopt techniques which keep part-playing clear. The performances make use of dynamics, albeit to different ends, and less obviously so in Richter's case. However, dynamic variety is perhaps less intimately connected to topic than is tempo or even articulation, so it is not surprising to find the greatest divergence in this single area.

Analytical data concerning the four performances of the gigue-fugue can be summarized as follows:

Gould, Hellaby, Hewitt, Richter
> Level 1: equal weight given to **authorship (score)** and **era (style)**
> Level 2: concluding fugal section, influencing some surface-level features (**genre**); gigue (**topic**) very important, directly influencing level three →
> Level 3: *vivace* manner (**topical mode**); importance given to downbeats (**characterizer**) →
> Level 4: dotted crotchet = 119–122, accommodating demisemiquaver passage (**tempo**)

---

[19] 'Allegro: frölich, lustig, wohl belebt oder erwedt; sehr offt auch: geschwinde und fluchtig; manchmal aber auch, einen gemässigten, obschon frölichen und belebten Tact' (Walther 1732: 27).

Gould
> Level 4: stable pulse but slows down for the last three bars and ends with a *ritenuto* (**duration manipulator**); genre-based textural clarity, mixed articulation inconsistently applied but favouring staccato, varied but voice-related dynamics moving towards a *forte* ending (**sonic moderator**)

Hellaby
> Level 4: mainly stable pulse with one increase of tempo and a *ritenuto* in the last bar (**duration manipulator**); genre-based textural clarity, mixed articulation consistently applied, varied dynamics but partially related to voice entries, averaging between *mf* and *f* (**sonic moderator**).

Hewitt
> Level 4: stable pulse with touches of *rubato* in four places, most noticeably the last two bars (**duration manipulator**); genre-based textural clarity, mixed articulation with some inconsistencies, varied dynamics but partially related to voice entries, averaging *mf* rather than *f* (**sonic moderator**).

Richter
> Level 4: stable pulse until the last two bars, where the pace is freer and ends with a *ritenuto* (**duration manipulator**); genre-based textural clarity, reasonably consistent use of mixed articulation, mainly *mf/f* dynamic, some limited projection of lower fugal voices (**sonic moderator**).

Due to the high level of interpretative agreement observed above, it is only necessary to show one reading graphically, and Hewitt's is depicted in Figure 3.2.

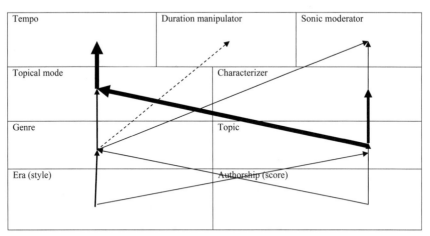

Dotted lines indicate weak emphasis; bold lines indicate strong emphasis.

Figure 3.2   Bach: Toccata in D major BWV 912, bars 177–277 (gigue-fugue); Hewitt's interpretation mapped on to the interpretative tower

Summary

At the beginning of this chapter, I anticipated that performances of a relatively 'thin' work are liable to demonstrate that performers' artistic prerogatives have been exercised in dissimilar ways. The first case study has tended to corroborate this prediction, and tower analysis has revealed varying emphases within the pianists' interpretative schemes, thus demonstrating disparity amongst the unique results of these. My analyses considered the possible influence of HIP, but any such influence proved hard to verify, so my analytical focus was therefore directed to the experience of the music as sound (the performer's acoustic trace), and to reading this as a statement of personal authenticity. As Angela Hewitt admits, after consulting two editions she added some of her own ideas (personal communication 21 June 2005).

If interpretative dissimilarity was anticipated, perhaps the degree of accord noted in recordings of the gigue-fugue, my second case study, comes as more of a surprise. It is as if the topical presence has 'thickened' the work's constitutive properties and narrowed the performance options. It could even be thought that the interpretations reflect the distant influence of HIP although, as argued, the evidence of the recordings cannot be taken to indicate a conscious assimilation of this influence on the part of the pianists but rather as a reflection of the work's musical informants. Nevertheless, the performers' traces are still unique, even if they tend towards convergence rather than divergence.

Afterword: From Suggestion to Prescription

It is an interesting thought that the interpretative tower's surface-level informants of tempo, duration manipulator and sonic moderator have not remained static but seem partly subject to fashion. This can be illustrated by comparing a typical modern *Urtext* with, for example, Czerny, Griepenkerl and Roitzsch's edition of Bach's *Italian Concerto*, in which metronome marks are added to each movement, a tempo direction is given to the first and barely a note is left without a dynamic, a suggested phrasing or articulation.[20] Here, the editors are presuming a brief that was later to transfer to the composer (and had largely done so in Czerny's own generation) but was, in Bach's time, that of the performer. As John Butt puts it, 'The dual role of the *practical* musician of Bach's time as both composer and performer is somewhat foreign to musical life today' (Butt 1999 [1990]: x). Czerny and his co-editors, acting on their own early Romantic understanding of the musical signals in the score, chose to translate these into performance

---

[20] Czerny *et al.* do, however, leave intact Bach's own dynamics, which reflect use of the harpsichord's 'soft upper manual' and the '*forte* of the lower keyboard ... to imitate tutti and soli groups in the orchestra' (Troeger 2003: 100).

directions that made sense to themselves and their own generation.[21] This is an instance of three interpreters presenting their joint perception of authorial intent and, in the process, manifesting 'the Romantic desire to link Bach with Beethoven' (Stauffer 1997: 207). Nowadays, the 'inauthenticity' of such offerings can offend and performers are, in part, restored to their original role, but only with continual backward glances to perceived 'performance practice'. This, in itself, creates an unbridgeable gap between the twenty-first-century and the eighteenth-century Baroque performer, especially as we now have contemporary taste (or historical situatedness) to deal with as well. As Taruskin says: 'performers can be counted on to flout historical evidence whenever it does not conform to their idea of "the truth"' (Taruskin 1995: 16).[22]

Ironically, similarity between performances of the Toccata in D BWV 912 might be greater had all protagonists used a Czerny edition, a view corroborated in part by the next chapter which focuses on a work which only exists in one edition. When score-based information provides only a little more than the notes, as with the Bach toccata, interpretative divergence seems often to be the result, but such divergence becomes increasingly discouraged when composers attempt to assume control of the interpretative aspects of their compositions. Where authorial performance prescriptions abound, the uppermost informants, those through which an artist can communicate a perception of a work's 'meaning', tend in performance to show signs of convergence. However, differences from artist to artist perhaps lessen but certainly do not altogether disappear. And so the *Werktreue* ideal, if ideal it is, remains both elusive and illusive.

---

[21]   The edition is still available from Peters. Another good example of editorial governance can be found in Augener's 1914 edition of the French Suites, edited by Franklin Taylor. The preface contains a note about varying sources, the need for accuracy of notes and the retention of Bach's original ornament signs, yet no word can be found in justification of the phrase, dynamic and articulation marks which are liberally added throughout. This naturally raises questions concerning the changing role of the editor, but these are outside the scope of my discussion.

[22]   He is referring, in particular to Frans Brüggen, Roger Norrington, John Eliot Gardiner and Malcolm Bilson.

Chapter 4
Messiaen: 'Première communion de la Vierge'

The Recordings and the Work

If Bach performance involves selection from a broad field of interpretative possibilities, especially with regard to higher-level informants, then Olivier Messiaen's music may appear to narrow this field very significantly – with perhaps only works like Boulez's *Structures* taking this yet further. I opened the previous chapter by ascribing some of Stephen Davies' constitutive properties of 'thinness' to the Bach toccata, so it may be appropriate now to ascribe the constitutive property of 'thickness' to Messiaen's 'Première communion de la Vierge' (from *Vingt regards sur l'Enfant-Jésus*).[1] By 'thickness', Davies means that 'a great many of the properties heard in performance are crucial to [the work's] identity ... the thicker the work, the more the composer controls the sonic details of its accurate instances' (Davies 2001: 20). My forthcoming analysis will, therefore, address the notion that the properties of a composition such as 'Première communion' 'must be reproduced in a fully faithful rendition of the work' (20).

Messiaen's score is full of detailed performance indications, or 'givens', and the three commercial recordings on which I am basing my case study each received the composer's approval. It may therefore be reasonable to suppose that there will be a high degree of accord between these acoustic traces and that the score will be more or less definitively projected into the performances. This suggests that a significant constraint may have been placed on the performers' freedom to exercise their artistic prerogatives, seemingly reducing their esthesic processes to a minimum. However, in most instances, experience does not lead the informed listener to expect interpretative uniformity, and it would be wrong at this stage to rule out the possibility that performances may 'differ in accordance with the way the players make the choices that are their prerogatives' (Davies 2001: 20). What has still to be investigated is just how much latitude of choice, if any, a thick work permits and to what extent the exercise of artistic prerogatives may be heard to operate within this stricture.

---

[1]   The use or otherwise of capital letters in French titles throughout this chapter is according to the published editions consulted.

Recording Artists

The artists whose recordings I shall be examining in this chapter all, in some way, had associations with the composer. Yvonne Loriod, the work's dedicatee, was the composer's wife and a long-time champion of his music. Clearly, Messiaen must have influenced her interpretations, but her pupil Pierre-Laurent Aimard suggests that 'the opposite is also true: one senses a radical enrichment of the composer's piano writing from the moment he met Yvonne' (Herpers 2000: 7). Peter Hill is in agreement: 'one sees the inspiring influence of Loriod, whose unquenchable powers enabled new complexities of thought, and liberated Messiaen's imagination (as he many times testified) from practical limitations' (Hill 1995a: 88). Certainly the CD re-release of her 1973 recording prompted admiration from Michael Oliver: 'Her virtuosity is formidable, her authority felt on every page, and her love for the music is urgent and passionate.' He also comments that 'this recording has the additional authority of having been produced by Messiaen himself' (Oliver 1994: 127–8).

Peter Hill prepared most of his own complete Messiaen cycle with the composer in Paris and, according to his CD of the *Vingt regards*, from the latter he received this compliment: 'Beautiful technique, a true poet: I am a passionate admirer of Peter Hill's playing.' David Fanning is equally enthusiastic:

> what Hill does is allow the listener to come to the music, rather than bring the music to the listener. In this sense his comparatively passive approach can be held up as a virtue, as can the literalness of his adherence to notated rhythm … and to the metronome markings … the most complex movements are … thoroughly prepared…while the lyrical effusions … have an inner calm and glow all their own. (Fanning 1992: 135)

Pierre-Laurent Aimard was, as mentioned, a pupil of Loriod's at the Paris Conservatoire, and he studied with her for a total of seven years. He was a regular companion of Messiaen and Loriod when they toured and, according to his *Vingt regards* CD cover notes, he received this eulogy from the composer himself: 'Pierre-Laurent Aimard was thoroughly admirable: technically superb, clear and rich in tone; outstandingly intelligent playing, always completely in control of the demands of the piece thanks to his flawless skill.' The same CD cover notes quote pianist Alfred Brendel: 'Pierre-Laurent Aimard's performance of Messiaen's *Vingt regards* at the London Barbican ranks among the truly exceptional piano recitals in my memory.' Michael Oliver appears to concur with this assessment of Aimard's interpretation:

> the power and excitement of Aimard's playing are indeed astonishing … Aimard's prodigious range of timbre and dynamic provide just the sound that Messiaen must have imagined … intense concentration, stillness and purity of colour … his dazzling technique and fabulous range of colour make this the most spectacular reading of *Vingt regards* yet. (Oliver 2000: 106)

I shall also be referring to my own CD of 'Première communion de la Vierge', recorded privately in January 2004 (CD, tracks 18–24).

As in the previous chapter, it is important to establish a frame of reference within which the performer operates, and against which the evidence of the recordings may be assessed. I therefore begin with some observations about the artistic context of Messiaen's work and of 'Première communion de la Vierge' in particular.

Messiaen's Performance Instructions in Context

Amongst Messiaen's immediate French predecessors, Debussy is often regarded as the former's most important mentor. Carla Bell believes that '[f]rom Debussy, [Messiaen] inherited the coloristic rather than the traditional (directional) conception of harmony' (Bell 1984: 14), enabling him to create 'a harmony existing in a state that is neither tension nor relaxation in a structure that does not seek progressions based on a principle of dissonance and resolution' (23). It is, no doubt, this shift from harmonic functionality towards harmonic colour that prompts Madeleine Hsu to write: 'Debussy and Messiaen … stress the sensuous side of music … Like Debussy, Messiaen strove for an iridescent music, one that delights the auditory senses with delicate voluptuous pleasures' (Hsu 1996: 138).[2] Thus the listener's auditory sense perception is directed towards 'the exquisite moment' (Hill 1995a: 73) rather than towards 'temporal articulation' (Pople, 1995: 19). Messiaen's performance directions attempt the fine control of the colouristic and sensuous effects of a performance, and it would be worth briefly comparing these directions with those typically supplied by Debussy.

An aspect of Debussy's and Messiaen's music that is of relevance to both performer and analyst is their association of a soundscape with parallel visual imagery. Debussy's inclination to suggest programmatic connections for the great majority of his piano works, either as titles or parenthetic subtitles, is symptomatic of this association. Messiaen not only supplies each of the *Vingt regards* with a title but elaborates it further with an aphoristic subscript. The music of 'Première communion de la Vierge', the eleventh of the *Vingt regards* cycle, was inspired by a painting depicting the Virgin kneeling in a contemplative pose and worshipping the Christ child within her. The subscript to the title of the piece leaves the player in no doubt as to the programme of the music: 'After the Annunciation, Mary worships Jesus within her … my God, my son, my Magnificat! – my love without the noise of words … .'[3]

---

[2]   Madeleine Hsu (1996) believes that Debussy's main influence on Messiaen is aesthetic, but that in other areas Bartók's influence is at least as important.

[3]   'Après l'Annonciation, Marie adore Jésus en elle … mon Dieu, mon fils, mon Magnificat! – mon amour sans bruit de paroles …' (*Vingt regards sur l'Enfant-Jésus*, Edition Durand, p.77).

Turning to more informant-specific issues, topical mode directions, when linked with appropriate musical passages, could be thought to explore some of the acoustic implications of a title, yet Debussy does not fill his scores with such directions. Amongst his preferred instructions of this type in both books of *Préludes* are '*doux*', '*très doux*' or '*doucement*', which he applies to several preludes, sometimes more than once. Also, '*expressif*' makes some appearances and, more rarely, '*gracieux*' ('La puerta del vino'), '*joyeux*' ('Les collines d'Anacapri') and '*scintillant*' ('Ondine').[4] If Debussy does not particularly rely on topical modes, Messiaen relies on them even less in *Vingt regards*. For example, in 'Première communion', which combines both mystical and ecstatic elements, it may seem reasonable to expect a considerable number of mood-related topical modes, yet '*enthousiasme haletant*' (bar 21) along with '*tendre*', '*intérieur*' and '*embrassement intérieur*' in the opening and closing bars are the only instances in the piece.[5] A likely reason for the two composers' reluctance to make many such petitions to the performer's imagination is that plentiful, much more precise top-layer information renders them partially redundant.

With regard to top-layer informants, Messiaen adopts Debussy's habit of indicating, as precisely as possible, every nuance of tempo, dynamic and articulation that he wants from the performer, but he is yet more precise in other respects. Debussy does not habitually provide metronome marks and, where he does, the single one at or near the outset of the piece is almost invariably the only one[6] despite numerous subsequent written instructions to modify the tempo. Messiaen's early *Préludes* prescribe many tempo adjustments but are wholly without metronome indications. By 1944, when *Vingt regards* was written, the composer had become more specific, supplying metronome marks at the head of all the movements and accompanying any significant tempo change within each piece by a further indication. In 'Première communion', there are eight metronome marks printed in the score.

Pedal instructions in Debussy's scores are surprisingly infrequent,[7] given the nature of his piano writing. Messiaen does provide more information for the

---

[4]   An interesting comparison can be made with a Romantic score such as Liszt's 'Les cloches de Genève', from *Années de Pèlerinage 1*, which is also a pre-echo of impressionism and equivalent in length to one of Debussy's bigger preludes. In this single piece alone, the following are employed: *Agitato, Animato, Cantabile, Cantando, Con somma passione, Dolce* (x 2), *Dolcissimo, Espressivo, Quasi arpa, Più dolce*.

[5]   I am treating appellations such as '*oiseaux*' (bar 7) and '*Battements du couer de l'Enfant*' (bar 61) as programmatic properties of the work rather than as performance directions.

[6]   'Et la lune descend sur le temple qui fut' from *Images*, Series 2 is an exception.

[7]   The majority of Debussy's piano music contains no pedal indications at all. Those supplied at a few points in, for example, *Estampes* are exceptions. Otherwise, there is the occasional instruction '*les deux pédales*' ('La sérénade interrompou' from *Préludes*, Book 1), '*laisser vibrer*' ('Mouvements' from *Images*, Series 1) or, even more rarely,

Messiaen: 'Première communion de la Vierge' 93

pianist but is still not unduly prescriptive. In 'Première communion', the composer indicates pedalling in several places, mainly in the later stages of the piece, but it is hard to imagine a performance which does not include use of the sustaining pedal over and above where marked, not to mention the *una corda* pedal. The implication of this, along with other pedal markings in the cycle, is that the composer makes a point of adding pedalling instructions only where he feels that the performer might otherwise misunderstand his wishes, or where he desires a particular effect.[8] At other times, he leaves this aspect to the performer's judgement even though, according to Hill, Messiaen as a teacher 'was punctilious over pedalling, and ... disliked any blurring of harmonies' (Hill 1995b: 279).

Messiaen's detailed use of dynamic indications in *Vingt regards*, as with the piano writing itself, is an extension of the impressionist practices from which it grew. This can be illustrated by comparing his practices in 1944 with those employed in the only slightly later work, *Cantéyodjayâ* (1948), in which, according to Hill and Simeone, 'the old and the new Messiaen collide' (Hill and Simeone 2005: 190). Perhaps reflecting his early experiments with integral serialism, the dynamic (and articulation) instructions in *Cantéyodjayâ*, though numerous, are more segmented. Thus separate voices and discrete units are partially defined by the dynamic marking, a practice that is especially evident in the passage running from bar 64 to 101, where pitch, duration and dynamic are integrated. A consequence of this is the relative scarcity of *crescendo* or *diminuendo* indications,[9] reflecting a break with concepts of phrasing or harmonic tension and release which gradual increases and decreases in dynamic levels have tended to reflect. However, this latter function is still, in part at least, ascribed to the role of dynamics in 'Première communion', as for example in the *crescendo* which accompanies the rising left-hand octaves and right-hand chordal work from bar 39, and which culminates in the climactic passage commencing at bar 43. The tension thus generated is released in the music of bars 61–72, where the customary intensifying function of a pedal note is reversed to produce a calming effect which is matched by a long *diminuendo*.

Messiaen is equally precise with regard to articulative markings, although he limits these throughout the *Vingt regards* almost entirely to three: the accent (>), the *marcato* line (-) and the *staccato* dot (.). All three appear in 'Première communion', occasionally with accent and staccato dot in combination (as in bar 28), although

---

'con sordina', as at the opening of 'Clair de lune' (from *Suite bergamasque*). Debussy's sonorities are fundamentally dependent on sensitive use of the pedal, yet he maintained that '[p]edaling [*sic*] cannot be written down, it varies from one instrument to another, from one room or one hall, to another' (Dunoyer 1999: 99).

[8]   For example, in 'Regard des prophètes, des bergers et des mages', Messiaen indicates that the pedal should be held unchanged throughout the first twenty-one bars and reinforces this by adding the words *'laisser résonner'*.

[9]   *Crescendo* and *diminuendo* (mainly the former) appear on only 9 out of the 25 pages of music in the Universal Edition of *Cantéyodjayâ*.

94   *Reading Musical Interpretation*

the latter does not feature prominently elsewhere. However, a pianist's observance of both accents and *marcato* lines can shape the acoustic effect of the music in performance and, as the forthcoming analyses will reveal, have a significant role to play in the interpretative profiles of the four recordings.

Analytical Strategy

Because performance elements of 'Première communion de la Vierge' are apparently 'fixed' to a very large extent by the score, the acoustic evidence of the selected recordings will be analysed in close relationship with the printed evidence of the score, and interpretations will be reconstructed layer by layer according to the interpretative tower, starting at level one and advancing to level four. Level four informants, those at the surface, will be referred to throughout because, as audible signs of interpretative involvement lower down the tower's hierarchy, they perforce remain my first points of reference. Symptomatically, they will receive the closest attention when the top three informants themselves are being scrutinized. My analytical focus will gradually shift from work to recorded performance, progressively viewing the former through the medium of the latter. Moving upwards from the objective 'facts' of the work into the more performer-dependent areas, that is from the ideal to the executive, may help to ascertain just how far performances of a 'thick' work may be perceived as predetermined.

As stated, my analysis concerns performances of 'Première communion', a movement of the *Vingt regards* which, along with other relative favourites such as 'Regard de l'Esprit de joie' and 'Le baiser de l'Enfant-Jésus', is regularly presented in recital as a free-standing movement. An examination of 'Première communion' in performance within the broader context of the complete *Vingt regards* cycle might affect the analytical findings as reflected in the interpretative tower, especially considering the movement's positioning between the celebratory virtuosity of 'Regard de l'Esprit de joie' and the powerful sonorities of 'La parole toute-puissante'. However, such an examination is outside the scope of this book and I shall therefore only make reference to movements other than 'Première communion' where relevant.

'Première communion de la Vierge' and the Interpretative Tower

Authorship (Score)

Starting at level one of the interpretative tower, Messiaen's role as author emerges as a compelling presence when compared to the relative distance of Bach's. The former's detailed performance instructions, such as those described above, have a degree of 'authority' lacking, to a greater or lesser extent, in eighteenth- and nineteenth-century scores. Messiaen's instructions are equally available to all performers and, with the presence of just one edition, the *mens auctoris* may appear to be relatively accessible. One detailed and more or less 'authoritative' score, representing a seemingly definitive authorial statement, could be thought to ensure a recognizable similarity of interpretation between any two performers with the necessary technique and musical skill to tackle the pieces in the first place.

This virtual proximity of the author is not only discovered through the agency of the score. As has been mentioned, all three principal performers under consideration studied the music with the composer himself or with his wife, so the influence of authorship in these cases operates at very close quarters. (I am clearly an exception.) The influence is likely therefore to be a more powerful presence in their interpretative set-ups than the more indirect influence of a long-dead composer who had the benefit of neither such precise notational conventions nor of supervision prior to recording.

The existence of supervised recordings also has repercussions in that they propagate an authorial 'voice' via a medium other than the score. The ones that I am using, excepting my own, act as interpretative documents with at least some claim to authority, due to the artists' relationships with Messiaen. Even bearing in mind Aimard's warning that '[Messiaen] was ... far too often satisfied by his performers' (Herpers 2000: 7), the recordings are documents which pianists, for many years to come, will be able to consult in the knowledge that the composer himself was involved in their formative stages. Messiaen did not actually live to hear Aimard's recording but it is probably safe to believe that it is not fundamentally different from the pianist's live performances which Messiaen did hear.

Era (Style)

Compared to the performance of more historical works, performances of recently composed music present the analyst with a different set of issues to address when considering era (style). Historical performance practice, despite its inevitably generalized nature, may be perceived to act as a powerful informant in Baroque, Classical and, to a lesser extent, Romantic music, in as much as it may partially substitute for a lack of audio evidence and score-based specificity. In the case of a piece such as 'Première communion de la Vierge', performance practice seems a much less thorny issue, in that the score provides a detailed testimony to the composer's ideas. Detective work regarding general trends and performance styles is therefore of less immediate concern, and the analyst can draw a direct comparison between performance and score.

In the context of the current discussion, one area where era possibly has relevance is that of piano sonority. Although one may still agree with William Leslie Sumner when he noted over forty years ago that 'modern cultured taste, concerning the tones of keyboard instruments, demands more and more clarity and brightness' (Sumner 1971 [1966]: 98), Messiaen was writing for an instrument that is thoroughly familiar to the contemporary pianist. Grand pianos and their capabilities in 1944 were not very dissimilar from those of more recent manufacture, if at all.[10] Consequently, where the composer appears to exploit the full dynamic and expressive range of the instrument, the pianist can take this at face value. Although touch sensitivity is paramount in such 'colourful' music as the *Vingt regards*, worries about whether a player's sonority and touch are appropriate for music originally written with a different keyboard instrument in mind seem unlikely to arise. In this connection, neither Peter Hill nor Philip Mead, both noted Messiaen exponents, regards the matter as any kind of an 'issue' (personal communications 18 August 2005 and 26 June 2005). My analysis of the sonic moderator category suggests that all four pianists take full advantage of the expressive potential of the respective instruments, despite timbral variations innate to each individual piano and the recorded sound of each CD.

With regard to music by a composer as recently alive as Messiaen, perhaps authorship (score) and era (style) become practically indistinguishable in the interpretative tower construct. It could be seen therefore as a historical process that authorship and era, so clearly divided and yet so mutually dependent in the Baroque period, have tended to converge as documentary evidence has become more detailed and compelling. This seems to modify the modern historian's view of the past, as described by Foucault. Where historians have had to make 'monuments'[11] out of documents to construct some sort of totality so that the 'document ... is no longer ... an inert material' (Foucault 1972 [1969]: 7), the Messiaen performer can regard the document as still sufficiently fresh to be a vital, active material, uniting author and executant with the era in which the product was born.

Genre

In 1924, Messiaen won first prize in the French government's music history competition. This reflects an early interest in history which may later have informed his developing compositional personality, one that Jane Fulcher describes as 'innovative, yet rooted in tradition' (Fulcher 2002: 467). As teacher, the composer identifies Couperin as a 'starting point' (Samuel 1994 [1986]: 177) for classes focusing on piano music, and French keyboard 'character' pieces which reach back to Couperin, Rameau (and beyond) could be seen to foreshadow the *Vingt regards*. Paul Griffiths suggests that *Vingt regards* 'can be used in the

---

[10]   Richard Lieberman goes so far as to claim that Henry Steinway built the first 'modern piano' and that 'it has not changed much since 1859. By the end of the century most of the major piano manufacturers in the United States and Europe were imitating Henry's construction' (Lieberman 1995: 29).

[11]   Foucault appears to be drawing on Friedrich Droysen's terminology. The latter describes 'monuments' as a hybrid of 'sources' which 'constitute a linguistic tradition [serving] our understanding of a linguistically interpreted world' and 'vestiges' which are 'fragments of a past world [which] assist us in the intellectual reconstruction of the world of which they are a remnant' (Gadamer 1977 [1964]: 99).

manner of a Couperin *ordre*, as a collection of character pieces' (Griffiths 1985: 117), and a number of Messiaen's movements, especially those with titles like 'Regard de la Vierge' or 'Regard des Anges', have an affinity with this genre. However, as the 'regard' of the title implies, an added element of contemplation may be perceived.

Although 'Première communion' may be seen as a character piece it needs also to be set in the context of Messiaen's devout Roman Catholicism. The composer said: 'I've always been a believer, pure and simple. Little by little ... I've strengthened my faith' (Samuel 1994 [1986]: 16), and his belief manifests itself throughout the *Vingt regards*. Thus the concept of 'religious character piece' draws together the various elements under discussion. The composer's theological reference points, from the 'interior' quality of the opening and closing measures to the 'enthusiasm' of the central episode, are clearly reflected in all four recordings, although this only becomes fully demonstrable once progress through the interpretative tower has enabled more detailed analysis.

As already suggested, the setting of 'Première communion de la Vierge' within a large-scale, interlinked, cyclical structure may have a bearing on how performers view the piece in relation to its neighbours, should they be playing the complete cycle, but, as previously stated, this matter lies beyond the scope of my analysis. However, the discrete macrostructure of 'Première communion' – which may be conveyed to the informed listener through an audibly recognizable distribution of the main musical elements and their related tempos, dynamics and moods – is clearly discernible in all four performances. The movement's episodic but essentially simple, truncated, ternary design is acoustically obvious, with observance of the pause mark in bar 20 – at the close of the first 'A' section – acting as a prominent structural marker, especially in Hill's interpretation.

Topic

Messiaen does not obviously draw on any pre-established topic in 'Première communion' but topicality may, nonetheless, be sensed. In five of the movements from *Vingt regards*, Messiaen incorporates a simple non-retrogradable *dhenkî* rhythm:[12] that is, quaver–semiquaver–quaver. Jean Marie Wu (1998) has accorded this idea a significant role in the cycle's final number, 'Regard de l'Eglise d'amour', but its role in 'Regard de l'Esprit de joie' is of more importance to the present discussion. Between bars 60 and 131, Messiaen uses the *dhenkî* idea (see Example 4.1) as the basis for an elaborate musical discourse, thus according it a topical status akin to that identified in Chapter 2.

---

[12] Messiaen identifies 'the very ancient Hindu *dhenkî* and the antique Greek *amphimacer*' as 'the first known non-retrogradable rhythms' (Wu 1998: 96). The *dhenkî* rhythm appears in a number of the composer's works before and after 1944, such as *Les Corps Glorieux* (1939) for organ.

Example 4.1 Messiaen: 'Regard de l'Esprit de joie', bars 60–61; *dhenkî* rhythm

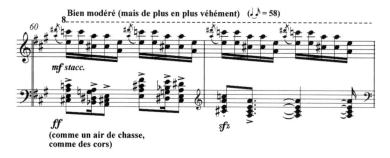

Although the localized affiliation of this passage is with a hunting song and horns, Messiaen's incorporation of the *dhenkî* rhythm into the *danse véhémente* character of 'Regard de l'Esprit de joie' establishes an association which, on the rhythm's reappearance at bar 21 of 'Première communion de la Vierge', is likely to be remembered by both performer and informed listener, especially as the two movements occur consecutively in the cycle. The interconnection is reinforced by metronome marks which, even if only loosely observed in performance, yield similar tempos. The indication for the former works out at quaver = 145, whilst that for the latter is given as quaver = 138, and where Messiaen ascribes a *véhément* character to the former, he accords one of *enthousiasme* to the latter. Thus, in 'Première communion', it could be said that Messiaen is further developing a personal topic which retains a strong dance character, and also conveys a distinct authorial presence in performance.

To some pianists, a rather more distant association may reinforce the dance topic. The ear schooled in Western art music may detect a suggestion of compound time in the left-hand rhythms. A dotted rhythm in compound time is associated with dance music in a number of topics, notably the siciliano, the forlana and the loure. Messiaen's use of *dhenkî* collapses the characteristic rhythms of these dances (see Example 4.2), creating a rather unsettled effect – hence perhaps the instruction '*haletant*' ('pantingly') – but this collapse may not be quite sufficient to dispel an association with pre-existing dance topics in the interpreters' minds, be they analysts or performers.

Example 4.2 Messiaen: 'Première communion de la Vierge', bars 21–23

Up to this point, the interpretations by Loriod, Hill, Aimard and myself appear to be similarly anchored, with the tower's lower-level informants retaining their largely ideal role, but different approaches to the passage under discussion are

detectable (manifested, like all lower-level informants, through the acoustic evidence of the recording). As David Fanning (1992) implies in his review, Hill is quite literal in his adherence to Messiaen's performance indications. He is meticulous in his observance of the *f* dynamic, the *marcato* and accent signs. In the absence of any instruction to the contrary, he adopts a more or less *legato* approach in which the pedal seems to be used as shown in Example 4.3. As a consequence of this, no strong sense of a dance topic can be deduced, even though Hill's tempo, as with all four recordings, is above the metronome marking (of which more later).

Example 4.3   Messiaen: 'Première communion de la Vierge', bars 21–23; Hill's pedalling

Aimard projects the dynamic and accents rather less than does Hill but adopts a less legato approach, pedalling only the initial quaver of each group and performing its complements in a detached manner, as shown in Example 4.4. Aimard's articulations are not marked in Messiaen's score, but, to the informed listener, they seem to evoke a characteristic dance-like articulation.

Example 4.4   Messiaen: 'Première communion de la Vierge', bars 21–23; Aimard's pedalling

Loriod's version, which also adheres to all dynamic, *marcato* and accent requirements, has much in common with Hill's with regard to articulation and pedalling, but more obviously separates the 10/16 bars from the 5/8 bars, as shown in Example 4.5.

Example 4.5   Messiaen: 'Première communion de la Vierge' Bars 21–23; Loriod's placement

My own recording likewise observes the composer's dynamic and articulation markings, but I apply pedal only to the first left-hand quaver. I subsequently hold the second quaver for its notated value and play the intervening semiquaver *staccato*. The outcome is thus a compromise between Hill's and Aimard's readings (CD, track 21).

If one accepts the notion of *dhenkî*-as-dance topic, then this can be perceived more in Aimard's account than in the other three, because Hill's and Loriod's more literal accounts offer less support for the notion. So, despite the detail in Messiaen's score, room seems to have been left for subtle differences of emphasis in performance. These differences illustrate that what may be regarded as a minor fissure in a work's 'thickness' opens up the interpretative field, here producing four acoustic traces which project a perceived topicality in varying degrees, even though the performance directions that are provided are observed to a greater or lesser extent by all.

Topical Mode

As mentioned earlier, Messiaen's only topical mode indications in 'Première communion' are '*enthousiasme haletant*' (bar 21), '*intérieur*' (bars 1 and 75), '*tendre*' (bars 2 and 76) and '*embrassement intérieur*' (bar 76). A response to the latter indications, with their suggestion of a rapt inwardness, may be expected to involve sensitively controlled layering of p and pp dynamics. Such playing is likely to be achieved via a close-knit spirit–mind–body connection which will be discussed in more practical terms under the duration manipulator and sonic moderator informant categories. With regard to the '*tendre*' of bars 2 and 76, all four pianists play the right-hand quaver dyads as requested by the composer: quietly, slowly, with a *legato* touch and according to the marked phrasing, factors which in themselves seem to convey the topical mode. However, Aimard's slight *ritenuto* towards the end of the phrase could be regarded as a more personal response to *tendre*.

The affective qualities suggested by *enthousiasme* and *haletant* appear to be embedded in the music anyway, thereby facilitating the performer's task. Enthusiasm is ensured largely by the dynamic and the speed, whilst the 'panting' character is conveyed by the irregular, distorted 'compound' rhythms and the asymmetrical accents. All artists observe the accentuation, although Aimard projects this aspect the least, to the extent that the right-hand accents in bar 23 are only just detectable. Hill's reading brings out the accents prominently, so, although he may not especially project any latent dance properties in the passage, he does realize its 'panting' quality. This is entirely consistent with his respectful approach to the details of the score in that the accents are requested by the composer himself whereas the dance topic is unspecified and its realization is much more dependent on the poietic/esthesic interactions between score, performer and analyst.

A topical mode cannot, by its nature, describe an exact sonic or durational quantity but rather suggests a manner of delivery: various characters and qualities must be imagined into a sonic event, requiring 'voluntary interpretation' (Cook 1992 [1990]) on the part of the performer. This informant's inherent vagueness and implied trust in the performer's judgement do not lie comfortably in a score that is as precise as Messiaen's. In fact, he has supplied so much detailed top-layer information that the topical mode's tendency to redundancy, noted earlier, may be witnessed as it is all but subsumed by the top-layer categories.

Characterizer

The characterizer category is, perhaps, less challenging to the performer's analytical powers in music such as this, in which everything is spelt out so exactly. Nevertheless, one section, running from bar 47 to bar 70, demands attention. The proportionally organized expanding note values which operate in bars 53–70 can be taken as characterizers. Messiaen writes under bar 53 in the score: 'Valeurs de 2 en 2, de 1–3 à 13–15' but there is little that the performer can do to demonstrate this feature other than to get it right. In this regard, the repeated left-hand semiquavers that run from bar 61 to 70 in my recording are accurate and, of the four under scrutiny, have the most percussive clarity. Aimard is also accurate but, in terms of audibility, Loriod is minus one semiquaver in bar 64 and Hill drops one at the end of 70.

Carefully calculated augmenting note values also appear in bars 47–51. The duration of the first chord of each bar augments from two semiquavers to three, to five, then to seven, and finally to eleven, so that each bar, with its unchanging crotchet, totals progressively 6, 7, 9, 11 and 15 semiquavers' length, as shown in Example 4.6.

Example 4.6 Messiaen: 'Première communion de la Vierge', bars 47–51

In Chapter 2 of *Technique de mon langage musical*, Messiaen issues this warning: 'in my music ... the values are always notated very exactly; hence whether it is a question of barred passages or not, the reader and the performer have only to read and execute *exactly the values marked*' (Messiaen 1956 [1944]: 14).[13] The problem in this instance is compounded by the fact that there is no

---

[13] In the preface to *Quatuor pour la Fin du Temps* (1942), Messiaen asks his performers to play the text, the notes and the values exactly, but does allow that the 'sense' of the values may suffice in unbarred stretches. In this connection, it is interesting to note

102 *Reading Musical Interpretation*

sounded semiquaver 'pulse'[14] as there is from bar 61, so the executant has to keep mental count. Amongst the recordings of the above passage, Hill and I achieve this exactly (CD, track 22, 16″). Both Aimard and Loriod manage 6, 6½, 7, 9 and 12 semiquavers, slightly collapsing the notated requirement and thus producing minor implications for the duration manipulator informant. It has to be conceded that these are only apparent when the analyst sits, accompanied by a score, and counts carefully through repeated hearings. In a more general sense, an informed listener may notice that Loriod and Aimard get through the passage a little faster than do Hill and I, but the additive nature of the rhythm is not audibly lost and the underlying 'spirit' may still be perceived in the performances.

The characterizer can be heard to inform all four performances but, because the durations are meticulously reproduced in those by Hill and myself, in this regard a strong underpinning authorial influence can be detected. It would be difficult, however, to justify describing Loriod's and Aimard's less precise versions as more 'subjective'. It is far more likely that – especially within the context of the topical mode, 'enthusiasm' – they just got their counting slightly wrong. And even here, the term 'wrong' is questionable partly because 'it is realized that there is a certain tolerance around ... [notated] ratios in actual performance' (Gabrielsson 2000 [1988]: 35–6), and also because the active performer does not always experience time in the same way as the critical listener. Psychological tension and adrenaline can have the effect of slightly shifting our perceptions or, to put it more negatively, as Andrew Steptoe does: 'A characteristic feature of musical performance anxiety is disruption of task-orientated cognitions' (Steptoe 2002 [2001]: 298).

Tempo

The use of metronome indications to accompany all main tempo changes in Messiaen's score bespeaks an attempt to achieve as much authorial control over tempo as possible. Nevertheless, this control can only be manifest if a performer rigorously adheres to the metronome marks that Messiaen so meticulously specifies. It would therefore be useful at this point to compare the composer's specifications with averages achieved in the respective performances of 'Première communion de la Vierge' by Loriod, Hill, Aimard and myself as shown in Table 4.1.

---

that Messiaen's recordings of his own music, when followed with the score, often sound far from rhythmically exact. For example, in his 1951 recording of *Quatre Études de rythme*, some note-values in 'Ile de feu 1' are cut slightly short whilst others are slightly extended and, in bars 13 and 14, crotchet values are not accurately converted into quaver values. In 'Neumes rythmiques', coupled semiquaver chords are played in a near-triplet rhythm and *dhenkî* rhythms are executed imprecisely, whilst Messiaen's recording of 'Modes de valeurs et d'intensité' sounds rhythmically approximate in many places.

[14] In the score, Messiaen describes these semiquavers as the 'Battements du cœur de l'Enfant'.

Messiaen: 'Première communion de la Vierge' 103

Table 4.1   Messiaen's metronome markings in 'Première communion de la Vierge' and average tempos adopted by Aimard, Hellaby, Hill and Loriod

Bar	1	7	9	17	21	43
Mm	**qu = 50**	**qu = 40**	**qu = 50**	**s'qu = 76**	**qu = 138***	**qu = 120**
Aimard	66	44	59	70	168	138
Hellaby	45	41	46	79	148	135
Hill	51	34	40	73	152	120
Loriod	60	44	61	54	168	137

Bar	73	75
Mm	**s'qu = 96**	**qu = 50**
Aimard	92	65
Hellaby	92	50
Hill	74	53
Loriod	96	62

Note

*   It was impossible to take a reliable reading for this passage using the tapping method. This reading, therefore, is deduced from the CD time-track at bars 31–33.

Table 4.1 shows that none of the performers actually ignores the composer's instructions but none fully adheres either. Some of this could be put down to 'human error' in as much as humans do not experience music metronomically. Gabrielsson notes: 'Even if an exact metronomic tempo is given, the performer often deviates from that, consciously or unconsciously … there is usually much more variation in tempo than is realized or consciously perceived' (Gabrielsson 2000 [1988]: 33). In any case, even though all of the recorded performances were done in studio conditions, the number of takes needed to ensure metronomic exactitude throughout would be prohibitive, especially in the case of Loriod's pre-digital recording, which was made without the sophisticated editing techniques of more recent years.

Loriod and Aimard generally play above Messiaen's markings, although both drop below at bar 17 and Aimard is very slightly under at bar 73. Hill is a little more changeable, especially as he does not always retain his initial tempos. For example, his opening quaver pulse in bar one rises slightly in bar 2 – a pattern which is repeated in bars 3–4 and again near the end, in bars 75–76. Also, he prolongs the first quaver of bar 73, delaying regularity of pulse until the second beat of the bar. Nevertheless, one perceives an intention to abide by Messiaen's wishes: Hill is often close to the very slow quaver markings, and it is worth remembering that very slow speeds are probably the hardest to match against a metronome and, more importantly, retain.[15] Having meticulously checked my own tempos against Messiaen's requirements, it was interesting, even a little surprising, to find myself below them at bars 1 (CD, track 18) and 9 (CD, track 19, 16″), but above at bar 43 (CD, track 22, 10″). These discrepancies may be explained by a strong desire not to hurry the music of the opening pages, with its *intérieur* quality, and to generate excitement at the climax. Nevertheless, as with Hill, the intention to adhere is apparent.

When semiquaver = 96 is requested at bar 73, Hill is furthest out of all, at 22 points below. Since this is uncharacteristic of the rest of his performance, one is tempted to look elsewhere for an explanation, and a clue could lie in the cadenza-like passage at bars 34–35, shown in Example 4.7.

Example 4.7   Messiaen: 'Première communion de la Vierge', bars 34–35

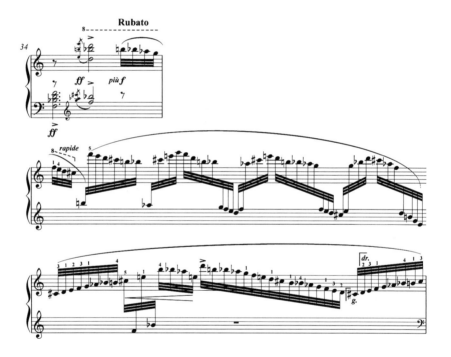

---

[15] In this connection, György Sándor offers an interesting insight: 'if the beat unit is slower than our pulse, we perceive the music as slow ... When we are on stage, our pulse may be faster than normal. Will this change affect our sense of timing and our rate of playing? Of course it will!' (Sándor 1981: 221). Although my comments concern studio rather than 'on stage' performance, the former can cause an adrenaline rush.

Here Loriod and especially Aimard play with great rapidity (the composer marks *rapide*). Aimard keeps the same velocity throughout, barely taking account of the marked accent on d‴, whereas Loriod introduces touches of *rubato* (as requested in the score) at the outset and around the accented d‴. Nevertheless, momentum is generated and sustained, creating a recognizably *bravura* character. Hill's motion is less rapid, and the shifting hand positions required to play the figurations produce a slightly variable rhythmic flow. He also opens the passage with an *accelerando*, and pauses slightly on the lowest note, c♯' (which is also played *marcato*), although these features could be accounted for by the *rubato* marking. Bearing this in mind, his slow tempo at bar 73 could be due to applied technique: semiquaver = *c.* 74 is Hill's choice for a speed at which he feels he can achieve optimum accuracy and clarity.[16] One is reminded of Carl Seashore's observation that '[t]he problem for the musician is not so much, "How fast can I move my fingers?" but rather, "How accurately can I make fine time distinctions in the movement?"' (Seashore 1967 [1938]: 93). It may also be this aspect that prompted David Fanning to suggest that 'in terms of drama and panache, it would be easy to find Hill wanting' (Fanning 1992: 135).

Aimard notably diverges from the text in the three sections which call for quaver = 50, where his performance is 16, 9 and 15 points higher, respectively. Although he plays 30 points and then 18 points higher at bars 21 and 43, this is in relation to a significantly faster tempo indication, and therefore the rise is proportionately smaller. One consequence of these generally faster tempos is that the analyst may sense a slight musical condensation and equalizing of the various elements within the work. Loriod, despite her intimate relationship with the composer, diverges from the text in a similar manner to Aimard. She is generally less extreme in exceeding the metronome markings than the latter, only once slightly topping his tempo, at bar 73, where she is actually on the marking (and he is very slightly below it). At bar 17 she plays, uncharacteristically, below the metronome mark (by 22 points) but, as the passage lasts only three bars, the analyst detects no major rearrangement of the music's perceived constitutional balance.

A difference between the French and the English performers may be observed at bar 39. At this point, in line with the absence of any authorial indication to the contrary, Hill and I (CD, track 22) retain our preceding tempos but both Loriod and Aimard reduce theirs to quaver = *c.* 130. This may be for dramatic intensification, to reflect the ensuing culmination in a climactic *ff*. However, by slowing the tempo well before a *rallentando* marked in bar 41, the approach to the climax is prolonged and the emotive effect of the topical mode (*enthousiasme*) is, for the listener, necessarily modified.

As noted, Hill generally adheres to the composer's markings, so his interpretation has consequences for the internal flow of the interpretative tower.

---

[16] Given the sophistication of digital technology and microphone placement, the acoustic of the recording location (St Paul's, New Southgate) is unlikely to be a significant contributory factor.

His 'passive' approach, to borrow David Fanning's epithet, suggests that the work (or score) is allowed largely to dictate the tempo aspect of the performance, bringing it strongly under the influence of the underpinning authorship informant. My recording likewise contains no really significant divergences from Messiaen's tempo indications, therefore also demonstrating 'passive' traits. In these instances then, the ideal axis of the tower achieves a hierarchically superior influence than may be observed in the analyses of the Bach performances or even the Brahms performances to be discussed in the next chapter.

The tempos in Aimard's and Loriod's recordings seem guided rather than determined by the composer's printed metronome markings, demonstrating the improbability of complete authorial control over tempo in the performance life of a work. Thus some intuitive decision-making emerges from the performances and a freer exercise of artistic prerogatives may be surmised.

Duration Manipulator

Regarding the duration manipulator informant, it could be thought that the very high degree of precise tempo information provided by the composer tends to undermine the role of this informant. As noted, all main tempo changes are accompanied by a metronome mark but Messiaen leaves the interpretative field a little more open where he specifies *rall.* at bar 41, two brief *ralls* at the ends of bars 19 and 73, and in the two cadenzas which are labelled *rubato* and *rapide* (bars 26–27 and 34–35). Also, *rubato* and *pressez* are requested in bar 42, and pause marks appear in bars 16, 20, 74 and 80. Although scrutiny of the score suggests that duration manipulation may be partially subsumed by tempo, this can only be the case in performance if the pianist is heard to adopt a literalist, *Texttreue*, approach.

Example 4.8 shows the passage commencing at bar 39 in which the composer stipulates *rall.* (bar 41), *rubato* and *pressez* (bar 42). Although, as noted, both Loriod and Aimard reduce their tempo at bar 39, the former nevertheless includes a *rallentando* from the point at which it is marked whereas Aimard leaves it to the third beat of the bar. Both ignore the *rubato* and *pressez* instructions which accompany the upward flourish in bar 42 and simply play it fast. Hill and I, on the other hand, do all that the composer asks for, although the response to *pressez* is more noticeable in Hill's performance than in mine. Nevertheless an apparently respectful attitude emerges from the recordings once again.

Loriod's and Aimard's uniformly fast rendition of bar 42 turns it into a sort of introductory anacrusis to the *modéré* of the next bar, especially as the caesura at the end of bar 42 is barely observed by either of them. Although Hill's observation of the composer's wishes in these bars may be thought to generate a sense of approaching climax – projecting a portentous, preparatory role at bar 42 – he also largely ignores the caesura, thereby affecting the sense of arrival at bar 43. Of the four, my own recording is the only one that more perceptibly incorporates this feature, using it as an acoustic marker which helps to define the climactic function of bar 43 for the listener (CD, track 22).

Example 4.8 Messiaen: 'Première communion de la Vierge', bars 39–43

Loriod introduces a personal touch during bars 61–70, where a repeated F⟋ pedal note evokes the infant Jesus' heartbeat. She gradually slackens the rate of the grace notes, according to the specification in the score, but additionally integrates her *diminuendo* from *ff* to below *pp* with a general *ritenuto* which she initiates at bar 64. Neither Aimard nor I adopt this idea but Hill, contrary to his normal more literal ways, does. He commences his retardation a bar later than Loriod and ends at quaver = *c.* 90, to her quaver = *c.* 100. In connection with this, Hill reports that he 'wasn't particularly aware of doing a rit … it happens naturally with the dynamics' (personal communication 09 Februrary 2005). In any case, an interpretative function is communicated in that, by bringing tempo into line with dynamic, the aural-structural attenuation of the passage is reflected, taking the music progressively from a topical mode of excitement to one of tranquillity. The listener is also witnessing the evolution of a performance history.

Sonic Moderator

Messiaen's music is well known for its colour associations. For the performer wishing to create an appropriate sound world, it therefore seems reasonable to assume that the sonic moderator informant acquires even greater significance

108 *Reading Musical Interpretation*

than with less 'colourful' music. Robert Sherlaw Johnson believes that '[i]t is not only harmonies and modes that give rise to colour associations but the totality of the music' (Sherlaw Johnson 1975: 19). The composer's own comments seem to support Sherlaw Johnson: 'When I hear music, and equally when I read it, [I] see inwardly, in the mind's eye, colours which move with the music, and I sense these colours in an extremely vivid manner' (Samuel 1976 [1967]: 16). So vivid was this sense that he extended it to composers other than himself, identifying music by 'atonal or serial composers' as 'black or gray, devoid of coloration' and associated 'gray-violet' and a 'mixture of orange and blue' with the Prélude to Debussy's *Pelléas et Mélisande* (Benitez 2000: 127–8). By the time he wrote *Couleurs de la Cité Céleste* (1963), he actually wrote colour associations into the score. However, precise colour connections in Messiaen's own imagination are unlikely to be precisely conveyed by a performer, a solo pianist in particular. As the composer admits: 'Perhaps my colours are unachievable' (Samuel 1994 [1986]: 64). Although Messiaen did not identify any exact colour affiliations in the score of *Vingt regards*, 'colourful' playing,[17] exploiting every tonal nuance of which the instrument is capable, seems to be required for this music to achieve its full impact – and it should be remembered that, as mentioned earlier, 'Première communion' was inspired by a painting.

A typical instruction for detailed tonal nuancing occurs during the opening measures of 'Première communion', in which the *Thème de Dieu* in the left hand is required to be dynamically a degree above the accompanying filigree of the right: *p* as opposed to *pp*. The right-hand quavers of the second bar at level *p* take over melodic significance from the left, as if the theme has transferred register. This construct is then repeated in bars 3–4. The first three *Thème de Dieu* chords also carry *marcato* indications, implying a very slight individual emphasis, with an accent on the fourth chord at the start of bar 2, as shown in Example 4.9.

Execution of the right-hand filigree, which accompanies the *Thème de Dieu*, seems an important feature in conveying the effect of the passage. Where Aimard and Hill sound on a par in terms of delicacy and crystalline clarity of articulation, Loriod's recording sounds clear but slightly percussive, although it has to be allowed that recording quality plays a part in this. The articulation in my recording is comparably clear, but the slower tempo perhaps reduces the 'sparkling' quality of the right hand (CD, track 18).

The only pianist that audibly manages all the features of this passage as indicated in the score is Aimard. Neither Loriod nor I really distinguish between *p* and *pp* and, whilst Hill achieves this in bar 1, his *p* in the right hand of bar 2 shows little, if any, increase in dynamic. Hill's playing suggests a *marcato*

---

[17] Of interest in this connection is the 'colour' scheme espoused by Sydney Vantyn, as applied to piano tone. Vantyn proposes 'a quality of tone which is clear, neat, and free, and which I should describe as *azure*'. Elsewhere the author writes: 'tone … will sound hesitating and flabby and will be the musical equivalent of *mauve*'. Also 'we shall obtain a very velvety tone which may be compared to a *bluish grey*' (McEwan and Vantyn 1917: 135–7).

Messiaen: 'Première communion de la Vierge'

Example 4.9   Messiaen: 'Première communion de la Vierge', bars 1–4

over the opening left-hand chords and reflects the accent mainly agogically, but Loriod's projects neither *marcato* nor accent. Aimard's effect here is partially achieved by his pedalling. Where Loriod and Hill use standard *legato* pedalling, Aimard achieves a very slight separation of the left-hand chords by applying direct pedalling, a technique which I also adopt in my recording (CD, track 18). Earlier, I indicated that Messiaen is less exact about his notated pedal requirements than with other performance parameters and here Aimard chooses a pedalling that could be thought to complement the markings that the composer has supplied. As previously mentioned, Aimard further personalizes the opening by applying a slight *ritenuto* to the quaver dyads of bars 2 and 4, thus suggesting discrete phrase units – an idea that is not apparent in the other recordings. So, as far as the introductory bars are concerned, Aimard's performance appears to be guided by information in the score as well as by intuition, and the analyst can perceive a merging of authorial decree and interpretative freedom with regard to the top-layer informants.

Turning now to the other end of the dynamic spectrum, it may be observed that all four pianists' recordings reflect the intensity of the climactic passage that runs from bars 37 to 61. Hill, Loriod and I observe the broad dynamic requirements of ***mf***, ***f***, ***ff*** and *crescendo* exactly as marked in the score but in Aimard's recording the dynamic is modified to a single ***f*** at bar 53 (relative to the ***ff*** at bar 45). The dynamic level then swells through bar 58, reaching ***ff*** at bar 59, just two bars before the 'deflation' of bars 61–70. This dynamic scheme necessarily modifies the affective impact of the passage, with its chordal 'insistence', as marked in the score, but could be taken to reflect the progressive harmonic intensification of the chordal repetitions and associated augmenting *valeurs*, to their point of release at bar 61 where the 'deflation' begins.

Projection of marked accents is not universally evident in the recordings and the simplest way to indicate the four artists' levels of observation is to tabulate them. Taking bars 37–51 of the score and numbering the right-hand accents 1–21, clear observance will be shown by a tick, non-observance by a cross, and weak observance by a circle (see Table 4.2).

Table 4.2   Messiaen: 'Première communion de la Vierge'; observance of marked right-hand accents between bars 37 and 51 by Aimard, Hellaby, Hill and Loriod (accent number given at the top)

	1	2	3	4	5	6	7	8	9	10	11	12	13	14	15	16	17	18	19	20	21
Aimard	O	O	✓	O	O	O	O	O	O	O	O	O	O	✓	✓	✓	✓	✓	✓	✓	✓
Hellaby	✓	✓	✓	✓	✓	✓	✓	✓	✓	✓	✓	✓	✓	✓	✓	✓	✓	✓	✓	✓	✓
Hill	✓	✓	✓	×	×	✓	✓	✓	✓	✓	✓	✓	✓	✓	✓	✓	✓	✓	✓	✓	✓
Loriod	O	O	✓	✓	✓	✓	✓	O	×	×	×	×	✓	✓	✓	✓	✓	✓	×	✓	✓

My own recording observes all marked accents equally (CD, track 21, 55"– track 22). Aimard observes all to a greater or lesser extent but more consistently strong ones come from Hill, despite his apparent loss of numbers 4 and 5. Loriod is the most inconsistent, and it is hard to understand how she avoids accents 9 to 12 because the augmenting chordal separation and concomitant somatic engagement naturally produces accentuation. A similar physical requirement occurs in bars 44–46 during which Messiaen does not ask for accents but the writing, with its chordal acciaccaturas onto adjacent chords within the context of registral changes, results in all artists providing continued (and interpretatively convincing) accentuation. Indeed, avoidance of such accentuation would require a strong act of mental and physical will, not to say one of musical eccentricity.

This raises the question of how far one can take the concept of applied technique: at what point does interpretative will have to give way to physical limitation? It may be that, contrary to my assumption above, Loriod's physical make-up meant that the considerable leaps involved before the performance of accents 9 to 12 produced a tensing of her psycho-motor equipment, so that the 'leap trajectory' (Parncutt 2002: 287) and subsequent 'freefall',[18] necessary to produce the accent, was inhibited. Personal experience as a piano teacher has acquainted me with tension-induced reduction in technical efficiency when faced by the need for super-control. As Alan Fraser puts it: 'Often the big movement "in" will be curtailed just as the hand reaches the keyboard: the pianist arrests the movement in the instant to assure an accurate attack, and we are deprived of

---

[18]   For further discussion of freefall technique, see György Sándor, *On Piano Playing* (1981), Chapter 4.

the big tone we have been led to expect' (Fraser 2003: 112). Nevertheless, had Loriod wished to change her interpretation to bring her accentuation in line with the score's markings, she could easily have recorded another take: tape splicing was a common enough practice in 1973. So, in line with the proviso expressed in Chapter 2, I will assume that the issued recording is indicative of artistic choice rather than physical necessity.

A pianist's technical mechanism is likely to shape an interpretation which involves a strong virtuoso[19] element even more than one which does not. Tremendous physical exertion inevitably occupies mental 'space' in that a significant part of a performer's concentration is perforce claimed by keyboard negotiation and 'our mind's first tendency is to succumb to the overwhelming nature of the experience' (Fraser 2003: 388). There are places where technical challenges may override other considerations or, indeed, may *be* the chief constituent of a performance. Any performance of, for example, 'Regard de l'Esprit de joie' which attempts to quell the pianistic bravura is in danger also of underplaying the '*esprit*' of the title. Samson claims that '[v]irtuosity presents rather than represents. It encourages us to wonder at the act rather than to commune with the work and its referents by way of the act' (Samson 2003: 84). But in this case, it can lead us directly to the work and its referents. The *esprit de joie* may be heard to inhere in the virtuosity itself. As Rosen writes: 'it would be a mistake to deny the dramatic interest of ... displays of physical prowess both in piano music and ballet, which have an artistic importance at the very least equivalent to the high altitude arabesques of the mad Lucia' (Rosen 2002: 5).[20]

'Première communion' does not belong to the super-virtuoso class of piano works, despite the taxing moments under discussion, but it is nonetheless at such points that the player's technique becomes of greater significance in the sonic moderator category. This could be one reason why Hill's concluding right-hand arabesques (bar 73) arguably do not quite fall within the dynamic containment of the score's '*pp*' instruction, especially when compared with the same passage in Aimard's recording. I have previously noted that Hill's tempo is here well below that which the composer asks for and my suggested explanation that this speed is his optimum for clarity and accuracy may well carry through into the dynamic field too. It would also be difficult to describe Loriod's dynamic at this point as *pp* but, because the notes move by more quickly, the lack of a real *pp* attracts less attention. But only in Aimard's performance can the analyst detect what is arguably an optimum 'colour' for this passage.

---

[19]   I use the term 'virtuoso' here in the sense which it acquired during the nineteenth century, when it became equated with 'speed, reach, strength, agility and endurance' and demanded 'little beyond admiration from its audience' (Samson 2003: 71–2).

[20]   Cumming, like Samson, overlooks this aspect of virtuosity when she writes: 'If [the virtuoso] seeks attention to his own virtuosity, he has drawn it away from the work' (Cumming 2000: 41).

112   *Reading Musical Interpretation*

Summary

Although the foregoing analysis has tended to focus on the performers' perceived areas of divergence both with the score and with each other, no major interpretative disagreement has been discovered and the authorship (score) informant emerges as a strong influence in all four recordings. Having said this, the performances do not actually sound very alike, and each has a distinctive personality. Each of the acoustic traces makes those 'subtle ... adjustments of tempo and dynamics on which expressivity depends' which 'have no sanction but personal feeling' (Taruskin 1995: 168).

So, having 'read' the performance traces and their relationship to Messiaen's score, I can now start to project my findings into an analysis trace. Because 'Première communion' contains extra-musical references, my summary will also interpret some of the 'expressive cues' (Juslin 2002 [2001]) that the performances might imply with regard to these programmatic elements.

With a total track time of 6'23", Aimard's is the fastest performance, and this is indicative of a complete technical mastery as well as of an impetuosity which takes the tempos above the quaver = 50 markings, thereby seemingly downplaying the adorational aspect suggested in the movement's subtitle.[21] However, both the broad dynamic capacity and the articulation in the *Magnificat* section lend this stretch an especially celebratory character. Loriod's recording, at 7'17" is nearly a minute longer overall and the slightly slower tempos for the quaver = 50 sections add a more perceptible sense of wonder. However, the lack of a truly refined *pianissimo*[22] affects the colouristic aspects of these moments, perhaps reducing the music's communication of 'the interior aspect of [its] object'[23] (Dahlhaus 1995 [1967]: 48) to the informed listener. Her playing generates life into the *Magnificat* passage but, with less sharply defined articulation and a very slightly slower tempo than Aimard, the performance does not seem to achieve quite the same sense of exaltation. My own reading, just a little slower than Loriod's, comes out at *c.* 7'25" and is probably the most literal of all. The very slow opening seemingly matches the *intérieur* quality requested by the composer, but the *Magnificat* section, although closest to Messiaen's quaver = 138, may be thought to have

---

[21]   Aimard's fast tempos accord with his performance of the cycle as a whole. Michael Oliver in *The Gramophone* comments that his 'overall timing is faster than most (nine minutes shorter than Messiaen's specified duration) and a few of his silences could have been held longer' (Oliver 2000: 106).

[22]   This could be caused partly by the CD transfer from the analogue sound source. The performance is accompanied by a persistent background hiss which is particularly distracting in the *pianissimo* passages in question.

[23]   Dahlhaus is critiquing Hegel's notion of music's 'objective' submergence in a content. The example given is of a Crucifixus in which music grasps 'the deep implications in the concept of Christ's passion, as his divine suffering, death and burial' (Dahlhaus 1995 [1967]: 48).

less of the *enthousiasme* heard in the other rather faster recordings. Hill, at 8′28″ adds yet another minute to Aimard's time and the proximity of his tempo to the composer's quaver = 50 effectively communicates a sense of stillness, as implied by '*intérieur*'. His virtuosity in the *Magnificat* is less obvious than it is in the French performances and because, as with 'Regard de l'Esprit de joie', virtuosity arguably *is* the expression of *enthousiasme haletant*, there are implications for the affective impact on the listener. The use of a Fazioli piano with its bright, bell-like sound also colours Hill's performance of the entire cycle.[24]

The above analytical data may now be summarized in a way that reflects my perception of the performers' varying interactions with score-based information evident in the four recordings.

All four artists:
> Level 1: **Era (style)** and **authorship (score)** combine to form an all-important base which influences the subsequent layers →
> Level 2: **genre** (religious character piece; clear structure) →

Aimard
> Level 2: **topic** (dance), detectable through articulation (sonic moderator) →
> Level 3: **topical mode**, few indications but reflected in performance as requested with some small personal adaptations slightly affecting tempo, charcterizer and duration manipulator, mainly subsumed by top-level indications; **characterizer**, strongly but not entirely author-influenced, some topical mode influence→
> Level 4: **tempo**, strongly but not entirely author-influenced, some topical mode influence; **duration manipulator**, little requested but slight topical mode influence; mainly subsumed by tempo; **sonic moderator,** requested by composer, supplied by artist but includes some personalization and adaptation, especially with regard to topical projection.

Hellaby
> Level 2: **topic** (dance), detectable through articulation (sonic moderator) →
> Level 3: **topical mode**, few indications but reflected in performance as requested with some small personal adaptations slightly affecting tempo, mainly subsumed by top-level indications; **characterizer**, entirely author-influenced →
> Level 4: **tempo**, almost entirely author-influenced, slight topical mode influence; **duration manipulator**, supplied entirely as requested, mainly subsumed by tempo; **sonic moderator**, requested by composer, supplied by artist but includes some adaptation especially with regard to topical projection.

---

[24]   The instrument used by an artist is obviously going to be an inescapable influence in the sonic moderator category.

Hill

Level 2: **topic** (dance), not a strong presence →
Level 3: **topical mode**, few indications but reflected in performance as requested with some slight personal adaptations affecting tempo and topical mode, mainly subsumed by top-level indications; **characterizer**, entirely author-influenced →
Level 4: **tempo**, almost entirely author-influenced, some topical mode influence; **duration manipulator**, little requested, once supplied significantly, some topical mode influence, mainly subsumed by tempo; **sonic moderator**, requested by composer, supplied by artist but includes some adaptation.

Loriod

Level 2: **topic** (dance), not a strong presence →
Level 3: **topical mode**, few indications but reflected in performance as requested with some slight personal adaptations affecting characterizer, tempo and duration manipulator, mainly subsumed by top-level indications; **characterizer**, strongly but not entirely author-influenced, some topical mode influence →
Level 4: **tempo**, strongly but not entirely author-influenced, some topical mode influence; **duration manipulator**, little requested, once supplied significantly, some topical mode influence, mainly subsumed by tempo; **sonic moderator**, requested by composer, supplied by artist but includes some adaptation.

As has been stated several times in the foregoing discussion, my own recording is the most literal of the four. I am neither a noted Messiaen exponent nor did I study the work with the composer, yet these two facts may help to explain my approach. Since all the other performers played the music to the composer and received his 'blessing', they may feel justified in including personal touches in their interpretations which do not appear to be explicitly sanctioned by the score. Without this 'blessing' my only authoritative source of reference is the score and, unless I were to feel strongly at odds with one or more of the performance directions, there is little reason to depart from authorial instruction. However, analysis of the Brahms variations (Chapter 5) will also reveal my strong inclination to be 'faithful' to the printed page.

The two most contrasting performances are probably my own and Loriod's and these are represented graphically in Figure 4.1. 'Contrasting' is a relative term here and, although differences are indicated, strong informant lines radiating outwards from authorship are characteristic of both graphs. This minimizes interpretative contrasts between the two recordings represented by this figure *in toto*, but maximizes contrast between this and other figures *in toto*, in which the graphs mainly show much stronger divergences between individual interpretative mappings.

(a) Artist: Loriod

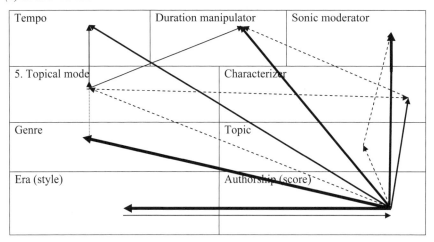

(b) Artist: Hellaby

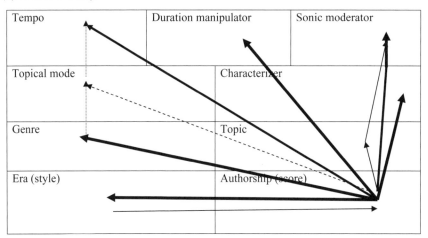

Dotted lines indicate weak emphasis; bold lines indicate strong emphasis.

Figure 4.1   Messiaen: 'Première communion de la Vierge'; interpretations by (a) Loriod and (b) Hellaby, mapped on to the interpretative tower

Again, it is not the purpose of this argument to determine which one of the four recordings is the 'best'. In my analysis I am concerned primarily with issues regarding the artists' interpretative outcomes in relation to the apparent 'givenness' of the score and how I, in turn, can read and interpret these outcomes. It will be observed that the interflow of the informants within the tower, when compared with that observed in Chapter 3, has adjusted to give primacy to authorship (score). A result of this is that the performance 'work of art' (Kivy 1995) can be heard in all cases to bear detailed similarities to the compositional work as reflected in the score and, as such, all four interpretative structures may be regarded as standing in close parallel with the work's conceptual and aesthetic structure. They have some affinity, therefore, with Charles Peirce's semiotic category of '*likenesses*, or icons which serve to convey ideas of the things they represent simply by imitating them'. Extending the metaphor, it is hard to take the Bach performances of Chapter 3 further than the category of '*indications*, or indices; which show something about things on account of their being physically connected with them'[25] (Peirce 1998 [1894]: 5).

Hermeneutic considerations regarding the historical situatedness of author, work, performer and analyst which seemed important when assessing Bach performance are, perhaps, of significantly less concern in this case. It is worth remembering that '[i]f we wish to invoke a code as a convention, we need to posit a reader whose competency includes that code' (Klein 2005: 54). In the case of contemporary musicians studying the work of a recently living composer, it is probably safe to assume that Messiaen's codes lie within the competency of all concerned and certainly within the competency of the pianists who studied with Messiaen himself. However, due to the malleability of musical signs 'even to those … born within the time and place of the historical work' (55), it is not possible to advocate either the inevitability or desirability of interpretative uniformity.

Interpretative uniformity amongst the four performances under discussion has clearly not been established. Tower analysis has shown the performances to be inextricably linked with textual performance information but has also demonstrated ways in which the performances reflect each performer's own personal authenticity. So, despite the work's 'thickness', it is not hermetically sealed, and opportunities for the exercise of artistic prerogatives have been shown to present themselves throughout the score. This is unlikely to be out of sympathy with Messiaen's own views on performance, even bearing in mind some of his written directives. In his preface to the *Quatuor pour la Fin du Temps*, Messiaen writes that his performance directions are there to 'produce a living and sensitive interpretation' (Messiaen 1942: IV),[26] implying something beyond literalism. This is corroborated by Hill: 'Above all he emphasized that, despite their meticulous clarity, his scores are not an end in themselves. For Messiaen the "music" was not in the notes, nor in the sounds they represent, but in the meaning which lies beyond and which through sound we hope to reveal' (Hill 1995b: 282).

---

[25] As discussed in Chapter 2, musical notation itself connects with Peirce's third semiotic category, symbols.

[26] 'Les nuances exagérées, les pressés, les ralentis … rend une interprétation vivante et sensible' (Messiaen 1942: IV).

Chapter 5
Brahms: *Variations and Fugue on a Theme by Handel* Op. 24

Some Background Issues

Structure and Performance

If the literature on Brahms's *Variations and Fugue on a Theme by Handel* can be taken as a gauge, it is the work's structural features that have overwhelmingly attracted critical attention, prompting favourable comments from writers as diverse as Karl Geiringer (1968 [1934]), Donald Francis Tovey (1967 [1944]), Michael Musgrave (1996 [1985]) and Malcolm MacDonald (1990). The formal aspect has also engendered a variety of analytical responses from, amongst others, Heinrich Schenker (1924), Hans Meyer (1928) and, more recently, Jonathan Dunsby. Dunsby's analysis of oppositional relationships considers only 'the first two bars of the Theme and selected variations' (Dunsby 1981: 7), on the assumption that 'the opening of each variation presumably declares the point of the whole variation' and that 'it is also a place where long-term relationships ... are strongly felt' (17).

Dunsby admits that 'consideration of the openings does not necessarily reflect the whole music' (17) and, as John Rink points out, such a method 'hardly captures what MacDonald calls "the grand sweep of the structure"' (Rink 1999a: 86). To ascertain an overview of this grand sweep, Rink, in a novel manoeuvre, takes his cue from the score's performance directives, firstly by tabulating a condensed version of them (see Table 5.1) and then by abstracting 'an intentionally simplistic' (87) 'dynamogram' which portrays the dynamic rise and fall of the music in graphic form. This provides visual evidence of 'the opposition and indeed juxtaposition of dynamic maxima and minima' which, he claims, 'makes the music's course so powerful' (88). The point is also picked up by Julian Littlewood, who charts the work's dynamic markings to highlight the absence of anything between *p* and *f*. This, he suggests, creates 'multiple, contrasting stable states' which produce 'the overriding effect of a discontinuous dynamic range' (Littlewood 2004: 93). Rink's graph and Littlewood's table seek to derive analytical insights from the score's performance directions, specifically those concerning dynamics. The implication is that Brahms's dynamic markings in the *Handel Variations* mirror the work's formal design or, at least, its 'intensity level' (Rink 1999a: 87) and may be read as signs of the work's 'shape' (86).

118   *Reading Musical Interpretation*

Table 5.1   Brahms: *Variations and Fugue on a Theme by Handel*; Rink's condensation of expression and tonality in variations 1–25 (Rink 1999a: 87). By kind permission of Cambridge University Press

Variation	Key	Dynamics and character	Articulation	Tempo
1	I	*poco f*		
2		*p animato*	*legato*	
3		*p dolce*		
4		*risoluto sf/f*	*staccato*	
5	i	*p espressivo*		
	♭			
6		*p sempre*	*legato*	
7	I	*p con vivacità* ⟨ *f*		
	♮			
8		*f/p/f/p*		
9		*sf* ⟩ *p*	*legato*	*poco sostenuto*
10		*f energico p/pp*		
11		*p dolce*		
12		*pp soave*		
13	i	*f espressivo*		Largamente, ma non più
	♭			
14	I	*sf/f*	*sciolto*	
	♮			
15		*f*		
16		*p ma marcato*		
17		*p*		Più mosso
18		[*p*] *grazioso*		
19		*p vivace*	*leggiero*	
20		*p* ⟨ ⟩ *espressivo*	*legato*	
21	vi	*p dolce, espressivo*		
22	I	*p* (> > > >)		
23		*p* ⟨ *f vivace*	*staccato*	
24		*p* ⟨ *f*		
25		*ff*		

Abstractions such as Rink's and Littlewood's provide an interesting structural slant on the work and can play an important role in helping the prospective performer to reach an interpretative solution. However, the question now arises as to whether tables and graphs based on the work's dynamic flux, as gleaned from the score alone, can relate to an informed listener's experience of the music in actual performance, especially as the aforementioned authors' abstractions do not address the issue of how a composer's dynamic (or other) indications may be conveyed to the listener by performers themselves.

Chapter 4 showed that drawing conclusions about how a performance will sound (rather than might, or even should, sound) from a score's performance directions, be they ever so detailed, is likely to be a flawed methodology in that it ignores a performer's interpretative mediation, or the exercise of what Rink (2004) himself has labelled 'artistic prerogatives'. Where Messiaen's score contains

Brahms: Variations and Fugue on a Theme by Handel *Op. 24* 119

detailed instructions to the pianist, Brahms's score, even for a nineteenth-century specimen, is relatively sparse, seemingly leaving plenty of interpretative 'space' for the executant. The picture is further complicated by certain well-investigated ambiguities concerning Brahms's status as a Romantic composer.

A Potential for Ambiguity

A work such as the *Variations and Fugue on a Theme by Handel* (1861) dates from a time when annotated performance details were becoming commonplace, seemingly limiting the interpretative parameters within which a performer can operate. Clive Brown explains that '[m]any composers ... came increasingly to regard accentuation and dynamic nuance as integral to the individuality of their conceptions and were unwilling to entrust this merely to the performer's instincts' (Brown 1999: 62). The result, according to Brown, was a 'general trend throughout the Romantic period ... for performers to stick more and more closely to the instructions contained in the score' (Brown 2002: 14). However, Brahms 'left much more to be decided by the performer' and 'regarded [instructions] as a necessary evil when a work was totally unknown to the performer ... once musicians were familiar with the piece, superfluous instructions were more likely to constrict their freedom of expression than to aid it' (16). This is borne out in the *Handel Variations*, in which Brahms is more economical with performance directions than some of his contemporaries or even predecessors. For example, in Beethoven's *Diabelli Variations* all but two variations carry tempo instructions, nearly one third of which are allied to topical modes. So, where Chapter 4 considered a 'thick' work and Chapter 3 a relatively 'thin' one, at risk of overworking sliced-bread terminology, this chapter's subject could be thought of as 'medium' (rather than 'medium thick').

Brahms also occupies a special place in the nineteenth century in that he shunned the thoroughgoing Romanticism of Liszt, through whom audiences could 'experience extremes of emotion vicariously' (Samson 2003: 78), and his antipathy to the Music of the Future was proclaimed in his Declaration of 1860, 'the one public outburst of his life' (Musgrave 2000: 59). Leon Botstein writes of Brahms's 'unique synthesis of musical Classicism and nineteenth-century expressiveness' and of 'the intensity and emotional immediacy we associate with late Romanticism, as well as the grace, clarity, symmetry and interior invention we associate with Classicism' (Botstein 1999: 24). Charles Rosen regards the *Handel Variations* as the composer's first piece to demonstrate Brahms's 'manipulation of the classical aesthetic' (Rosen 2000: 172), but he also allows that it displays the 'Romantic tradition of the grotesque' (174).[1] This possible bifurcation of

---

[1]   Rosen bases his use of the term 'grotesque' on 'the importance of the awkward for Brahms' (Rosen 2000: 174). The definition of the term found in Chamber's Dictionary contains elements which seem to justify its application to the *Handel Variations* more persuasively: 'extravagantly formed, fantastic ... incongruous' (Kirkpatrick 1983: 553).

120   *Reading Musical Interpretation*

elements within Brahms's idiom (in Meyer's sense) could be what provides points of reference for both romantic and classical performing temperaments.

It is perhaps symptomatic of the composer and of this work in particular that Brahms borrowed from Handel for his thematic prototype, and produced in the *Variations and Fugue on a Theme by Handel* his most self-consciously neo-Baroque piano work. Quasi-Baroque ornamentation, relatively sparing use of the keyboard range, stylized dance music and the 'learned style' of the fugue all duly make their appearances. The very fact that Brahms used this very little known theme[2] demonstrates a level of interest in Handel unusual at the time of the work's composition. Yet, as Rosen's comment above suggests, the variations also abound in thoroughly nineteenth-century thinking, 'guiding the listener from the Baroque to the Romantic' (Littlewood 2004: 93).

It would seem, then, that there are a number of historical and contextual perspectives from which both pianist and analyst can view the performance directions that appear in Brahms's score, suggesting that assumptions made concerning interpretative outcomes via a direct mapping from score to virtual performance are likely to be deficient. As demonstrated in the previous two chapters, a score's performance directions, should they appear at all, represent only the 'tip of the iceberg' and that the way this tip is shaped in performance connects to interpretative factors lying behind the audible surface level of a recording. Furthermore, because the interpretative tower is set up precisely to analyse the performance of a work, it is a useful mechanism by which to examine how far the literal reading of a score can accord with actual performance, or how far this can be shown to be a theoretical conceit.

For my case studies, I have selected five contrasting, strategically placed variations from the set, and begin by considering the relevant performance information supplied by the composer, a summary of which is shown in Table 5.1. Based on this information, I construct, as prelude to my investigations, a virtual *Texttreue* reading which will be useful as a comparative performance model or point of reference. I then examine how the information appears to be reflected in recordings made by a number of different pianists. Where apparent discrepancies with the score and between the recordings are observed, I attempt to account for these by investigating the evidence of the recordings through the medium of the interpretative tower. This three-way projection back and forth between work, recording and analyst will naturally embrace all the informant categories of the

---

[2]   The source is Handel's Suite No. 1 in B♭ major HWV 434, the third movement of which is an *Aria con Variazioni*. It is this aria that Brahms uses as the basis for his variations. According to Musgrave (1996 [1985]), the suite was published by John Walsh of London in 1733 and had only just been reprinted when Brahms wrote his piece. Musgrave elsewhere gives the date of Walsh's publication as 1723, and states that at the time of Brahms's *Handel Variations*, 'no modern edition existed' (Musgrave 2000: 168). In any case, Brahms's most likely contact with the music came through his association with Friedrich Chrysander, who had begun a complete Handel edition in 1858.

tower, but also take into account the historical positioning of the recording artist, especially as recordings of the Brahms–Handel *Variations* have a long history, spanning several generations of interpretative evolution. The case studies will not yield an overview of the entire work in performance but, given my earlier comments regarding the work's formal properties, it is appropriate also to give consideration to the position of the selected variations within the work as a whole, and to ascertain whether this may justifiably be thought of as an interpretative influence in the recording.

Editions

An analytical comparison of different artists' recordings which uses the score as a common point of reference must be based on the certainty that analyst and artists do, indeed, have a common point of reference. To this end I have scrutinized a substantial cross-section of editions by various publishers of the *Handel Variations*. These include the first edition and a number of twentieth-century publications (see Appendix 1 for a complete listing). Only a very few minor discrepancies are apparent, none of which are at odds with the information presented in Table 5.1, apart from the solitary omission of '*espressivo*' from the beginning of Variation 5 in Simrock. Where discrepancies between editions have a possible bearing on the forthcoming case studies, I deal with these as they arise. My own chief source of reference is the Könemann *Urtext* (1999).

Recording Artists

The *Variations and Fugue on a Theme by Handel* has quite a long recorded history, starting in 1930 with the shellac discs made by Benno Moiseiwitsch, followed eight years later with another shellac set by Egon Petri. To reflect the size and variety of the recording catalogue which has subsequently accumulated, my case studies will draw on a larger number of recordings than did the previous chapters. The following discussion will consider selected variations from complete recordings by Egon Petri (1938), Claudio Arrau (1963), Steven Kovacevich (1968) and Jorge Federico Osorio (1988), all of which have attracted critical approval. Benno Moiseiwitsch's recording is included because of its historical position in the recorded legacy of the work. The following critical reviews from *The Gramophone* helpfully illustrate the field.

Despite the pioneering status of Moiseiwitsch's recording, the anonymous reviewer, whilst saluting the pianist's 'wonderful fingers', found the playing possessing only 'a little feeling, which never goes deep' and lacking 'a brooding poetic feeling' without which Brahms is 'not fully nourishing' (Anon 1930: 24). Petri's performance met with a more favourable response from another anonymous source: 'The performance is undoubtedly a fine one ... Only a virtuoso of the highest class can hope to make a success of it and this Petri does from every point of view' (Anon 1938: 200). Arrau's live radio broadcast from 1963 appears not to have been reviewed in *The Gramophone* on its CD release in 1990, but his somewhat more ponderous 1978 account still attracted favourable comment from Max Harrison, who claimed that the pianist tended 'to see the work as a whole', applauded the 'force and weight' of his performance, and confirmed his status in the field by concluding that 'Brahmsians will know all about Arrau' (Harrison 1979: 352).

The recordings by Kovacevich (then known as Steven Bishop) and Osorio produced some of the most laudatory reviews of all. Max Harrison describes Kovacevich's performance as

> some of the most sensitive Brahms playing in the catalogue ... Bishop's response to this music is such that it would be possible to comment on felicities in almost every bar, certainly in every phrase ... relations between the different variations of Op. 24 ... are most beautifully judged ... it is striking how closely this performance reflects the way that Brahms drew full value from the discipline to which he submitted his musical thought ... Nobody who cares about Brahms or about fine piano playing ought to miss this record. (Harrison 1969: 976)

Almost as enthusiastic was the reception accorded to Osorio's account by James Methuen-Campbell: 'This is one of the most distinguished discs of Brahms's piano music that I have heard in recent years ... one is assured of [Osorio's] sense of style and his disciplined yet pliable approach to tempo ... a major artist who can draw on a panoply of pianistic resources with which to express his musical thoughts' (Methuen-Campbell 1988: 812–16).

Alongside case studies taken from the catalogue recordings, I will also be critically appraising relevant parts of my own recording of the complete work (see attached CD, tracks 1–13). In line with the Bach and Messiaen chapters, I will only refer to my intentions where relevant, especially if they seem in opposition to the evidence of the recording itself.

As the following discussion will be using recorded performances by pianists from an earlier generation than has so far been represented, a few biographical details will be supplied at relevant points so that a historical context is established. It would be worth stating at this point that my own training under the pianist Denis Matthews and later at the Royal Academy of Music falls firmly within the British tradition which, in the late 1970s/early 1980s, was still dominated by the *Texttreue* view of score as final arbiter. This influence has already been detected in my Messiaen recording and will continue to be observed in the forthcoming studies. My book does not, of course, primarily deal with the changing face of twentieth-century performance practice but, as it does concern perceived interpretative outcomes, this cannot be entirely disregarded.

Variation 5: Case Study

Two particular elements shown in Table 5.1 make Variation 5 interesting as a case study for performance. Firstly, it is the antecedent in a pair of tonic minor variations, which is in itself significant because the *Variations and Fugue on a Theme by Handel* as a whole strongly favours the tonic major, and there are only four minor-key variations in all. These are strategically placed at roughly a quarter of the way through (numbers 5 and 6), halfway through (number 13), and three-quarters of the way through (number 21) the set of 25 variations. Only Variation 21 abandons a tonic grounding, being cast in the relative minor. The second interesting feature shown in Table 5.1 is the use of the term '*espressivo*'. This is the first of only four applications of this topical mode throughout the entire work, including the fugue, three of which coincide with the minor-key variations 5, 13 and 21.

A closer look at the score suggests that a *Texttreue* performance of Variation 5 will not only be *piano* and *espressivo* (of which more later) but will be played in a *legato* manner, as suggested by the phrase marks in both left-hand and right-hand parts. The phrasing will largely be felt in half-bar units but with some sense of emphasis in the fourth and/or second beats of the bar, as indicated by the hairpin nuances and accentuation marks. There will be a *crescendo* from bar 5^3, perhaps to complement the relative chromaticism of the music at this point, followed by a rapid *diminuendo* from the end of bar 6^4 to the second quaver of bar 7^1, and the close of each binary half of the variation will be signalled by a *diminuendo*. As there is nothing to indicate a change of speed, this hypothetical *Texttreue* performance will retain the tempo of the theme.

It could be thought that, with its general *piano* level, modified by undulating dynamic nuances and subtle offbeat accentuations, the virtual performance sketched above is *espressivo* enough, rendering further expressive gestures redundant. But there are two possible complications to consider. The first concerns the wider implications of the topical mode *espressivo*, and the second concerns the music's apparent deviations from a 4/4 norm, as suggested by Brahms's dynamic markings. So before examining how Variation 5 is actually handled in performance by three pianists, it is worth discussing both these possible complications to ascertain whether further expressive gestures from performing artists may be implied by the score or anticipated by the analyst.

Topical Mode – Espressivo

The Italian performance direction '*espressivo*', translating directly into English as 'expressive', suggests that *espressivo* and the concept of expression in performance, as discussed in Chapter 1, are indivisible. An important point in this connection is that 'expression' is associated with romantic music in its broadest sense: music that is 'dreamy' or 'poetic' or 'sentimental' or strongly characterful, and mostly slow (hence involving the tempo informant). It is as

124   *Reading Musical Interpretation*

improbable that Liszt should write '*presto furioso*' and then add '*ed espressivo*' at the top of 'Wilde Jagd' as it is that a critic would judge X's performance of the study to be 'expressive'. On the other hand, in the case of Liszt's 'Ricordanza', which Busoni designates a 'bundle of faded love letters from a somewhat old-fashioned world of sentiment' (Busoni 1965 [1909]: 162), the composer requires the left hand to play *espressivo* when presenting the opening theme. Similarly, the first two of Chopin's Op. 9 nocturnes call for an *espressivo* manner. These associations tend to be matched by the research outcomes of Patrik Juslin, who discovered that, when presented with a variety of musical parameters, his sample listeners found 'legato articulation, soft spectrum, slow tempo, high sound level and slow tone attacks' (Juslin 2002 [2001]: 317) to be the most 'expressive' combination. An association with Romanticism – and here, era is important – is also supported by the fact that the term '*espressivo*' or, rather, '*con espressione*' is only infrequently found in the pages of Haydn or Mozart.[3] So *espressivo*, by its double referencing of romantic playing and Romantic 'rules' (Meyer 1989), may well lure the performer into manipulating features such as duration, dynamics and balance – that is, the areas of tonal beauty, melodic line and expressive *rubato* that I equated with a romantic manner of performance in Chapter 2 – to reflect a perceived emotional character.

An association, noted above, between *espressivo* and the nocturne is worth examining a little further. The nineteenth-century nocturne is a fully worked-out piece and, with its emphasis on a right-hand *cantabile*, is one that has acquired haptic implications for the pianist in terms of creating a suitable sound and mood. Thus, according to the parameters that I established in Chapter 2, it qualifies as a topic. Variation 5 allies *espressivo* with music that tends towards the conventionally lyrical: right-hand *legato* lines comprising rising arpeggios and undulating step-wise dactyls, supported by a mostly arpeggiated left-hand accompaniment. These factors combine to produce writing which, although simpler, is reminiscent of the characteristic texture in many of Chopin's nocturnes. Additionally, by adopting a tonic minor modality, the variation achieves a 'prevailingly "dark" tone-colour [which] seems to attract nocturnal imagery' (Kramer 2002: 33). It is therefore worth incorporating the concept of the nocturne-as-topic within the orbit of *espressivo*.

If, as implied in Chapter 1, expression in performance is derived from features within the musical work, it is logical to assume that the composer, consciously or unconsciously, would provide a suitable means for expression and would not label a passage *espressivo* unless the musical setting seemed to justify it.

---

[3]   Exceptionally, Mozart writes *Andante con espressione* as the heading for the second movement of the Sonata in D major K 311 and *Andante cantabile* with sub-heading *con espressione* for the second movement of the Sonata in A minor K 310. Haydn's use is equally rare, although he does write *Andante con espressione* as the manner for both opening movements of the two-movement sonatas in D major Hob XVl/42 and C major Hob XVl/48. Significantly all of these instances of *espressione* occur in the context of slow movements. Also, they are headings and not localized instructions within the movement.

The analytical case studies that Clarke uses (see Chapter 1) are of musical miniatures, both of which lend themselves, in contrasting ways, to 'expressive' treatment. For example, Chopin's Prelude in E minor Op. 28/4 is slow, harmonically rich, texturally varied and melodically intense, and a romantic performance is supported at all interpretative levels, from authorship and era, through genre and so to the upper informant levels. With this degree of expressivity already latent in the musical work, it is certainly true that the task of the performer to be expressive is greatly facilitated. Juslin *et al.* identify this aspect as one of the five main sources of expressivity in performance: 'Generative features may increase the emotional impact of the music, but do so mainly by enhancing the expression that is inherent in the structure of the piece' (Juslin *et al.* 2004: 253).

As has already been noted, Brahms uses the term '*espressivo*' only very sparingly but, when it does appear, its use matches the considerations described above. Of its four appearances, three are associated with the more lyrical or 'poetic' variations (all of which are in minor keys) and its fourth occurs in the context of the harmonically unsettled Variation 20, 'an endlessly moving chromatic line' (Littlewood 2004: 96). In addition, at least two of these, including Variation 5, feature rhythmic deviations from a norm.

Example 5.1   Brahms: *Variations and Fugue on a Theme by Handel* Op. 24, Variation 5, bars 1–2

Brahms's dynamic markings, shown in Example 5.1, suggest an asymmetrical demarcation of the bar. Where the theme of the variations, 'a dapper little tune, in two four-bar periods' (Macdonald 1990: 179), conforms to a Baroque common-metre type, with a strong downbeat and secondary emphasis on beat 3 complemented by weak second and fourth beats, Variation 5 sometimes appears to emphasize the second and fourth beats. This is not, however, consistent, offset as it is by more standard phrasing in bar 1^{1-2}, bar 4, bar 5^{1-2}, and bar 7^{1-2}. The score shows accents over the second quaver of bar 1^4, bar 2^2 and so on, which throw the strongest part of the bar not only on to traditionally weak beats, but also on to offbeats within them. Despite the possible ambiguity of these accent signs,[4] the

---

[4]   Beethoven and Schubert's use of accents can be ambiguous and some scholars have taken these signs to indicate both accent and *diminuendo*. Sandra Rosenblum calls these 'accent-*diminuendo*' signs and states that 'Schubert and, later, Brahms used the small hairpin as an accent-*diminuendo* sign fairly often' (Rosenblum 1991 [1988]: 88). The

126 *Reading Musical Interpretation*

implied musical syntax of the passage may therefore be understood as a potential performance feature (a characterizer in the interpretative tower), and as a focus for the type of expressive manipulation described above.

Given the cluster of properties to which *espressivo* refers in this setting, it is perhaps reasonable to expect that topical mode will emerge as an important interpretative factor. However, by placing Brahms's topical mode specification within the conceptual context of the interpretative tower, the analyst can appreciate ways in which the informant interacts with the remaining ones in shaping the acoustic outcomes of the performances. This may also account for interpretative divergences ranging from close textual adherence to significant textual departure, as reflected in the recordings. My analytical investigation opens by comparing recordings made by Claudio Arrau, Stephen Kovacevich and myself (CD, track 4).

Variation 5 in Performance

Claudio Arrau was Chilean-born but trained in Berlin under Martin Krause, a pupil of Liszt. Arrau regarded Krause as is his only real teacher, which is presumably why Harold Schonberg sees him as a representative of the German school, one whose chief characteristics he identifies as: 'scrupulous musicianship, severity, strength rather than charm, solidity rather than sensuosity, intellect rather than instinct, sobriety rather than brilliance' (Schonberg 1987 [1963]: 446). Schonberg does, however, admit the pianist's 'decidedly romantic piano sound' (454). Stephen Kovacevich, on the other hand, represents a younger generation and, although later studying with Myra Hess in London, he was initially trained in the USA. Writing in 1963, Schonberg saw American pianism as 'a relatively new phenomenon' and he characterized its main features as being 'clear in outline, metrically a little inflexible, tonally a little hard' (1969 [1963]: 429). He also claimed that American pianists 'tend to be literalists who try for a direct translation of the printed note. In a way they are junior executives, company men, well trained, confident and efficient, and rather lacking in personality' (429).[5]

As Schonberg's two accounts might suggest, the expressive manner in the two recordings is quite different, although his association of Arrau with the German school does not perhaps prepare the listener for the abundance of expressive gestures evident in the Arrau performance. His playing engages considerable amounts of *rubato*, to the extent that only a very approximate overall metronome measurement of crotchet = c. 60 can be determined. For example, there is a *ritenuto* from bar 2^2 second quaver, through to the end of 2^3, another *ritenuto*

---

arrangement of the hairpin signs in the first (1862) edition of the *Handel Variations* by Breitkopf & Härtel do look more like *diminuendo* than accent signs.

[5]   By 1987, Schonberg had come to view these qualities as characteristic of 'today's international school' – but with their roots in American pianism (Schonberg 1987 [1963]: 496).

from bar 3^4 to 4^2 and yet another through bar 6^4, with an obvious lengthening of the second quaver, maybe to highlight the apparent accent. Arrau, in his own way, certainly heeds the markings, as he emphasizes the accents both dynamically and agogically, thus end-loading much of the phrasing. The dynamic (marked '*p*' by Brahms) is full in the right hand, projecting a sustained, 'singing tone'[6] and supported by a sonorous texture in which pedal changes mostly correspond with the bass-note progression in the left hand.

Kovacevich's recording presents a very different view. The tempo is basically slower than Arrau's, but, whereas the latter's is variable, Kovacevich holds a fairly consistent crotchet $= c.$ 55 throughout, employing a hint of *ritenuto* to mark the cadence points of the two halves – an index of closure and one of the most conventional of all performance codes. Hints of *rubato* occur occasionally, usually in conjunction with the offbeat phrase peaks such as those at bars 1^4 second quaver, bar 2^2 second quaver and at analogous passages in bar 3. However, accentuation is avoided, thus these characterizers are not strongly projected; indeed, on the evidence of bar 1^4, it is possible that Kovacevich reads the apparent accents as *diminuendo* signs, but his approach here is very subtle and not consistent throughout. The dynamic is subdued, a real *p*, and even where the score calls for a general *crescendo* in bar 5^3–6, the effect is very discreet. He applies a slight, earlier than marked, *crescendo* in bar 5 but omits this on the repeat, and a *diminuendo* is applied through bar 6. Pedal changes are more frequent than Arrau's – mostly per crotchet, resulting in a clearer texture. Although Kovacevich's recording may be heard as 'cooler' and less intense than Arrau's, more flowing and less governed by *rubato*, the gentle dynamics, slow speed and projection of the right-hand line come across as persuasive interpretative features. The impression that the performance is authentically *espressivo* lends support to the idea that expressive, compositional devices can 'speak for themselves' and that the pianist, with seemingly minimal personal intervention, can convey these to a listener. Perhaps this exemplifies the apparently paradoxical case of 'inexpressive' performance yielding 'expressive' music-making. Despite Alfred Brendel's assertion that music 'cannot speak for itself' (Brendel 1976: 25), Kovacevich's recording suggests that it can.

The interpretative polarities apparent in Kovacevich's and Arrau's recordings seem to mirror differing perceptions of the performer's role that also existed in Brahms's time, and there is evidence to suggest that Kovacevich's style may have accorded with Brahms's own. The composer's English biographer, Florence May, from her own studies with Brahms, reveals that: 'Whatever the music I might be studying ... he would never allow any kind of "expression made easy"' (May 1948 [1905]: 19). On the other hand, Arrau's playing seemingly concurs with Eduard Hanslick's assessment of the performer's interventionist role. After hearing Brahms in a recital which included the recently composed *Variations and Fugue on a Theme by Handel*, Hanslick wrote of the composer–performer: 'Prompted by the desire to let the composer speak for himself, he neglects – especially in the

---

[6] For a discussion of this metaphorical term, see Naomi Cumming (2000), Chapter 3.

128   *Reading Musical Interpretation*

performance of his own pieces – much that the player should rightly do for the composer. His playing resembles the austere Cordelia, who concealed her finest feelings rather than betray them to the people' (Hanslick 1988 [1862]: 85).

In terms of underlying tempo, my recording is closer to Arrau's than to Kovacevich's, in that it moves at crotchet = *c.* 64, but in 'spirit' is probably nearer to the latter's. *Rubato*, although not employed in the manner of Kovacevich, is still minimal, being confined to pauses on the anacruses that introduce the two halves and a *poco ritenuto* to conclude each playing of the first half. Pedal is more restrained still, with none used until halfway through bar 1, and then changed according to the harmony. Passages in which the left hand has scalic rather than arpeggiated figures are mainly unpedalled and textures are always clear. Where the reading has some accord with Arrau's is in its projection of the offbeat accents, which are achieved both dynamically and agogically,[7] resulting in similar phrase contours. Dynamics are all observed as indicated in the score (CD, track 4).

On the evidence of the performers' acoustic traces, the informants are emphasized according to three distinct interpretative schemes. Moving from Arrau, through Kovacevich to Hellaby, the role of authorship progressively assumes supremacy but produces some perhaps surprising outcomes along the way. In the case of Arrau's recording, the underpinning emphasis on era (Romantic) and its perceived implications for a romantic delivery seems all-important. The bold surface-level gestures are, in part, the result of a strong projection of the rhythmic characterizers and a traditionally romantic interpretation of the topical mode, *espressivo*, with its double referencing, noted above, of romantic playing and Romantic rules. Both of these are supported by connections to the nocturne-as-topic and an emphasis on affective variety within a nineteenth-century variation context. The acoustic outcomes at the surface level of Arrau's recording can therefore be traced more markedly to a particular view of era (style), rather than to authorship (score). This emphasis is perceived to influence all the informant layers above, cutting an especially marked path from topical mode to duration manipulator and sonic moderator.

Kovacevich's acoustic trace comes across rather differently. A grounding in the authorship (score) informant may be inferred, with its wider implications of tasteful restraint, perhaps in accord with Brahms's own manner of performance, described above. The biggest surface-level gesture is the reduction in tempo to a speed significantly below that of the preceding variation. This may be accounted for, at a lower hierarchical level, by a perception of genre and a related tendency towards tempo changes in a variation context, reflecting in particular the expressive-structural implications of the music's shift to the minor key in Variation 5. However, the topical mode, characterizer and topic informants exert only a weak influence in the interpretative outcomes of Kovacevich's performance. So, if authorship is given pride of place, it is only in the general sense of, as Hanslick once put it,

---

    [7]   This is a feature that I would probably not have incorporated, had I seen the 1862 Breitkopf & Härtel edition before making the recording.

Brahms's 'Mozartian blood' (1988 [1878]: 158), because the recording does not follow the composer's performance directions in every particular.

Close observance of Brahms's performance directions in my own recording make it relatively easy to trace a path backwards to authorship (score) as the essential informant in the interpretation. In a sense, topical mode and characterizer and any associated nocturnal properties are allowed to 'speak for themselves' in as much as they are reflected through more-or-less faithful adherence to the score's performance markings. The tempo differential between Variation 4 and this one is less than in the other two recordings,[8] implying a perception of genre which, supported by the absence of any authorial indication that the tempo should change, emphasizes the musical continuum rather than any potential variety within this.

The above analyses may be summarized as follows:

Arrau:
> Level 1: romantic manner **era (style)** overriding **authorship (score)** →
> Level 2: variation, with interpretation maximizing variety **(genre)**; nocturne **(topic)** →
> Level 3: individually expressive style **(topical mode)** linked to projection of **characterizer** influencing →
> Level 4: relatively slow pace **(tempo)**; plentiful *rubato* and fluctuating tempo **(duration manipulator)**; singing right-hand tone, richly pedalled texture, exaggerated dynamic gestures **(sonic moderator)**.

Kovacevich:
> Level 1: **authorship (score)** implying disciplined romantic manner **(era (style))** →
> Level 2: variation scheme implied mainly by a significant drop in tempo from Variation 4 **(genre)**; nocturne **(topic)** – suggested by default rather than positive projection →
> Level 3: expressive style allowed, as far as possible, to speak for itself **(topical mode)** with **characterizer** unprojected and barely detectable aurally, reflected in →
> Level 4: slow pace **(tempo)**; minimal *rubato* and a fairly constant pulse **(duration manipulator)**; smooth melodic lines, clear pedalling and limited dynamic gestures **(sonic moderator)**.

Hellaby
> Level 1: **authorship (score)** accorded supremacy (all performance directions observed) but not at the expense of all romantic gesture **(era (style))** →

---

[8] Arrau's and Kovacevich's tempo for Variation 4 is crotchet = *c.* 87; mine is crotchet = *c.* 81.

Level 2: variation scheme implied mainly by a drop in tempo from Variation 4, but small enough to preserve a sense of continuity (**genre**); nocturne (**topic**) – presence by default rather than positive projection →

Level 3: expressive style allowed largely to speak for itself although some extra expressive devices are employed (**topical mode**) linked to projection of **characterizer** →

Level 4: relatively slow pace (**tempo**); small amounts of *rubato* plus agogic accents to reflect characterizer and topical mode but a fairly constant pulse (**duration manipulator**); smooth melodic lines, clear pedalling and well defined dynamic gestures reflecting scored dynamics, topical mode and characterizers (**sonic moderator**).

In diagrammatic form the above summaries are shown in Figure 5.1.

The relative appearances of the three diagrams graphically illustrate, at a glance, the boldness of Arrau's interpretation through to the restraint of Kovacevich's. The latter's recording is, on the face of it, the more detached and impersonal of these two in actual effect, as is evidenced by the rather unmarked top-level categories in his tower, but this need not imply any lack of interpretative commitment. Whereas Arrau's perceived starting point is era (style), Kovacevich's favours authorship (score), and these differences of emphasis at the base level carry implications all the way through the interpretations to the audible surface level. The interpretative features in Arrau's account seem the more obviously projected of the two and are reminiscent of Fontanier's description of 'spiritual' meaning: 'The spiritual meaning, the diverted or figurative meaning of a group of words, is that which the literal meaning causes to be born in the spirit by means of the circumstances of the discourse, by tone of voice, or by means of expressed connections between … relationships' (Ricoeur 2000 [1975]: 51). By extension, Arrau's performance, through use of tone and highlighting of structural connections, is heard to draw as much 'meaning', or 'expression' as possible out of the musical discourse.

Kovacevich's recording, on the other hand, retreats from even the performance instructions that Brahms does provide and so does not even appear to be embracing Fontainier's 'literal meaning'. My own recording of the variation projects a 'literal meaning' and, by paying heed to the characterizers in particular (hence the relatively bold lines through characterizer to duration manipulator and sonic moderator), acquires more expressive gestures than does Kovacevich's. There is some irony here. Through apparent literalism, the potentially Romantic properties of the score are more strongly projected than they are in Kovacevich's account, which means that in effect (or affect), my performance lies somewhere between the seeming 'coolness' of Kovacevich's and the expressive conceit of Arrau's. All of which stresses the complexity and elusive nature of 'expression'.

So the virtual, sonic *Urtext* performance that I drafted earlier in this chapter is not adequate, largely because it does not take into account all the complexities that 'voluntary interpretation' (Cook 1992 [1990]) involves and which tower analysis can help to reveal. But it was not entirely wrong either. It provided a 'neutral'

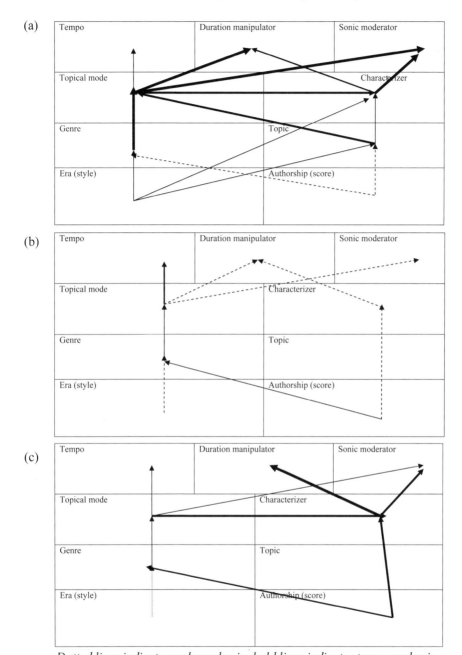

Dotted lines indicate weak emphasis; bold lines indicate strong emphasis.

Figure 5.1   Brahms: *Variations and Fugue on a Theme by Handel* Op. 24, Variation 5; interpretation by (a) Arrau (b) Kovacevich and (c) Hellaby, mapped on to the interpretative tower

model with which others can be compared. Perhaps unsurprisingly, my own near-*Texttreue* performance comes closest in effect to this virtual model, with seemingly opposing *espressivo* outcomes placing Arrau's and Kovacevich's performances on either side of this middle point.

Variation 5 perhaps presents a special case in that its expressive qualities, as described earlier, suggest a certain musical instability which may be variously read by pianists and variously conveyed and received in performance. It would now, therefore, be worth examining a more apparently stable variation to ascertain whether a sonic *Urtext* prediction can be any more accurate under different conditions.

Variation 7: Case Study

With its *con vivacità* heading, repetitive figurations and tonic major orientation, Variation 7 makes an interesting vehicle for interpretative comparison with Variation 5.

A *Texttreue* reading of the score of Variation 7 suggests that the pianist will play in a lively manner (*con vivacità*), which is highly likely to result in a quicker tempo than that adopted in the previous variation, even though no direct tempo instruction is supplied. In the absence of any indication to the contrary (or indeed musical implication), the selected tempo will be held steadily. The dynamic pattern of the variation's first half will work from a basis in *piano* but will rise to *forte* during bars 3 and 4, and this pattern will be repeated in the second half. Most on-beat quavers will be accented but offbeat quavers at bars 1^4, 2^4, 3^4, 5^4 and 6^4 will also be accented, especially the latter two which are marked '*sf*'. All semiquavers will be executed *staccato* but quavers will be held for their full value. The overall effect will be lively, detached, rhythmically pointed and *rubato*-free.

Despite its literalism, the above account may seem uncontroversial and in accord with most listening experiences of the variation in performance. However, before testing this hypothesis against some real performances, it would be worth identifying other performance clues in the score that could interact with an interpretation.

Topic and Genre in Variation 7

Michael Klein employs the notion of an 'economy of … musical sign[s]' when proposing that music, nineteenth-century music in particular, may 'participate in more than one topic' (Klein 2005: 56) and he cites the finale of Schubert's Piano Sonata in C minor D 958 as invoking both the tarantella and the 'horse topic' (57). A similar duality may be found in Variation 7, which can be heard to evoke the technical study and the galop, both of which are specifically era-related topics.

Several of the variations in the Brahms–Handel set seem to relate to the technical drills of many early nineteenth-century piano studies. The early 1800s witnessed

Brahms: Variations and Fugue on a Theme by Handel *Op. 24*   133

the first great flowering of piano pedagogy, and with it came a proliferation of studies, pieces with which Brahms grew up and was thoroughly familiar. Under his first piano teacher, Otto Cossel, 'the pianistic fare was limited, largely to the studies of Czerny, Clementi, Cramer and Hummel' (Musgrave 2000: 17). In Op. 24, Variation 4 focuses on consecutive octaves, Variation 13 on consecutive sixths, and Variation 7 on chordal repetition, loose models for the last of which can be found in Czerny's *Forty Daily Studies* Op. 337/18 and *School of Virtuosity* Op. 365/44.

If this referencing of the technical study topic suggests a focus on clarity and discipline, then the referencing of the galop topic may combine with this to influence tempo. Raymond Monelle (2000) has written on the notion of the horse-as-topic in nineteenth-century music, observing its influence in works as disparate as Schubert's *Erlkönig*, Wagner's *Ride of the Valkyries* and Brahms's setting of 'Keinen hat es noch gereut' from his *Magelone* songs. Despite the breadth of Monelle's topical field, he makes no mention of the dance bearing the name of 'galop', which became fashionable in nineteenth-century European ballrooms and was characterized by the contemporary Ludwig Rellstab as wild and wanton (Kramer 2002: 83). According to Andrew Lamb, the galop (French; German: Galopp) is 'a quick lively dance in 2/4 time' and 'was one of the most popular ballroom dances of the 19th century. It derived its name from the galloping movement of horses ... The galop rhythm has also been used to provide a rousing finale to orchestral showpieces, as in Rossini's *Guillaume Tell* overture' (Lamb 1980: 132–3). Elaine Sisman refers to the galloping figurations[9] of Variation 7 (Sisman 1999: 170), and certainly its resemblance to Variation 15 in Beethoven's *Diabelli Variations* and to the galop in Rossini's *William Tell* overture is striking, even though Brahms writes dactyls rather than anapaests. It is, therefore, the evocation of this dance topic and its potential tempo implications, as distinct from any specific evocation of a galloping horse (although the one is index to the other), that is of relevance in the present context.

One further consideration that may influence a performer's engagement with both tempo and topical mode relates, once more, to the genre informant and, in particular, the schematic placement of Variation 7 within the work. This variation follows and maximally contrasts with the tonic minor pairing of Variations 5 and 6 which are marked, respectively, '*espressivo*' and '*legato*'. Variation 7 leads seamlessly into Variation 8, the latter of which develops the musical and technical ideas established by its antecedent, producing an early point of climax in the work's overall design. The pause mark over the double bar at the conclusion of Variation 8, in conjunction with the new, chromatically ponderous style of Variation 9, suggests that Variation 7 and its natural companion, Variation 8, operate rather in the manner of an Act One *finale*.

The above account of the variation, with its explanation of certain referential and contextual factors, is not opposed in any obvious way to the chapter's opening

---

[9]   Sisman incorrectly refers to the dactyls as anapaests.

134   *Reading Musical Interpretation*

virtual *Texttreue* account, which made no reference to them. So I will now consider recordings by Benno Moiseiwitsch, Jorge Federico Osorio and myself (CD, track 5) to determine whether the very different styles of these pianists offer any alternative perspectives.

Variation 7 in Performance

An analysis of the surface properties of the three recordings reveals a similarity of response with regard to the tempo and duration manipulator categories, so I will start by considering these. The slowest reading is mine at crotchet = *c.* 110 and the fastest, at crotchet = *c.* 117, is Moiseiwitsch's. Almost exactly in between these is Osorio's which moves at crotchet = *c.* 113.[10] Compared with tempos adopted for Variations 5 and 6, all of these demonstrate a notable increase but, more significantly, the tempo in all three instances is above that adopted for the previous 'fast' variation, number 4, where the metronome readings are, respectively, crotchet = *c.* 81, crotchet = *c.* 100 and crotchet = *c.* 85 (*r*). The tempo that each artist adopts for Variation 7 remains very largely unaffected by duration manipulation. Moiseiwitsch applies none, Osorio holds back fractionally during bar 8^{1-2} (both times) and I insert a barely detectable fermata between the end of the first playing of bar 8 and the second of bar 5, which accommodates a drop in dynamic level. By thus displaying the greatest amount of unrestrained motion and activity in the variations so far, the three performances under discussion illustrate the sense of an Act One *finale*, suggested above by my score-based projections. This also connects strongly with the topical mode *con vivacità* which Brahms employs only twice again (as *vivace*) during the course of the variations — even more sparingly than he uses *espressivo*.

A few differences between the performances emerge in the characterizer and sonic moderator categories and, since the former is reflected through the latter, I will deal with them together. In my recording, all semiquavers are played *staccato*, as are the pair of quavers that fall on the fourth beats of bars 1, 2 and 3. The articulation and dynamic markings of the quaver pairs in bars 5 and 6 are played as indicated in the score. Accents (rhythmic characterizers) are observed as marked but those falling on downbeats are not very pronounced, their effect being achieved as much through duration as through dynamic: the quaver is held almost for its full duration but very slightly detached from its semiquaver companions (see example 5.2). The dynamic outline of the variation is played as indicated in the score but within a fairly narrow range. Moiseiwitsch's articulation varies between all-*staccato*, as in bar 1, semi-*staccato* quavers at bar 4^1 and 4^2 (on the repeat), and observance of the marked articulations in bars 7 and 8. He tends to accent the downbeats but to ignore offbeat accents, except those marked '*sf*', and the dynamic is generally quite loud, the only obvious *crescendo* occurring during the repeat of

---

[10]   Arrau's and Kovacevich's tempo for Variation 7, crotchet = 112, and Petri's crotchet = 110 are also close.

bar 3. Much of Osorio's articulation is similar to mine, although he executes bars 1 and 2 *staccato* throughout. The marked accents are incorporated, if not very prominently, although he does not play *sf* in bars 5 and 6. As with Moiseiwitsch, the general dynamic level is fairly loud and is thus unable to accommodate any significant *crescendo*, although a small one is detectable in the repeat of bar 1.

Example 5.2 Brahms: *Variations and Fugue on a Theme by Handel* Op. 24, Variation 7, bar 1, as played by Hellaby

Despite the differences in sonic moderation described above, the effect of all three recordings of Variation 7 is remarkably similar in that the tempo is roughly the same, the articulation is essentially detached, albeit with minor discrepancies, and the dynamic range is narrow, favouring ***mf/f*** levels. In music which strongly and audibly interfaces with era-related topics and which has such an obvious strategic placement within the work's design, a perception emerges that the authorship (score), era (style), genre and topic informants are fused together into such a solid base that the exercise of the performer's artistic prerogatives, as heard in the recordings, seems confined to toying with surface details, thus ensuring strong interpretative similarities. In this setting at least, topic has a role to play that is almost equal in importance to that played by the gigue in Bach's Toccata BWV 912.

The evidence of the recordings is that the above interpretative and technical concerns have been synthesized in similar ways, so it is possible to provide a summary of analytical findings which has general application in most areas of the performances:

> Level 1: **authorship (score)** and **era (style)** (suggestion of technical exercise) equally important, although tempo implied by a combination of factors rather than spelled out →
> Level 2: contextual/structural setting of variation helps suggest tempo and manner (**genre**); **topic** (galop-study synthesis) identified as prime informant, again especially for tempo and manner →
> Level 3: lively style and articulate execution (**topical mode** – *con vivacità*); offbeat accents variously observed (**characterizer**) →
> Level 4: topic and topical mode reinforce fastest reasonable pace (**tempo**); constant pulse – required by topic – so **duration manipulator** less important; dynamics variously observed (**sonic moderator**).

This can be represented visually as in Figure 5.2, although, in this generalized graph, the characterizer and sonic moderator informants have been left deliberately vague, since these are the areas of greatest divergence amongst the three readings.

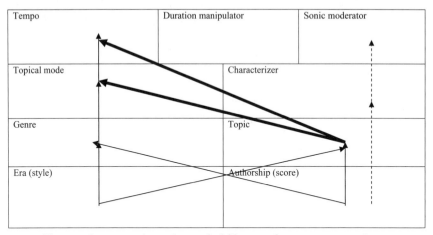

Dotted lines indicate weak emphasis; bold lines indicate strong emphasis.

Figure 5.2 Brahms: *Variations and Fugue on a Theme by Handel* Op. 24, Variation 7; 'general' interpretation mapped on to the interpretative tower

One general observation is, perhaps, still necessary and it concerns applied technique. Despite the close tempo match achieved between the three performers, a metronome mark in the range of crotchet = *c*. 110–*c*. 117 is not particularly fast, especially if one takes Rellstab's depiction of the galop as wild and wanton into account, and remembers that one of the most famous of all galops, that from Rossini's *William Tell* overture, can comfortably be taken at the composer's marking of crotchet = 152. This is, however, where the second topical reference, the technical exercise, exerts a moderating influence. Whilst the galop figurations urge the fastest achievable tempo, the performer's physical engagement with the keyboard necessarily imposes an upper limit on this. The technical exercise element in this variation is primarily chordal (see Example 5.2), requiring wrist rather than finger movement and, because pianists operating at the level of professionalism exemplified by these recorded performances will probably have velocity limits which are not dissimilar, tempo outcomes are likely to be close. The technical writing has two more related effects. Firstly, fast chordal repetition cannot be articulated other than *staccato* so Brahms's *staccato* dots are merely reflecting the unavoidable. Secondly, fast wrist work is harder to manage at a *piano* than at a *mezzo forte/forte* level, especially if accents are also required, which accounts for the generally raised dynamic level of all three artists. Perhaps Brahms's request for *piano* is unrealistic, at least on a twentieth-century grand piano.

Dynamics aside, the performance indications for Variation 7 could be thought to have a certain redundancy in that they merely reflect what is in any case required by the music, as discussed above. This is also probably a reason why the hypothetical account that I provided at the beginning of this study turned out to be a near match for the real performances, which may be positioned in close proximity to this *Texttreue* model. Only one significant divergence was noted, in the area of dynamics and, as explained above, this too is partially built into the performative demands of the music.

If Variation 7 presents a relatively straightforward case study, suggesting that topic can, in a nineteenth-century setting, be a strong and interpretatively decisive informant, I will now turn to a later variation in which topical association could be thought to reflect some of the ambiguities described at the beginning of this chapter.

Variation 19: Case Study

Writers on the Brahms–Handel *Variations* have often noted the neo-Baroque cast of Variation 19. Sisman regards the siciliano as one of the 'generalized Baroque elements' (Sisman 1999: 170) upon which Brahms models this variation, and, more specifically, Musgrave (1996 [1985]) and Littlewood (2004) note its evocation of the French siciliano, in particular 'the French school of Couperin whose music [Brahms] edited' (Musgrave 1996 [1985]: 53). The scene, therefore, is apparently set for a very different listening experience from that provided by Variation 7. But before examining the traces of either the work or the performers, I will first describe a possible *Texttreue* reading.

Such a description will not take long because, congruent with the Baroque influences noted above, Brahms has provided very few performance instructions, bars 1 and 5 (see Example 5.3) containing almost all of them. Drawing on this information, the hypothetical pianist will play the music lightly and quietly, with no obvious dynamic changes and, in accordance with the *vivace* indication, rather quickly. There will be a generally lilting rhythm, reflecting the syntax of the ever-present trochees.

Example 5.3 Brahms: *Variations and Fugue on a Theme by Handel* Op. 24, Variation 19, bars 1 and 5

Topic and Genre

If a performer reads Variation 19 as an invocation of the siciliano, or pastoral topic, then Brahms's request for *vivace* seems contradictory, since the general perception of such music is that it is gentle in nature.[11] With the presence of this potential dichotomy, the acoustic effect of the variation seems likely to be much more performer-dependent than is the case with, say, Variation 7. To develop the point further, it is worth considering Hatten's notion of the pastoral topic in Beethoven's Piano Sonata in A major Op. 101, since some of the performance issues arising from his discussion are also relevant in the present case.

Hatten regards Beethoven's Sonata in A major Op. 101 as a manifestation of the pastoral topic – or the 'pastoral expressive genre' (Hatten 1994: 91) to use his exact words. He does not mention performance, yet a pastoral basis could almost be lost in a rendition which failed to recognize this element. The projection of the topic may be modified by an interpretation of the tempo and topical mode informants supplied at the head of the score. The tempo direction of the first movement is '*Allegretto ma non troppo*', which is followed by the subheading: '*Etwas lebhaft und mit der innigsten Empfindung*' ('somewhat lively and with innermost feeling'). It would be quite possible for a performer to emphasize the *allegretto* and *lebhaft* elements of the headings and adopt a tempo that does not accord with Hatten's pastoral reading. Earlier examples of the topic usually come with slower tempo indications. For example, '*Larghetto*' is associated with the Pastoral Symphony and 'He shall feed His flock' from Handel's *Messiah*; '*Andante grazioso*' is the designated tempo/ topical mode for the first movement of Mozart's Sonata in A major K 331 (all three movements of which are topic-based). As Beethoven does not actually write the word '*pastorale*' at any point in the Op. 101, the case is by no means a closed one and leaves scope for divergence within the interpretative field. A performance in which a pastoral influence is detected as the backdrop for the musical drama of the Beethoven movement (or, indeed as Hatten claims, the whole sonata) would betoken a different version from one in which it is not apparent. And 'version' is not too strong a term, because if Hatten's interpretation is correct, a performance which audibly misses the pastoral aspect is tantamount to a misrepresentation. One is here reminded of the bewilderment once described by Artur Schnabel who, on consulting a programme note for one of his recitals, read: 'And now follows a jolly rondo', referring to a piece which he felt displayed 'unmistakably an atmosphere of despair and feverish suffering' (Schnabel 1988 [1961]: 134).

Returning to Brahms, the pastoral implications of Variation 19 seem more compelling still than those found in Beethoven's sonata movement. The variation's reference to the French siciliano is also strengthened by other references, in that a very similar style of writing occurs in both the Handel and Mozart pieces, mentioned above. There are even loose similarities between the melodic lie of

---

[11]   Türk's opinion that a siciliano is 'played in a caressing manner and in a very moderate tempo' (Türk 1982 [1789]: 396) is of interest in this connection.

Mozart's theme and the Brahms variation, as shown in Example 5.4. Despite all these seemingly rather obvious clues concerning the nature of the variation, Brahms, like Beethoven in Op. 101 and Mozart in K 331, does not supply either the designation 'pastorale' or the label 'siciliano' anywhere in the score, so the performer is left with a siciliano-like variation labelled '*vivace*'.

Example 5.4   (a) Mozart: Sonata in A major K 331, Andante grazioso, bars 1–2 (transposed) and (b) Brahms: *Variations and Fugue on a Theme by Handel* Op. 24, Variation 19, bar 1

This possible contradiction is compounded by the genre-related issue of Variation 19's placement in the work's overall scheme. Where Variation 5 is the first of a strategically placed tonic minor, *espressivo* pairing, and Variation 7 is the first of a counterbalancing *vivace* pair, Variation 19 appears as a 'one-off'. Wedged in between the self-evident interlinkage of variations 14–18 and the 'home-straight' of variations 23–25, Variation 19, along with numbers 20, 21 and 22, displays 'the individual character of the ... single variations' which 'contain some of the most striking of [Brahms's] inventions' (Musgrave 1996 [1985]: 55). But the variation's 'single' status deprives it of a clearly defined, immediate context, thus leaving the performer with fewer interpretative signposts than were found in Variation 7 or even Variation 5.

So, with the seeming ambiguity of topic versus topical mode, and no clearly defined formal context with which to correlate or oppose, the music of Variation 19 suggests a spacious interpretative field in which solutions to the challenges posed by the relative uncertainties within its informants are likely to be diverse. To investigate some of the acoustic outcomes from within this interpretative field I now turn to performances of the variation by the same trio of pianists on whose recordings I based my previous study (Moiseiwitsch, Osorio and myself), thus drawing a direct comparison.

Variation 19 in Performance

Where the three artists' tempos are close in Variation 7, in Variation 19 there is considerable divergence. Moiseiwitsch's tempo is variable but averages out at dotted crotchet = *c.* 71 across the variation. My tempo (CD, track 9) is a more-or-less steady dotted crotchet = *c.* 73, but Osorio's is considerably slower at dotted crotchet = *c.* 58. When compared to the tempo of the immediately surrounding variations, this data can be taken to signal something about the relationship of this variation to its immediate neighbours and its strategic place within the work as perceived in the recordings. Moiseiwitsch's recording, with surrounding tempos of crotchet = *c.* 110 for number 18 and crotchet = *c.* 78 for number 20, makes no obvious attempt at a tempo alignment, and seems to grant Variation 19 the single status ascribed to it by Musgrave. On the other hand, in Osorio's account, the tempo in Variation 19 relates to that for the ensuing Variation 20, converting the dotted crotchet = *c.* 58 into crotchet = *c.* 58. Sandwiched between significantly faster tempos in Variations 18 and 21, the consistency of pulse in numbers 19 and 20 creates a slower binary episode. My performance appears to promote a tempo continuum, in that dotted crotchet = *c.* 73 in Variation 19 is followed by crotchet = *c.* 72 in Variation 20, thereby avoiding a slower episode, since the tempos of Variations 18 and 21 are also similar.

My 'no nonsense' approach is reinforced by a regular adherence to the adopted tempo, employing no perceptible *rubato* until the last two beats, and here there is only the merest hint. In Osorio's performance durational modifications seem to be made according to perceived structural segments: in bars 1–8, Osorio applies a *poco ritenuto* at the end of the first and third two-bar segments, and a bigger *ritenuto* in the second half of bars 4 and 8, reflecting an assimilation of the shorter segments into the greater four-bar span. This is less consistent in bars 9–16, during which a *ritenuto* (rather than *poco ritenuto*) appears at the end of the first, third and fourth two-bar segments but not the second, and the overall tempo drops slightly to dotted crotchet = *c.* 56. Moiseiwitsch's reading is the least stable in tempo, and it ranges from high points of dotted crotchet = 108 down to below 30 in the most substantial *ritenuto*. Generally the first half, with an average pulse of dotted crotchet = 80, is taken faster than the second in which the average is 64.5. *Ritenuto* is applied to the end of the first four bars, then to the ends of bars 6 and 8, and an elongated *ritenuto* affects all of bar 10, most of bar 12 and all of the last four bars. The overall impression is that the second half deflates the momentum of the first and that duration manipulation seems to reflect a mixture of the artist's intuition and sense of structural design.

My recording remains a largely uninflected *piano* throughout, but the other two pianists engage significant levels of sonic moderation. In bars 1–8, Osorio employs a slight *crescendo/diminuendo*, apparently to reflect the contours of a perceived two-bar phrase structure. In the second half of the variation, the statements of bars 9–10 and 13–14 are more strongly laid forth, allowing for *piano* answers in bars 11–12 and 15–16, in line perhaps with his seemingly structural approach to interpreting the variation.[12] Moiseiwitsch is also heard to follow some personal idiosyncrasies,

---

[12]   The dynamic scheme adopted by Osorio between bars 9 and 16 is indicated in Mayer-Mahr's 1925 edition of the *Handel Variations* for Simrock (which is still available from Lengnick), as well as in Sauer's *c.* 1939 edition for Peters, which is also still available.

Brahms: Variations and Fugue on a Theme by Handel *Op. 24* 141

often starting the phrases *mp* and tapering them off to *pp*. At the end, he reverses Osorio's statement/answer arrangement by augmenting to *mf* through bar 15. It appears, in this case, that stability of pulse begets (or is begotten by) dynamic stability and that dynamic variation is the natural companion to a variable pulse.

From the evidence of the recordings, the inherent ambiguities of the variation, discussed above, do indeed seem to have yielded diverse interpretative outcomes. Osorio's reading can hardly be seen as either *vivace* or especially *leggiero*. With a consequent shift in topical mode to *poco serioso*, perhaps reflecting something of the 'Romantic tradition of the grotesque',[13] it would seem that in his case era (style) supports a generally sober manner of performance. Topical association tends to override other considerations where tempo is concerned and the demarcation of two-bar units through either duration manipulation or sonic moderation is sufficiently regular to qualify as a characterizer. Brahms's topical mode instruction '*vivace*' is certainly reflected in Moiseiwitsch's recording but, with its broad dynamic scope and liberal *rubato*, *leggiero* is only intermittently sensed and topical projection sounds inconsistent. However, with its relative extremes of sonic moderation and duration manipulation, the performance matches an early twenty-first-century analyst's notion of archetypical romantic playing, thereby connecting more closely to a perception of era (style) than to authorship (score) at its base. This observation suggests a particular relationship between Moiseiwitsch's historical situatedness, his perception of the work as heard in the recording and its reception by an informed, contemporary listener. It also concurs with Harold Schonberg's rather less circumscribed opinion that the pianist 'represented the last vestiges of romanticism ... which means pliancy ... and a free approach to the notes' (Schonberg 1987 [1963]: 331).

Authorship (score) again clearly underpins my reading and a very disciplined view of era (style) emerges. The '*p, leggiero*' instruction is honoured throughout and a rather clipped, unitary or beat-by-beat phrasing is employed, which aids the suggestion of a dance topic and thereby generates a consistently applied characterizer. The moderately fast tempo brings it close to a *vivace* reading but not sufficiently so to lose all sight of the topic. Thus my own somewhat *Texttreue* performance of this variation seems conceptually distant from Moiseiwitsch's account and, indeed, from that of Osorio.[14]

The two most contrasting recordings (Osorio's and my own) may therefore be interpreted as follows. The sonic moderation and duration manipulation heard in Osorio's recording connect with the two-bar phrase structuring (characterizer), also evident in the recording. This in turn suggests a particular understanding of the music's syntax (authorship). The slowish tempo reflects a topical mode, *poco*

Most editions do not include these dynamic suggestions, so it seems reasonable to treat Osorio's interpretative accord with Mayer-Mahr and Sauer as an interesting coincidence.

[13] According to the dictionary usage, rather than Rosen's (see Chapter 5, footnote 1).

[14] It is intereting to note that Osorio studied with, amongst others, Wilhelm Kempff, one of the least *Texttreue* pianists of the twentieth century.

serioso, rather than the given '*leggiero e vivace*'. This is further supported by a perception of the variation as pastoral topic and by use of the slowish tempo as means to achieve variety in a variation context (genre). The base-level informants of era (style) and authorship (score) appear both to be influential, although non-observance of the authorially indicated topical mode is of significance. Thus era (style) tends to support features related to tempo and mood, whereas authorship (score) tends to influence the (structurally derived) expressive elements. In keeping with my other recordings, my own account avoids obvious personal intervention or romantic pianism, again strongly favouring authorship (score) over any overtly expressive notion of era (style). What little sonic moderation there is reflects the lilt (characterizer) of the dance topic, but the *vivace* tempo, following Brahms's direction, brings the topic closer, perhaps, to the forlana than the siciliano. The alignment of this variation's tempo with that adopted in the surrounding units demonstrates both a holistic concept of the complete work (genre) as well as a reluctance to introduce variety without authorial sanction.

These findings are summarized below and graphically depicted in Figure 5.3.

Osorio:
> Level 1: romantic ('serious') manner **era (style)** and **authorship (score)** roughly equal but personalized →
> Level 2: variation coupled through tempo to Variation 20, creating a 'slow' episode **(genre)**; siciliano pace **(topic)** →
> Level 3: *poco serioso* rather than *leggiero e vivace* **(topical mode)** and some projection of **characterizer** as two-bar units (direct link to authorship/score) →
> Level 4: relatively slow pace **(tempo)**; structurally related tempo fluctuations **(duration manipulator)**; generally a full sound, some changes structurally related **(sonic moderator)**.

Hellaby
> Level 1: **authorship (score)** accorded supremacy (very little added to the relatively 'clean' score) and **era (style)** sense developed from this →
> Level 2: variation form continuum implied by tempo retention with neighbouring variations **(genre)**; **topic** detectable, if its precise nature is ambiguous →
> Level 3: *leggiero e vivace* as indicated **(topical mode)** with projection of beat-by-beat 'lilt' **(characterizer)** →
> Level 4: fastish pace **(tempo)**; no significant *rubato* **(duration manipulator)**; negligible dynamic variety **(sonic moderator)**.

In contrast to Variation 7, where the hypothetical *Texttreue* performance turned out to be in close accord with actual performances, the *Texttreue* reading of Variation 19, lacking as it did the deeper influence of the lower-level informants, has proven to be very inadequate, with only my own reading again showing some alignment.

The situation is also more complex than that presented by performances of Variation 5 which were shown to be either more overtly 'expressive' (Arrau) or less overtly 'expressive' (Kovacevich) than a *Texttreue* account, enabling their oppositional placement along an *espressivo* axis. In the case of Variation 19, with its seemingly inherent ambiguities, each performance is heard to emphasize certain informants in contrasting ways, sometimes at the expense of others, so that the character of the music is individually and variously realized, but without producing any oppositions as such.

(a) Artist: Osorio

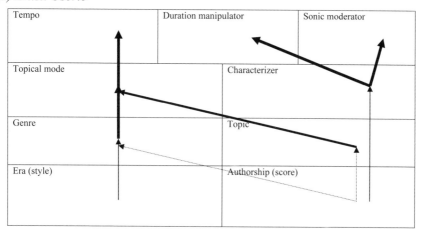

(b) Artist: Hellaby

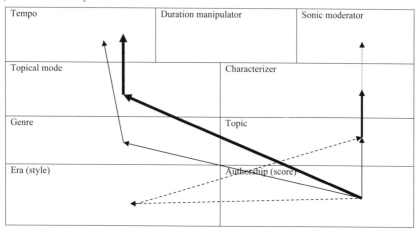

Dotted lines indicate weak emphasis; bold lines indicate strong emphasis.

Figure 5.3   Brahms: *Variations and Fugue on a Theme by Handel* Op. 24, Variation 19; interpretations by (a) Osorio and (b) Hellaby, mapped on to the interpretative tower

144   Reading Musical Interpretation

This diversity in the exercise of artistic prerogatives and resultant performers' traces will also impact on the wider issue of the complete work's overall 'shape' in performance, in that any projections based on dynamic or tempo data in the score cannot take into account deviations in these areas by individual performers. An examination of the subsequent variation, number 20, and its handling by a different trio of artists will serve to illustrate the point further.

Variation 20: Case Study

In Variation 20, Brahms moves far away both melodically and harmonically from Handel's simple aria, resulting in 'Romantic chromaticisms' (Sisman 1999: 170).[15] The variation's harmonic complexity, combined with a lack of obvious topic or tempo informant and an *espressivo* injunction in bar 11, seems likely to prompt a varied response in performance, especially as it is also another of those variations that Musgrave characterizes as 'single'. However, before evaluating the evidence of selected recordings of the variation, I will describe another virtual performance based on a literal reading of the score. Example 5.5 shows bars 1–8 of Variation 20, the performance indications of which are replicated in a fairly similar fashion throughout.

Example 5.5 Brahms: *Variations and Fugue on a Theme by Handel* Op. 24, Variation 20, bars 1–8

In the absence of any authorial instruction to the contrary, the hypothetical *Texttreue* performance will retain the tempo adopted in the work's opening aria. The tempo will be held steadily, although some *rubato* may be introduced in bar 11 to reflect the marked '*espressivo*', and there may be a slight *ritenuto* at

---

[15] Littlewood describes Variation 20 as 'aggressively "modern"' (Littlewood 2004: 93).

the end of bar 16 as a gesture of closure. Phrasing will be executed irregularly, commencing with a four-and-a-half-beat unit and thereafter ranging from one- to five-beat units, according to the marked slurring. The touch will be *legato* throughout and the dynamic will remain *piano*, but will include small fluctuations to reflect the rise and fall of the melodic contour. On two occasions, in bars 4 and 8, this slight dynamic flux will emphasize the first downward step in the right hand's melodically descending chromatic line. Pedal is likely to be employed on a largely beat-by-beat basis to achieve the necessary *legato*.

The most controversial aspect of this virtual performance account probably concerns tempo because the account disregards a common perception of Variation 20 as slow. A brief examination of the other variations where a slower tempo is indicated by Brahms may help, at least in part, to explain this common perception of Variation 20. Table 5.1 shows that Brahms only requests a reduction in tempo for Variations 9 and 13, and pianists invariably present broadly paced performances of these two, thus highlighting their strategically placed contrast with the variations that surround them. Variation 9 acts as a respite from the mainly active character of the music up to this point, which culminates in the two 'galop' variations, numbers 7 and 8. Despite its slow passage, Variation 9 is not lacking in dynamic energy and this subsequently finds an outlet in the *energico* of its successor. Variation 13, the numerical half-way point of the variations, comes as a moment of dark, tonic minor, drama, which stands alone between the preceding *dolce* and *soave* of Variations 11 and 12, and the energetic pianism of numbers 14, 15 and 16.

Performance tradition has added Variation 20 to this small, if weighty, collection of slow units. Structural placement may again be a reason for this in that, like Variations 9 and 13, number 20 provides another anchor point, in this instance coming before the final stretch in which the variations build up to the fugue. But the tempo, as with the other two variations, also seems to be embedded in the musical substance. Chromatic right-hand chordal lines, often in contrary motion with the mainly octal left hand allied to a tendency to explore the lower register of the keyboard, seem to suggest a measured rather than a rapid pace and a topical mode of sobriety.

My investigation of Variation 20 is based on contrasting recordings by Arrau, Kovacevich and myself (CD, track 10) and will open with a consideration of tempo, but the analysis will inevitably develop with reference to the interpretative tower's other informants.

Variation 20 in Performance

The most extreme tempo response to the variation comes from Arrau, who drops from dotted crotchet = *c.* 76 in Variation 19 to crotchet = *c.* 43 (*r*) in Variation 20, although the latter is more easily experienced by the analyst as quaver = *c.* 86 (*r*). Kovacevich also slows down significantly, moving from dotted crotchet = *c.* 70 in the previous variation to crotchet = *c.* 52. Of the three recordings, only my own retains equivalence across the two, with the dotted-crotchet pulse of *c.* 73 in

146   *Reading Musical Interpretation*

Variation 19 closely matching the crotchet pulse of *c.* 72 in number 20. It is worth mentioning that this feature was the result of a conscious, rather than intuitive, decision on my part.

All three pianists' tempos are affected by duration manipulation, which often seems to be influenced by Brahms's irregular phrase marks, or characterizers. Use of *rubato* is, unsurprisingly perhaps, the most extreme in Arrau's recording, and the slow tempo appears to lend added significance to the expressive device. Most of the *rubato* delineates phrase ends and beginnings, thus aligning characterizer with tempo and duration manipulation. Phrase peaks which coincide with beats 2 and 4 are also highlighted, although this is not entirely consistent. Even within the slow tempo, the *ritenuto* at phrase ends is substantial, especially in the second half. Kovacevich's recording contains significantly less duration manipulation, its use being largely confined to infinitesimal pauses around phrase peaks during beats 2 and 4 in the first half, and again at the very end, where a *ritenuto* is also applied. My own recording follows Brahms's marked phrasing although a very slight *ritenuto* in bars 4 and 8, suggesting greater four-bar spans up to the half-way point, is evident. Thereafter *ritenuto* is apparent in bar 10 and, a little more substantially, at the end of the variation.

Regarding sonic moderation, Arrau, Kovacevich and I all follow Brahms's *legato* specification but in both Arrau's and Kovacevich's recordings, dynamics appear to be based on a perceived musical (authorial) syntax rather than on authorial performance indications in the score. The score's notated 'hairpin' nuances are mainly unrealized, with both interpretations presenting a broader dynamic view. In Arrau's interpretation, the second half of the variation rises dynamically from bar 8^4 (second quaver) to bar 11^1, as if all one phrase, and is then complemented by a *diminuendo* through the consequent 'phrase' to bar 12^4 (see Example 5.6). This pattern is repeated in the closing four bars of the variation.

Kovacevich's interpretation, so different from Arrau's in most other respects, can be heard to adopt a similar scheme, allowing the sonic moderation to reflect a broader phrase sense than the one that Brahms has marked.[16] However, since both pianists do make *rubato* or agogic gestures around the composer's marked phrase peaks, this can be taken as a solution to combining larger- and smaller-scale views of the structure, blending authorial decree with interpretative discretion. My own recording of Variation 20 follows the dynamics supplied by Brahms, and is in fact the only one of the three to do this. However, the dynamic rise and fall evident in the three recordings extends well beyond any realistic conceptual containment of *p*, and reaches, in all three cases, a weighty *mf*, especially at phrase peaks in the second half. The absence in the score of any markings between *p* and *f* is the basis for Julian Littlewood's notion of the work's 'dynamic discontinuity'.

---

[16]   Augener's edition (*c* .1928) and Sauer's for Peters (*c.* 1939) make some alterations to Brahms's phrasing but, as neither Arrau nor Kovacevich shows any sign of adherence to these suggestions, they need not be of concern here.

Example 5.6 Brahms: *Variations and Fugue on a Theme by Handel* Op. 24, Variation 20, bars 8^4–12^4, as phrased by Arrau

Despite allowing for 'local swellings' (Littlewood 2004: 93), his notion is not borne out by the evidence of these recordings of Variation 20.

Projecting back from the performance to score, it may be deduced that the strongly marked surface-level features of Arrau's recording bespeak a level-three topical mode of *gravitas* and a characterizer that broadens the score's indicated phrase structure. This is supported at the level beneath by a sense of the variation's significance in the overall scheme of the work (genre) and the interpretative edifice as a whole seems to be underpinned by an equal allegiance to era (style) and authorship (score). Kovacevich's perception of the variation appears to have much in common with Arrau's, although this commonality is conveyed to the listener by more restrained top-level informants. My own interpretation places more emphasis on authorship (score) than on era (style), which results in a sense of the variation's place within the overall musical continuum (i.e. it does not slow down) and in relatively little adaptation of the informants at levels three and four.

The foregoing analyses may be summarized as follows:

Arrau:
>Level 1: **authorship (score)** and **era (style)** of similar importance. Authorship influence deduced from the notation rather than by explicit instruction. Romantic gesture equally important →
>Level 2: variation context important in helping to determine breadth of tempo and related phrase perception **(genre)**; **topic** (not relevant) →
>Level 3: **topical mode**: none indicated but grave solemnity deduced; phrasing, though not as marked, strongly influencing duration manipulator and sonic moderator informants **(characterizer)** →

148 *Reading Musical Interpretation*

Level 4: very slow speed linked to authorship, genre and topical mode (**tempo**); extensive *rubato* and agogic accentuation employed for structural purposes (**duration manipulator**), complemented by dynamics used to project a broad view of the phrase structure and not circumscribed by *p* (**sonic moderator**) – Brahms's nuances substituted by agogic accents from the previous informant.

Kovacevich:
Level 1: **authorship (score)** and **era (style)** of similar importance. Authorship influence deduced from the notation rather than by explicit instruction. Romantic gesture minimized, implying discipline rather than 'indulgence' →
Level 2: variation context important in helping to determine tempo and phrasing (**genre**); **topic** (not relevant) →
Level 3: **topical mode**: none indicated but solemnity can be deduced; phrasing, though not as marked, influencing duration manipulator and sonic moderator informants (**characterizer**) →
Level 4: slow speed linked to authorship, genre and topical mode but characteristically less extreme than Arrau's (**tempo**); discreet *rubato* employed around marked phrase peaks as substitute for Brahms's dynamic nuances (**duration manipulator**); dynamics used to project a broad view of the phrase structure and not circumscribed by *p* (**sonic moderator**).

Hellaby:
Level 1: **authorship (score)** given preference over **era (style)**. Authorship influence followed explicitly, with romantic gesture confined to minimal *rubato* →
Level 2: variation context important in helping to determine tempo, here resulting in related tempos from Variation 18 through to 22 (**genre**); **topic** (not relevant) →
Level 3: **topical mode**: none indicated and none strongly projected; phrasing realized as marked in the score (**characterizer**) →
Level 4: flow of the surrounding variations retained in the absence of any instruction to the contrary (**tempo**); discreet *rubato* employed around some phrase ends (**duration manipulator**); dynamics realized as marked in the score although not circumscribed by *p* (**sonic moderator**).

The above analysis suggests some conceptual similarity between Arrau's and Kovacevich's performances but, as observed in the performance analysis of Variation 5, Arrau's manner exaggerates the interpretative points far more forcibly than does Kovacevich's. Indeed, it is probable that Kovacevich's more disciplined gestures are what prompted the comment in Max Harrison's *Gramophone* review: 'it is striking how closely this performance reflects the way that Brahms drew full value from the discipline to which he subjected his musical thought' (Harrison

1969: 976). However, by relying much more heavily on authorship than on era at its base, my own interpretative map contrasts with the other two and again reflects the most 'literal' approach. The two most contrasting interpretations are represented graphically in Figure 5.4.

(a) Artist: Arrau

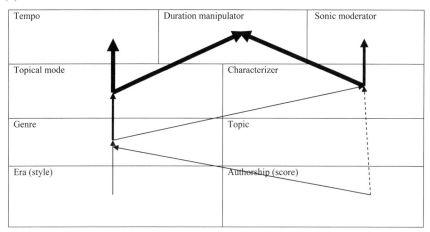

(b) Artist: Hellaby

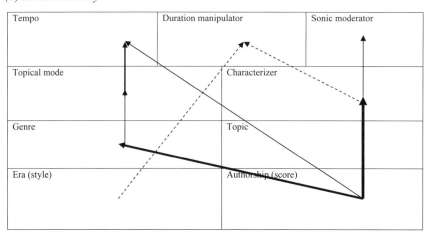

Dotted lines indicate weak emphasis; bold lines indicate strong emphasis.

Figure 5.4   Brahms: *Variations and Fugue on a Theme by Handel* Op. 24, Variation 20; interpretations by (a) Arrau and (b) Hellaby, mapped on to the interpretative tower

150 *Reading Musical Interpretation*

Whilst lacking the complex ambiguities of Variation 19, Variation 20, with its chromaticisms and uncertain tempo character, has been heard to prompt vigorous and varied interpretative responses from the three artists, even if my interpretation may seem a less mediated extension of the composer's poietic act than is the case with either Arrau's or Kovacevich's. Thus the *Texttreue* performance which prefaced this case study is at least as inadequate as that proposed for Variation 19, although it does have some affinity with my own performance. Nevertheless, even my reading includes personal touches in the areas of both duration manipulation and sonic moderation.

As in Variation 19, interpretative discrepancies in Variation 20 continue to affect the overall formal balance of the work as experienced by the listener. In fact at these two points the work seems particularly malleable and thus performer-dependent for its acoustic effect. By way of contrast, I will conclude my short series of studies by investigating performer responses to a variation which seems to serve a more obvious structural function within the work's schema.

Variation 23: Case Study

The schematic context of Variation 23 can briefly be described as follows. After variations 19–22, a set of more or less discrete entities or 'singles', Variation 23 initiates the 'home straight', the 'massive "crescendo" towards the fugue' (Rink 1999a: 87). The musical figures and ideas of Variation 23 are retained in Variation 24 but elaborated melodically and pianistically to create a virtuoso number, rather in the manner of 'model and *double*' (Littlewood 2004: 95). This process culminates in a climactic outburst of energetic pianism in Variation 25, now stripped of the minor-key allusions so characteristic of the compositional dialogues so far, to produce music of unreserved affirmation. Thus, the schematic import with which Variation 23 is apparently loaded seems hard for a performer to ignore.

Another feature of some significance is the variation's evocation of the gigue topic. With its simple 12/8 *staccato*, it resembles, in particular, Meredith Little and Natalie Jenne's 'giga II' designation which includes, amongst other things, 'tripleness at the pulse level' and an absence of 'sautillant' figures (Little and Jenne 2001 [1991]: 168). Regarding the execution of a gigue, Türk, writing in 1789, comments: 'The *gigue* (*giga*, *gique*) is executed in a somewhat short and light fashion. Its character is for the most part one of cheerfulness, and consequently the tempo must be fast' (1982 [1789]: 394). The performance data provided by Brahms for Variation 23 corresponds to this surprisingly closely: '*p vivace e stacc.*', greater dynamic variety appearing in the second part (see Example 5.7).

Before discussing the recordings, I will, once more, construct a hypothetical *Texttreue* reading based on the performance indications, shown above. In response to the marked topical mode '*vivace*', the tempo will be faster than that adopted for Variation 22 and probably for the original theme; this tempo will be held steadily throughout and will not feature any *rubato*. The touch will be *staccato*

Example 5.7 Brahms: *Variations and Fugue on a Theme by Handel* Op. 24, Variation 23, bars 1 and 5

as indicated both by the dots and the written instruction, and, to aid this, pedal will not be applied at any point. The opening dynamic will be *piano* but, in the first half, this will incorporate small 'hairpin' nuances and a slightly bigger and longer *crescendo/diminuendo* in bars 3[4]–4. Accents will emphasize the second, third and fourth beats of bars 2 and 4. In the second half, the hairpin *crescendos* will rise steeply to *forte*, and bars 7[4]–8 will be *forte* throughout, although bar 8 could commence at a *mezzo-forte* level because the hairpin *crescendo* through beat one leads to only a single *f* marking.

The virtual performance that I constructed in response to the topic-based Variation 7 turned out to bear close similarities to the actual performances that were analysed and, in Chapter 3, the presence of a gigue topic was observed to bind four very different pianists into relative interpretative conformity. On the other hand, Brahms's apparent evocation of the siciliano topic in Variation 19 of the *Handel Variations* was heard to produce no such accord. So I now compare recordings of Variation 23 by another diverse trio of pianists, Egon Petri, Steven Kovacevich and myself (CD, track 12), to discover whether topic and genre, in combination with the remaining informants, yield similarity or dissimilarity of interpretative response, and whether any alignment with my earlier *Texttreue* account is evident.

Variation 23 in Performance

The recorded performances under consideration do, in fact, show significant differences, diverging in a number of areas, although the three artists' tempo choices tend to be moderate rather than headlong, probably because an over-ambitious tempo for Variation 23 would lead to problems with control and clarity in Variation 24, even for the finest technique. The tendency towards a moderate tempo is especially evident in my own recording. Table 5.2 lists the pianists' adopted tempos for Variation 23 as well as for the preceding 'music box' variation. A comparison of the two provides a reference point for the analyst to assess how any new musical 'direction' implied by Variation 23 is reflected in performance.

152   *Reading Musical Interpretation*

Table 5.2   Brahms: *Variations and Fugue on a Theme by Handel* Op. 24; tempos adopted by Hellaby, Kovacevich and Petri in Variations 22 and 23

	Variation 22	Variation 23
Hellaby	quaver = *c.* 136	dotted crotchet = *c.* 98 (CD, tracks 11 and 12)
Kovacevich	quaver = *c.* 136	dotted crotchet = *c.* 121
Petri	quaver = *c.* 118	dotted crotchet = *c.* 122

The biggest difference in tempo between Variations 22 and 23 occurs in Petri's recording, but the effect is coloured by a semi-*staccato* touch on the quavers and a near disregard of marked dynamics: most accents (characterizers) and hairpin nuances within beats are absent, and the 1938 recording quality cannot be accountable for this, since there are clear dynamic contrasts elsewhere. The second half starts *mf* and rises to *f* by bar 7^4, the texture thickened with pedal from bars 6^4 to 8^1. The performance directive in the score is '*vivace e staccato*', which seems conceptually to link topical mode with sonic moderator, the latter being reinforced by the addition of *staccato* dots to the quavers. Petri's tempo certainly suggests *vivace*, and is indicative of a new musical direction leading to the approaching climax, even though this approaching stretch is condensed by his amalgamation of Variation 23 with Variation 24, where the two halves of the latter are played as repeats (or '*doubles*') for the former. However, a *staccato* touch is not audibly apparent, and so the sonic moderation acquires a personal character.

Kovacevich's reading follows Brahms's performance directions fairly closely. Apart from the marked accent (characterizer) in bar 4^4 and the crescendo from *p* to *f* in bar 5, all dynamic markings are observed. Pedal is applied only to bars 7^4 and 8^2, otherwise the texture is dry and crisp. The *staccato* is consistent and buoyant, creating a genuine *vivace e staccato*, as requested, and certainly sounding as close to a dance as the music might allow.

My own recording of this variation is dryer still, eschewing the sustaining pedal altogether, in accord with the double *staccato* instructions. With the exception of the accents at 4^{3-4} and any dynamic drop to reflect the *p* at 7^3, dynamics are all observed as indicated. Table 5.2 shows that, of the three recordings, my tempo differential between Variation 22 and 23 is the smallest, which implies that tempo stability is being favoured over contrast as a guiding principle. It can be added here that, as in the previous study, this was a conscious rather than an intuitive decision. However, the tempo is slowish (approximately 23 points below the next slowest), and there is a hint of introductory 'easing in' at the opening. These features do not actually deprive the variation of its capacity to signal the launch of a 'grand finale' but they barely generate *vivace* and therefore have implications for both topical and authorial links. The tempo does, however, allow for continuity of momentum and articulative clarity in variation 24.

Brahms: Variations and Fugue on a Theme by Handel *Op. 24*   153

In sum, the tempo and sonic moderation in Petri's account present a puzzling case. On the one hand, tempo can be traced back through the *vivace* component of the topical mode to both the motion of a gigue (topic) and the variation's strategic placement within the work's macrostructure (genre), all of which may be derived from authorship (score). On the other hand, the sonic moderation seems to have no such derivation, appearing to be in opposition to the *staccato* dots, as well as to the *staccato* component of the topical mode, the characterizers (emphatic accents) and traditional gigue-like articulation. It could thus be perceived to have some sense of dislocation from authorship (score), especially given the collapsing of Variations 23 and 24 which, to an extent, also counterbalances the genre links noted above. A personal style emerges but, as it is difficult to relate this to either a romantic or a disciplined view of the era (style) informant, it is best described as 'neutral'. By way of contrast, the surface-level features of Kovacevich's recording signal adherence to both topical mode (*vivace e staccato*) and characterizer, further suggesting an appreciation of topic (gigue) and the variation's strategic position in the work (genre). As is customary with this pianist's interpretations, authorship (score) rather than era (style) may be read as a primary informant. My own performance, with its close observation of authorial performance directions, clearly favours authorship (score) over era (style), and it may be thought that the interpretative synthesis of the genre, topic, topical mode and tempo informants underemphasizes any Romantic elements latent in this music.

The foregoing analyses may be summarized as follows:

Petri:

> Level 1: **authorship (score)** of some influence; personal, if 'neutral' sense of **era (style)** developed from sonic moderator →
>
> Level 2: context of variation used to influence tempo and manner; commingling of Variations 23 and 24 has implications for the structural effect of the passage (**genre**); dance **topic** (gigue) only partially identified as an informant →
>
> Level 3: lively style but semi-detached execution, so **topical mode** (doubling up with sonic moderator) only partially observed; accents not observed, so **characterizer** by-passed →
>
> Level 4: fast pace suggested by topic and topical mode (**tempo**); semi-*staccato* touch and loose observation of marked dynamics generate a personal style, seemingly breaking the link with topic and topical mode (**sonic moderator**). (Constant pulse so **duration manipulator** not relevant.)

Kovacevich:

> Level 1: **authorship (score)** favoured over **era (style),** implied by a largely strict observance of performance directions →
>
> Level 2: context of variation used to influence tempo and manner (**genre**); dance **topic** (gigue) →

154   *Reading Musical Interpretation*

> Level 3: lively style and detached execution (**topical mode** doubling up with sonic moderator); accents observed as marked (**characterizer**) →
> Level 4: fast pace derived from levels 2 and 3 (**tempo**); *staccato* touch (despite occasional pedal use) and most dynamics observed as marked (**sonic moderator**). (Constant pulse so **duration manipulator** not relevant.)

Hellaby
> Level 1: **authorship (score)** favoured over **era (style)**, implied by an almost strict observance of most performance directions and an eschewing of bravura effect →
> Level 2: context of variation used to influence tempo (preserving stability) and manner (**genre**); dance **topic** (gigue) a little weak due to slowish tempo →
> Level 3: fairly lively style and very detached execution (**topical mode** doubling up with sonic moderator); accents observed as marked (**characterizer**) →
> Level 4: moderate pace derived from levels 2 and 3 (**tempo**); *staccato* touch and almost all dynamics observed as marked (**sonic moderator**). Slight easing in of opening triplets as if introducing topic and topical mode (**duration manipulator**).

The two most contrasting interpretations (Petri's and my own) are shown graphically in Figure 5.5.

The *Texttreue* performance with which I opened this case study clearly does not exactly match any of the actual performances, but bears some affinity with both my own and Kovacevich's readings. It also serves to highlight the more idiosyncratic engagement with a number of the informants evident in Petri's reading. So some convergent tendencies, as well as divergent ones, can be observed.

A Case for Performer Dependency

Throughout this chapter, I have presented what I have called *Texttreue* readings of each variation, in order to supply a point of reference for my discussions of individual performances. That the former rarely accord with real performances is unsurprising because 'otherwise, performing works would be akin to minting coins' (Godlovitch 1998: 85). However, the *Texttreue* readings appear to accord with performances of some variations more than with others. There is, as noted, a tendency for performances of Variation 7 to show some remarkable affinities with the *Texttreue* account, for those of Variation 19 to display very few, and for those of Variation 23 to lie somewhere between these extremes. Despite these variables, to which I will return, a comparison between the models and the real performances has, in all cases, revealed that the effect of a work in performance is ultimately in the hands of each individual pianist. Without necessarily agreeing

Brahms: Variations and Fugue on a Theme by Handel *Op. 24* 155

(a) Artist: Petri

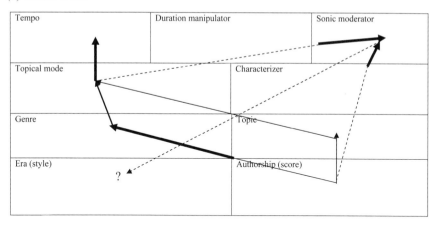

(b) Artist: Hellaby

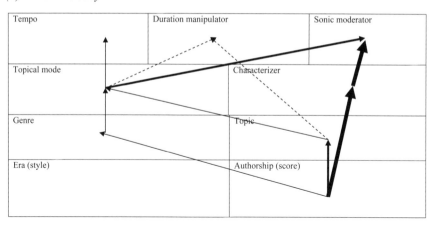

Dotted lines indicate weak emphasis; bold lines indicate strong emphasis; dotted lines leading to bold lines indicate strong emphases that seem to have a weak link with the layer below. Question mark indicates neutrality.

Figure 5.5   Brahms: *Variations and Fugue on a Theme by Handel* Op. 24, Variation 23; interpretations by (a) Petri and (b) Hellaby, mapped on to the interpretative tower

with Christopher Small (1998) when he claims that a musical work exists only in performance, one may conclude that a musical work's existence as heard in multiple performances is distinctly protean.

So how does this conclusion, based on a series of semi-discrete entities extracted from the context of a major composition, impact on a larger view of the work? As with Dunsby's structural analysis, my highly selective performance analysis 'gives only a limited picture of the *Handel Variations*' (Dunsby 1981: 7). However, the variations that I used for tower analysis are sufficiently contrasted in their characters, piano styles and formally strategic significance that, from a combined view of their executive outcomes, some conclusions may be drawn about performances of the work as a whole.

If interpretations of individual variations are broad in their range of effective and affective outcomes, it is very likely that interpretations of the complete work will, as I have intimated already, reflect this on a larger scale, especially in a piece whose constituent properties I earlier characterized as 'medium'. Analysis of performances by means of the interpretative tower has demonstrated that, in the relatively few instances where the musical informants appear to be largely unambiguous, interpretative outcomes are convergent, but where there is a seeming ambiguity such outcomes are varied, sometimes maximally so, according to the level of informant ambiguity. The inference is that pianists are heard to play the complete work with varied interpretative emphases, leading mainly to interpretative diversity but occasionally to relative concurrence.

This brings me back to the starting point of this chapter where I asked whether tables and graphs based on the work's dynamic flux (or possibly tempo flux), as gleaned from the score alone, can relate to a listener's experience of the music in actual performance. Just as my *Texttreue* constructions that prefaced each case study turned out largely to be unable to accommodate the actuality of performance, a larger-scale *Texttreue* projection is almost certainly going to suffer the same fate as a small-scale one. I earlier acknowledged that John Rink's 'dynamogram' and Julian Littlewood's table present a fresh and interesting analytical slant and, in presenting a type of *précis* of the work, are of value to the performer. However, it is now probably safe to affirm that such abstractions serve primarily as Wittgensteinian models, that is, as objects of comparison to which reality need not correspond.

The above case studies strongly suggest that post-performance data concerning recordings of the complete *Variations and Fugue on a Theme by Handel* would result in contrasting graphic depictions of both dynamic and tempo outcomes. Such graphs may be worthwhile in conveying an overview of the work's intensity levels and shape, as reflected in these parameters and as managed by individual artists. Whilst providing some potentially useful comparative information for the performance analyst, such graphs would merely present but would not explain, whereas the conceptual framework of the interpretative tower is set up to enable the analyst actively to seek explanations for interpretative results, to examine aspects of performance within their wider setting. This method derives from my belief that a work's overall shape in performance is the result of an artist's personal response not merely to surface-level informants but also to deeper levels within the work, as symbolized by the various informant categories and levels of the interpretative tower.

Afterword: The Tolerance Factor

The foregoing analyses suggest that contrasting performances of the Brahms–Handel *Variations* from contrasting pianistic styles and temperaments have emphasized some of the lower-level informants in preference to others, thereby producing top-level features that reveal alternative interpretative approaches, ultimately presenting authorship (score) and era (style) through a personal filter. These can be observed visually in the tower graphs, amongst the most telling of which depict Variations 5 and 19.

It is possible that these contrasts would not have worried the composer himself. Sherman points out that Brahms 'appreciated interpreters of widely varied sorts' and may have been 'concerned more with a performer's ability to convey musical content than with adherence to specific performance practices' (Sherman 2003: 3). Walter Frisch identifies two oppositional 'schools' of Brahms performance amongst conductors and characterizes these as 'restrained–interventionist, Apollonian–Dionysian, classic–romantic' (Frisch 2003: 279). The outcomes of this chapter support a perception of similar oppositional tendencies in 'schools' of piano playing.

This duality seems to be accommodated by a work such as the Brahms–Handel *Variations*, which invites both classical and romantic realizations. There is sufficient expressive material in the music to prompt characteristic responses from more overtly emotional artists such as Moiseiwitsch or Arrau, whilst there is enough disciplined and regularized music to elicit responses from more restrained players such as Kovacevich or myself. Yet both styles, and several in between, have generated critical admiration, which demonstrates that in performance this music invites disparate responses from the critical listener too, and that 'performers can communicate successfully with listeners without compromising their unique playing styles' (Juslin and Persson 2002: 237). By processing the interpretative results of these unique playing styles through the tower, emphasis of one informant over another becomes apparent and helps to explain why the end results sound the way that they do. And when a divergence of emphasis can be traced to the base level of the tower, the contrasts are revealed at their most striking.

Chapter 6
Conclusion

The Journey So Far

At the beginning of this book I suggested that an essential mystery lies at the heart of musical performance and that, although useful investigative inroads have been made, no glib solutions – fortunately, perhaps – have been forthcoming. As another investigative inroad, I have developed a means of analysis which focuses on interpretative outcomes within the broad context of performance, performer and work, and which draws on a wide range of related concerns. It would now be timely to assess whether this inroad, as represented by the interpretative tower, has achieved any further demystification of the performer's art.

Chapter 2 presents the tower framework as an ordered series of performance-related 'informants', thereby developing a means by which to analyse interpretations of Western art music in terms of a particular set of insights. Chapters 3, 4 and 5 demonstrated the tower in operation, testing its efficacy in the context of three different eras, three prototypical works from each era, and a broad range of pianistic styles. What emerges is a framework which seems to have the flexibility to cater for such diversity and has the capacity to transmute successive acoustic events into visual co-existence.[1] There are, of course, some areas that are only touched on or not broached at all, and these may be fruitful sources for future research. But before looking at these it would be worth summarizing a few issues that have arisen with some regularity during the case studies, and also returning to the questions I raised in Chapter 1.

By constructing the interpretative tower and seeking analytical results through its conceptual framework, answers to the first four questions that I posed near the beginning of Chapter 1 are suggested. Firstly I asked whether there are any identifiable factors by which an interpretative compound heard in the performance of a work may be elucidated and how an interpretative scheme, as reflected in the final 'product' (or acoustic trace), might be understood. Both these questions can be addressed by the deconstructional–reconstructional approach demanded by the tower. The tower is conceptually based on identifiable factors within performances and works, where the factors have a direct bearing on compound interpretative formations. By means of a hierarchical investigation, according to these identifiable factors – the tower's informants – the analyst can engage an esthesic/poietic process in response to the surface-level features of recordings.

---

[1]   Kant writes that '[d]ifferent times are not co-existent but successive (as different spaces are not successive but co-existent)' (Kant 2004 [1781]: 54).

160 *Reading Musical Interpretation*

This process can yield perceptions regarding the informants' interaction in a sub-surface interpretative scheme, thus elucidating the complex connections between acoustic trace and score. Wittgenstein's law of projection, as discussed in Chapter 2, has been useful in clarifying this nexus of relationships.

I then asked why some interpretations are heard to emphasize certain aspects of a work at the expense of others and why it is that no two recordings of the same work seem to offer exactly the same interpretative solutions. Again the two questions are interlinked. By identifying interpretative categories and evaluating acoustic outcomes within the context of these hierarchically arranged informants, prominent features at the perceptible level may be shown to connect with lower-level emphases in the overall interpretative scheme. For the informed listener, this interlinkage can promote a deeper appreciation of a work's capacity to support alternative emphases in performance and to produce artistic diversity. Tower analysis, as witnessed in my case studies, has thus also confirmed that some degree of interpretative divergence between performers is the invariable result of these variable emphases.

Authenticity Issues and the Interpretative Tower

Interpretative divergence between different artists is implicit in Kivy's notion of personal authenticity. I indicated in the first chapter that a theory of interpretation necessarily embraces the question of authenticity in its wider as well as in its *Texttreue* or HIP senses. The interpretative tower is not primarily set up as a tool to determine whether or not a performance is 'authentic', but its capacity to demonstrate how various kinds of authenticity are reflected in performance, or even to suggest boundaries beyond which the concept flounders, is admissible nonetheless. In the rare case of a performance appearing to reflect none but authorship (score) of the tower's informants, it is probable that a case for 'inauthenticity' could be made. The foregoing case studies do not present any such extreme situations, but some listeners may question the 'authenticity' of Gould's recording of the first movement of Mozart's Sonata in A major K 331, discussed in Chapter 2. However, value judgements concerning the rights and wrongs of authenticity or inauthenticity remain outside the scope of the tower's analytical brief.

Negative value judgements may be directed towards *Texttreue* performances as much as towards perceived inauthenticities. Symptomatic of the former is Kivy's elaboration of the sonic *Urtext*. He applies this concept particularly to period instrument performances of the 1950s and 1960s which were '"merely playing the notes" with no musicality whatever in evidence. They were bad performances, nor did they serve any useful musical purpose' (Kivy 2001: 16). I stated in Chapter 2, however, that 'deadpan performance' (Friberg and Battel 2002: 201) need not necessarily be regarded as invalid. The *Texttreue* account with which I prefaced each of the Brahms case studies served primarily as a point of reference, but it also raises another issue: performances which appear merely to be conforming to a

Conclusion 161

score's printed instructions can, in fact, be shown to be the result of interpretative decisions just as much as those which display a more obvious personal authenticity. Of the pianists under discussion in the case studies, my own readings manifested the highest degree of score-based literalism, yet tower analysis has not shown these or similar performances to be 'shallower' in terms of their informant properties than any other. What it has shown, however, is that the interpretative scheme of such performances tends to display, at base level, strong affinities with authorship (score) rather than with era (style).

The interpretative tower can provide insights into why recorded performances sound as they do, and its analytical function may well enable listeners to confirm or deny their own evaluations of the merits, drawbacks or neutralities of a performance. Tower analysis can reveal artistic preference but what it cannot do, and this has been stressed several times, is yield judgements concerning the artistic merit of a performance. Such judgements must remain the critical prerogative of each individual listener.

Explanatory Functions of the Interpretative Tower

The fifth question I raised in Chapter 1 asked why some types of music are heard to promote greater similarity of interpretation than others. The tower framework helps to explain why certain works, or passages within them, can be thought to urge a high degree of interpretative accord, whilst others yield considerable variance. For example, the analytical results of the case studies generally support the notion that slow music tends to allow for greater interpretative divergence than does fast music, and also strongly suggest that perceived ambiguities within the properties of a work's informants are another significant factor in producing such divergence. These phenomena were especially highlighted in the analyses of the Brahms variations. The case studies also demonstrate that interpretative similarities may sometimes be achieved through apparent recognition of the topic informant, especially where dance types are concerned. All of the studies show that if certain topics, implicit in the score, are audibly identified by the executants (as in the livelier dance episodes), then interpretative convergence is promoted, particularly in the area of tempo. Perhaps even more significantly, if unsurprisingly, the case studies have confirmed that the greater the authorial urge to control performance through precise directions in the score, the greater is the ensuing tendency towards interpretative accord. The relative confluence of all four Messiaen performances discussed in Chapter 4, when compared to the Brahms and, especially, the Bach *con discrezione* performances, clearly illustrates the point.

As interpretative similarities are most noticeable in twentieth-century music in which authorial control attempts to 'fix' performance, it may be that this is, significantly, co-existent with a diminishing diversity of playing styles. As Robert Philip comments, 'there is great pressure for musicians who wish to succeed in the international market to model themselves on the international standard' (Philip 2004: 245). A result of this, he suggests, is that '[b]y the beginning of the twenty-first century, we have reached the point where it is difficult to tell the difference between instrumentalists' (23). Tower analysis seems to provide some confirmation of this, in that perhaps the most personalized (or overtly 'subjective') interpretations are shown to come from pianists of an earlier generation, such as Arrau and Moiseiwitsch. This suggests a positive answer to the sixth and final question raised in Chapter 1, in which I asked if training and fashion play a part in the interpretative profile of a work as heard in performance. Although the issue of changing performance styles and whether they tell us more about fashion than about authenticity has not been central to this book, early indications are that general trends in performance practice can be observed and appreciated through the agency of the interpretative tower.

The Role of the Tower

The foregoing discussion again emphasizes the analytical role of the interpretative tower, so it is worth repeating that the tower is intended to reflect the acoustic evidence of a performance (as fixed by a recording) rather than to supply a blueprint for performance. It is not an attempt to define a pre-set route by which performers may safely feel that they have discovered the 'real' meaning of a work. As explained, the framework is designed for the performance analyst rather than the performer, even though the informant categories are drawn from and intimately bound up with performance practices in a Western art-music setting. The structuring and categorizing of the informants is therefore to achieve analytical workability rather than to suggest a rigid series of stages to the performer.

Working with the interpretative tower's informants necessitates repeated, detailed hearings of the same work in different recordings. Given that the tower is not designed as an agency for assessing artistic quality in performance, the listening act has to be carried out dispassionately, aside from the analyst's own artistic preferences. From a personal perspective, practising such artistic detachment has enabled me to accept a performance on its own terms, rather than to evaluate it in terms of my preconceptions as to how the work 'should' be played. Another paradoxical result of such disciplined listening is that I now feel artistically freer as a performer. At the end of this project, I find that my own playing is less score-bound, that I am more willing to take risks based on my engagement with the music as sound as opposed to the music as print. The research experience has therefore broadened my receptivity as a listener and expanded the interpretative scope of my own performance.

Future Directions

Expanding the Brief and Achieving Flexibility

As a first step in applying and testing my interpretative construct, I have used case studies that exclusively concern solo piano performance and deal mainly with relatively short musical spans. The second case study examines interpretations of an entire piece, Messiaen's 'Première communion de la Vierge', rather than a section within a bigger one, the results of which seem promising. However, other problems may need to be addressed when analysing performances of larger compositions and works for other instrumental or vocal media. If the interpretative tower is to accommodate the analysis of, for example, chamber, orchestral, choral or operatic performances, then adaptations to its structure may be necessary.

Where performances are given by more than one performer, the issue of textural balance assumes importance and may not, in some instances, be easily accommodated by the sonic moderator category as it currently functions. For example, in Vladimir Horowitz's 1951 recording of Rachmaninov's Piano Concerto No. 3 in D minor Op. 30 with the RCA Victor Symphony Orchestra under Fritz Reiner, the semiquaver passagework in the piano part of the first movement during bars 27–51 is played quite forcefully and with great articulative clarity, dominating the orchestral cello melody, which seems to be accorded a very secondary role. By contrast, Moura Lympany's 1952 recording of the same passage with the New Symphony Orchestra of London under Anthony Collins allows the cello melody much greater prominence and the piano part is heard as an accompaniment to this, with a roughly equal musical dialogue emerging where melodic fragments receive greater projection from the pianist between bars 38 and 44. These contrasting acoustic results – which may be an amalgam of the producers' and recording engineers' as well as the performers' artistic judgements – seem to go beyond the relatively straightforward issues of dynamics, articulation and voicing. Whilst such issues still lie within the broad remit of sonic moderation, it may be necessary to create a subcategory to indicate the significance of ensemble balance in the analysis of a recorded performance.

Another area of potential significance at the tower's surface level is pitch variability, as manifested in the use of instrumental or vocal vibrato, HIP-influenced pitch or 'expressive intonation' (Johnson 2004). Again this area arguably falls within the sonic moderator category and links with the tower's level three informants in that pitch variation techniques are likely to be used (or not used as the case may be) to project musical character and affect, or, at a deeper level, era (style). Thus when comparing, say, the 1989 (historically informed) performance of Bach's Violin Concerto in A minor BWV 1041 by Catherine Mackintosh and the King's Consort under Robert King with the 1962 recording by David Oistrakh and the Royal Philharmonic orchestra under Eugene Goossens, an informant subcategory to represent pitch manipulation may be helpful.

164   *Reading Musical Interpretation*

Another aspect of performance that may be worth taking into account concerns Italian opera, where the importance of performance tradition – 'the network of relationships between different performances' (Cook 2007: 185) – has been highlighted by José Bowen. He suggests that if 'one knows a Puccini aria from performances and recordings, the printed score can often look rather foreign' (Bowen 1999: 444). My analyses have been of instrumental performance in which both the analyst's and the performer's engagement with a score are central but, in the case of a Puccini aria, the tower framework may need to give greater space to aural tradition, perhaps allowing it a presence alongside topical mode and characterizer in that it can directly influence a singer's shaping of surface-level expression but still lies hierarchically above the levels of topic, genre, authorship and era.

More fundamental adaptations to the tower structure may be necessary when analysing performances of music by very early composers such as Léonin and Pérotin. Since the scores for this music provide clues rather than clear instructions, at least to a twenty-first-century performer, the authorship (score) category, though still a root cause, is unlikely to be of great practical significance to either performer or analyst. A 'reconstructive' category may therefore be an appropriate addition, alongside that of era (style), so that the listener can analyse interpretations in the light of 'archaeological' evidence.

More problematic still would be any attempt to analyse performances of indeterminate or chance music such as Stockhausen's *Aus den sieben Tagen* (1968), where the 'score' is no more than a set of written instructions, some of which seem 'deliberately and fanatically impracticable' (Smith Brindle 1975: 96). Whilst performances of such works can still theoretically be traced back to authorship (score), the highly structured approach to performance analysis that is offered by the interpretative tower seems incompatible with the unstructured freedom of interpretation invited by a text-score. A framework that is dependent on at least some invariables in performance against which the analyst can assess interpretative variability probably collapses when confronted by a performance in which almost no invariables (other than perhaps the recognizable sounds of the instruments or voices being used) can be detected.

The areas discussed above show some of the possible limitations of the interpretative tower in its current construct and there are, no doubt, many more especially as I have not considered its applicability to jazz or rock – but that would be another book! Adaptations to the tower may therefore be required to accommodate areas outside the interpretation of solo piano repertoire, although too many categories are liable to make the framework over-complex and unwieldy. Nevertheless, my hope is that further research may usefully be able to adapt, develop and expand the initial concept.

If flexibility in the structure of the tower framework may prove advantageous, it is also possible that flexibility regarding graphic depictions of performances is desirable, even necessary. The graphs shown in Chapters 3, 4 and 5 are based on my own perceptions and responses to the traces left by both works and performances.

As analyst, I therefore occupy a subjective position and must allow for other subjective positions.[2]

However, my guess is that, although other analysts' projections may yield alternatives, it is unlikely that their completed graphs would be radically different from my own. One is reminded that in Schenkerian analysis the same musical work can engender more than one graphic representation.[3] Varying perceptions may well complement rather than contradict and, as I have stressed, musical meaning is neither static nor absolute.

Semiotics

As noted several times throughout this book, it is a performer's engagement with the top-level informants that is the starting point for the analyst's investigation. These surface-level informants, as interpretative signifiers, suggest a semiotic process. Earlier chapters have touched upon semiotic ideas, particularly those of Charles Peirce, but have not dwelt on them or developed any particular theoretical perspective. However, further work addressing the signification of surface features heard in a musical performance may be productive. The semiotic nature of the interpretative tower is complicated by the fact that we are not dealing with one sign and its referent but simultaneous, multiple, interwoven signs (defined by all varieties of sonic and temporal properties) with simultaneous, multiple, interwoven referents. Perhaps Cumming points the way forward when she writes: 'in cases of complex signification, more than one *kind* of sign is at work ... an analysis of distinct kinds of signs allows for the possibility that their effects upon one another can be pursued, as effects that are automatically "synthesized" in acts of hearing the work' (Cumming 2000: 225). By developing these ideas, it may be possible to amalgamate signs and informants into an analytical framework, although the potential complexities of this should not be underestimated.

Topic theory has featured prominently within the field of semiotic studies and has been used to ascribe meaning to Beethoven's music (Hatten 1994), to music by mid-nineteenth-century composers (Klein 2005; Monelle 2000), and to music by Shostakovich (Sheinberg 2000). The authors very largely ignore performance, although Klein does observe, with regard to the finale of Schubert's Piano Sonata in C minor D 958, that ' [a]lthough the tempo of the movement is only Allegro, a performer may well decide to take a topical clue and push the music toward a more frenzied pace' (Klein 2005: 56). The implications of Klein's almost throw-away remark are significant. Most topical theorists seem to work directly from the score, although it is conceivable that their views

---

[2] The issue of the analyst's subjectivity and how this relates to interpretation is addressed in Chapter 2.

[3] Allen Forte and Steven Gilbert's analysis (1982) of Bach's C major Prelude from Book One of the *Well-Tempered Clavier* modifies the one supervised by Schenker himself (1969 [1933]), yet the work can accommodate both.

166   *Reading Musical Interpretation*

may be supported (perhaps unconsciously) by sympathetic performance. In Chapter 5, my studies of Variation 23 and, in particular, of Variation 19 from the Brahms–Handel *Variations* demonstrated that a composer's apparent topical references will not necessarily be projected or heard in the same way in different performances. My own inclusion of topic as an informant within the tower framework is circumscribed, as described in Chapter 2, so as to give it a very performative function, but this can be extended and developed within or outside the tower framework. There is thus a strong suggestion here that topicality as heard in performance could be a very productive area for future research.

Hermeneutics

If topical theory seeks a way of finding meaning in music, then it is located within the broader ambit of hermeneutics. Early in my book I drew on Gadamer's writings to explain the relativism of my own analytical framework, embedding this construct in the notion that 'the work of art is the absolute present for each particular present, and at the same time holds its word in readiness for every future' (Gadamer 1977 [1964]: 104). Further to this idea, I drew on Wimsatt and Beardsley's Intentional Fallacy to explain why performance analysis avoids the ascription of intentions to either composer or performer other than as received and understood by the informed listener. Performance analysis is, therefore, a slippery business in which the analyst attempts to negotiate between the 'horizon of understanding in which [he] has to move' (210) and that of the composer and performer. This concept has inevitably resurfaced at certain points throughout my book but, although it has made the discussions in one sense 'meaningful', I have generally avoided the use of ekphrastic[4] language, in as much as attributing figurative meanings to performances is difficult and probably unhelpful in the present context.

Nevertheless, the ascription of figurative meaning to music, be it through topicality or other hermeneutic methods, remains a musicological concern, so that Kramer (2002) can read Schubert's *Moment Musical* in A♭ as a trope of syphilis, Beethoven's *Moonlight* Sonata as significant in the 'history of musical meaning and the history of sexuality' (Kramer 2002: 29), and Schumann's *Carnaval* as symbolic of cross-dressing, gender-crossing and female mirror-gazing. These hypotheses incidentally reveal a great deal about Kramer's own historical situatedness but, once again, his arguments ignore these works' variability in performance. This omission may point to another fruitful line of research. How far could such specifically attributed musical meanings actually be projected through performance, or do Kramer's hermeneutics derive solely from his contextual understanding of the score?

---

[4]   Ekphrasis is the 'literary representation of a pictorial representation' (Kramer 2002: 16) which Lawrence Kramer applies to the 'verbal paraphrase of musical expression' (16).

Conclusion

Last Words

This brings me back to one of my points of departure: the question of words and music. The tower structure draws on the communicative power of words to convey a cluster of properties to both analyst and performer. When appearing in the context of a specific composition, the meaning of a word may be narrowed so that, to most interpreters, the respective contexts of Mozart and Liszt affect the meaning of *espressivo* in era-related ways. However, this circumscription of a musical word's meaning can never be total, because it always admits space for interpretation – as Nicholas Cook wittily sums it up, 'you can't play it as you say it' (Cook 1999b: 11). Thus a performance 'blueprint' can never be established.

The interpretative tower framework has proved to be sufficiently flexible to allow for divergent interpretative profiles and personal authenticities. The analytical method employed acknowledges the artistic freedom of an interpretation, graphically capturing the dynamic flow of the tower's informants as perceived in multiple readings of the same and different works. These multiple readings are continually heard subtly to redefine the informants' meanings, thereby feeding an evolutionary process which adds progressively to Wittgenstein's 'family of meanings' (Wittgenstein 1978 [1953]: 36). The informants may guide us to a deeper understanding of performance but can never express its totality – and so its essential mystery remains.

Appendix 1

Editions consulted in connection with Brahms's *Variations and Fugue on a Theme by Handel* **Op. 24**

Alfred Lengnick & Co. Ltd, no date given; reprint of Simrock, 1925
Augener's Edition, *c.* 1928; no editor given
Breitkopf & Härtel, 1862 (first edition)
Breitkopf & Härtel, 1927; edited by Eusebius Mandyczewski
Breitkopf & Härtel, 1981; reprint of the 1927 edition
Dover, 1971; reprint of Breitkopf & Härtel, 1927
G. Henle Verlag, 1978; edited by Sonja Gerlach
International Music Company; no date or editor given, but identical to
    Mandyczewski
Könemann Music Budapest, 1999; edited by Enikő Gyenge
Peters, *c.* 1939; edited by Emil von Sauer
Peters, 1976; edited by Seemann/Stephenson
Schirmer, 1951; no editor given
Schirmer, no date given; reprint of Peters, *c.* 1939
Simrock, 1925; edited by Moritz Mayer-Mahr

Appendix 2

Attached CD track listings

Brahms: Variations and Fugue on a Theme by Handel *Op. 24*

1. Theme and variation 1
2. Variations 2–3
3. Variation 4
4. Variations 5–6
5. Variations 7–8
6. Variations 9–12
7. Variation 13
8. Variations 14–18
9. Variation 19
10. Variations 20–21
11. Variation 22
12. Variations 23–25
13. Fugue

Bach: Toccata in D major BWV 912

14. Bars 1–10
15. *Allegro*, bars 10–111
16. *Con discrezione*, bars 111–126
17. Bars 127–277

Messiaen: 'Première communion de la Vierge'

18. *Très lent*, bars 1–6
19. *Un peu plus lent*, bars 7–16
20. *Plus lent*, bars 17–20
21. *Modéré, un peu vif*, bars 21–38
22. Bars 39–60
23. Bars 61–72
24. *Très lent*, bars 73–78

Julian Hellaby – piano

Bibliography

ABRSM (Associated Board of the Royal Schools of Music), *Rudiments and Theory of Music* (London: ABRSM Publishing, 1958).

Agawu, Kofi, 'The Challenge of Semiotics' in Nicholas Cook and Mark Everist (eds), *Rethinking Music* (Oxford: Oxford University Press, 1999).

Agay, Denes, 'Style in Composition and Performance' in Denes Agay (ed.), *Teaching Piano*, volume 2 (New York: Yorktown Music Press, Inc., 1981).

Anon, 'Brahms/Variations and Fugue on a Theme by Handel/Benno Moiseiwitsch', *The Gramophone* (June 1930): 24.

Anon, 'Brahms/Variations and Fugue on a Theme by Handel/Egon Petri', *The Gramophone* (October 1938): 200.

Anthoni, Nalen, 'Beethoven/Piano Sonatas/Kovacevich', *The Gramophone* (August 2003): 56.

Audi, Robert (ed.), *The Cambridge Dictionary of Philosophy* (Cambridge: Cambridge University Press, 1999).

Avins, Styra (ed.), *Johannes Brahms, Life and Letters* (Oxford: Oxford University Press, 1997).

Bach, Carl Philipp Emanuel, *Essay on the True Art of Playing Keyboard Instruments*, English translation by William J. Mitchell (New York and London: W.W. Norton & Co., 1949).

Badura-Skoda, Paul, *Interpreting Bach at the Keyboard* (Oxford: Oxford University Press, 1995).

Barthes, Roland, *Image – Music – Text* (New York: Hill and Wang, 1999).

Bazzana, Kevin, *Glenn Gould: The Performer in the Work* (Oxford: Oxford University Press, 1997).

Beardsley, Monroe and Wimsatt, William, 'The Intentional Fallacy', *The Sewanee Review*, 54 (1946): 468–88.

Beardsley, Monroe, 'Intentions and Interpretations: A Fallacy Revived' in Peter Lamarque and Stein Olsen (eds), *Aesthetics and the Philosophy of Art – The Analytic Tradition* (Malden, Oxford and Victoria: Blackwell Publishing, 2004).

Bell, Carla, *Olivier Messiaen* (Boston: Twayne Publishers, 1984).

Benedict, Ruth, *Patterns of Culture* (Boston: Houghton Mifflin, 1934).

Berry, Wallace, *Musical Structure and Performance* (New Haven: Yale University Press, 1989)

Benitez, Vincent, 'A Creative Legacy: Messiaen as Teacher of Analysis', *College Music Symposium*, 40 (2000): 117–39.

Bohlman, Philip, 'Ontologies of Music' in Nicholas Cook and Mark Everist (eds), *Rethinking Music* (Oxford: Oxford University Press, 1999).

Boorman, Stanley, 'The Musical Text' in Nicholas Cook and Mark Everist (eds), *Rethinking Music* (Oxford: Oxford University Press, 1999).

Botstein, Leon, 'Introduction' in Leon Botstein (ed.), *The Compleat Brahms* (New York and London: W.W. Norton & Co., 1999).

Bowen, José, 'Finding History in Musicology: Performance History and Musical Works' in Nicholas Cook and Mark Everist (eds), *Rethinking Music* (Oxford: Oxford University Press, 1999).

Bowman, Wayne, *Philosophical Perspectives on Music* (Oxford: Oxford University Press, 1998).

Brendel, Alfred, *Musical Thoughts and Afterthoughts* (London: Robson Books, 1976).

Brendel, Alfred, *The Veil of Order* (London: Faber and Faber, 1976).

Brown, Clive, *Classical and Romantic Performing Practice 1750–1900* (Oxford: Oxford University Press, 1999).

Brown, Clive, 'Notation and Interpretation' in Anthony Burton (ed.), *A Performer's Guide to Music of the Romantic Period* (London: ABRSM Publishing, 2002).

Burton, Anthony (ed.), *A Performer's Guide to Music of the Baroque Period* (London: ABRSM Publishing, 2002a).

Burton, Anthony (ed.), *A Performer's Guide to Music of the Classical Period* (London: ABRSM Publishing, 2002b).

Burton, Anthony (ed.), *A Performer's Guide to Music of the Romantic Period* (London: ABRSM Publishing, 2002c).

Busoni, Ferruccio, 'Sketch of a New Esthetic of Music' in *Three Classics in the Aesthetic of Music*, English translation by Theodore Baker (New York: Dover Publications, Inc., 1962).

Busoni, Ferruccio, *The Essence of Music*, English translation by Rosamond Ley (New York: Dover Publications, Inc., 1965).

Butt, John, *Bach Interpretation* (Cambridge: Cambridge University Press, 1999).

Butt, John, *Playing with History* (Cambridge: Cambridge University Press, 2002).

Chaucer, Geoffrey, *The Wife of Bath's Prologue and Tale*, James Winny (ed.) (Cambridge: Cambridge University Press, 1965).

Clarke, Eric, 'Expression in Performance: Generativity, Perception and Semiosis' in John Rink (ed.), *The Practice of Performance* (Cambridge: Cambridge University Press, 1995).

Clarke, Eric, 'Generative Principles in Music Performance' in John Sloboda (ed.), *Generative Processes in Music* (Oxford: Clarendon Press, 2000).

Clarke, Eric, 'Listening to Performance' in John Rink (ed.), *Musical Performance, A Guide to Understanding* (Cambridge: Cambridge University Press, 2002).

Clarke, Eric, *Ways of Listening* (Oxford: Oxford University Press, 2005).

Coltman, Rod, *The Language of Hermeneutics* (Albany: State University of New York Press, 1998).

Cone, Edward, *Musical Form and Musical Performance* (New York and London: W.W. Norton & Company Inc., 1968).

Cook, Nicholas, *A Guide to Musical Analysis* (London: J.M. Dent & Sons Ltd, 1987).

Cook, Nicholas, *Music Imagination and Culture* (Oxford: Oxford University Press, 1992).

Cook, Nicholas, *Beethoven: Symphony No. 9* (Cambridge: Cambridge University Press, 1993).

Cook, Nicholas, 'Analysing Performance and Performing Analysis' in Nicholas Cook and Mark Everist (eds), *Rethinking Music* (Oxford: Oxford University Press, 1999a).

Cook, Nicholas, 'Words about Music, or Analysis Versus Performance' in Nicholas Cook, Peter Johnson and Hans Zender, *Theory into Practice: Composition, Performance and the Listening Experience* (Leuven: Leuven University Press, 1999b).

Cook, Nicholas, 'Between Process and Product: Music and/as Performance', *Music Theory Online*, 7/2 (2001): 1–20, www.societymusictheory.org/mto/issues/mto.01.7.2/mto.01.7.2.cook_frames.html (accessed May 2003).

Cook, Nicholas, 'Music as Performance' in Martin Clayton, Trevor Herbert and Richard Middleton (eds), *The Cultural Study of Music* (New York and London: Routledge, 2003).

Cook, Nicholas, 'Prompting Performance: Text, Script, and Analysis in Bryn Harrison's *être-temps*', *Music Theory Online*, 11/1 (2005): 1–9, www.societymusictheory.org/mto/issues/mto.05.11.1/mto.05.11.1.cook_frames.htmlc (accessed February 2007).

Cook, Nicholas, 'Performance analysis and Chopin's mazurkas', *Musicæ Scientiæ*, X1/2 (2007): 183–207.

Cooke, James Francis, *Great Pianists on Piano Playing* (New York: Dover Publications, Inc., 1999).

Crist, Stephen, 'The Early Works and the Heritage of the Seventeenth Century' in John Butt (ed.), *The Cambridge Companion to Bach* (Cambridge: Cambridge University Press, 1997).

Crombie, David, *Piano* (London: Balafon Books, 1995).

Cumming, Naomi, *The Sonic Self* (Bloomington and Indianapolis: Indiana University Press, 2000).

Czerny, Carl, *Complete Theoretical and Practical Piano Forte School* (Part III) (London: Messrs R. Cocks & Co., 1839).

Dahlhaus, Carl, *Esthetics of Music* (Cambridge: Cambridge University Press, 1995).

Davidson, Jane, 'Developing the Ability to Perform' in John Rink (ed.), *Musical Performance, A Guide to Understanding* (Cambridge: Cambridge University Press, 2002).

Davies, Stephen, *Musical Works and Performances* (Oxford: Oxford University Press, 2001).

Day, Timothy, *A Century of Recorded Music* (New Haven and London: Yale University Press, 2000).

Desain, Peter and Honing, Henkjan, *Music, Mind and Machine* (Amsterdam: Thesis Publishers, 1992).

Dibben, Nicola, 'Musical Materials, Perception, and Listening' in Martin Clayton, Trevor Herbert and Richard Middleton (eds), *The Cultural Study of Music* (New York and London: Routledge, 2003).

Dummett, Michael, *Frege: Philosophy of Language* (London: Duckworth, 1981).

Dunoyer, Cecilia, 'Debussy and Early Debussystes at the Piano' in James Briscoe (ed.), *Debussy in Performance* (New Haven and London: Yale University Press, 1999).

Dunsby, Jonathan, *Structural Ambiguity in Brahms* (Michigan: UMI Research Press, 1981).

Eisert, Christian, *J.S. Bach Toccaten* (Vienna: Wiener Urtext Edition, 2000).

Epstein, David, *Shaping Time* (New York: Schirmer Books, 1995).

Fanning, David, 'Messiaen/Vingt regards sur l'enfant-Jésus/Peter Hill', *The Gramophone* (September 1992): 135.

Forte, Allen and Gilbert, Steven, *Introduction to Schenkerian Analysis* (New York and London: W.W. Norton and Company, 1982).

Foucault, Michel, *The Archaeology of Knowledge*, English translation by Alan Sheridan Smith (New York: Pantheon Books, Random House Inc., 1972).

Foucault, Michel, 'What is an Author?' in Robert Con Davis and Ronald Schleifer (eds), *Literary Criticism: Literary and Cultural Studies* (New York: Longman, 1998).

Fraser, Alan, *The Craft of Piano Playing* (Lanham and Oxford: The Scarecrow Press, Inc., 2003).

Frege, Gottlob, *The Foundations of Arithmetic*, English translation by John Langshaw Austin (Oxford: Basil Blackwell, 1959).

Friberg, Anders and Battel, Giovanni Umberto, 'Structural Communication' in Richard Parncutt and Gary McPherson (eds), *The Science and Psychology of Music Performance* (Oxford: Oxford University Press, 2002).

Frisch, Walter, 'In Search of Brahms's First Symphony: Steinbach, the Meiningen Tradition, and the Recordings of Herman Abendroth' in Bernard Sherman and Michael Musgrave (eds) *Performing Brahms* (Cambridge: Cambridge University Press, 2003).

Fulcher, Jane, 'The Politics of Transcendence: Ideology in the Music of Messiaen in the 1930s', *Musical Quarterly*, 86/3 (2002): 449–71.

Gabrielsson, Alf, 'Timing in Music Performance and its Relations to Music Experience' in John Sloboda (ed.), *Generative Processes in Music* (Oxford: Oxford University Press, 2000).

Gabrielsson, Alf and Lindström, Erik, 'The Influence of Musical Structure on Emotional Expression' in Patrik Juslin and John Sloboda (eds), *Music and Emotion* (Oxford: Oxford University Press, 2002).

Gadamer, Hans-Georg, *Philosophical Hermeneutics*, essay compilation and English translation by David Linge (Berkeley: University of California Press, 1977).

Bibliography

Geiringer, Karl, *Brahms: His Life and Work* (London: George Allen and Unwin Ltd, 1968).

Godlovitch, Stan, *Musical Performance* (London and New York: Routledge, 1998).

Godowsky, Leopold, 'The Real Significance of Technic' in James Francis Cooke (ed.), *Great Pianists on Piano Playing* (New York: Dover Publications, Inc., 1999).

Goehr, Lydia, *The Imaginary Museum of Musical Works* (Oxford: Oxford University Press, 1992).

Goehr, Lydia, *The Quest for Voice* (Oxford: Oxford University Press, 2004).

Griffiths, Paul, *Olivier Messiaen and the Music of Time* (London: Faber and Faber, 1985).

Hanslick, Eduard, 'Brahms' in Henry Pleasants (ed.), *Hanslick's Music Criticisms*, English translation by Henry Pleasants (New York: Dover Publications, Inc., 1988).

Hanslick, Eduard, 'Brahms's Symphony No. 2' in Henry Pleasants (ed.), *Hanslick's Music Criticisms*, English translation by Henry Pleasants (New York: Dover Publications, Inc., 1988).

Harrison, Max, 'Brahms/Variations and Fugue on a Theme by Handel/Steven Bishop (Kovacevich)', *The Gramophone* (December 1969): 976.

Harrison, Max, 'Brahms/Variations and Fugue on a Theme by Handel/Claudio Arrau', *The Gramophone* (August 1979): 352.

Hatten, Robert, *Musical Meaning in Beethoven* (Bloomington and Indianapolis: Indiana University Press, 1994).

Herpers, Ulla, *Pierre-Laurent Aimard*, English translation of CD liner note by Stewart Spencer (Hamburg: Teldec 3984-26868-2, 2000).

Heywood, Andrew, *Politics* (Basingstoke: Macmillan Press Ltd, 1997).

Hill, Peter, 'The Piano Music I' in Peter Hill (ed.), *The Messiaen Companion* (London: Faber and Faber Ltd, 1995a).

Hill, Peter, 'Messiaen as Teacher' in Peter Hill (ed.), *The Messiaen Companion* (London: Faber and Faber Ltd, 1995b).

Hill, Peter and Simeone, Nigel, *Messiaen* (New Haven and London: Yale University Press, 2005).

Hofman, Josef, *Piano Playing* (New York: Dover Publications, Inc., 1976).

Horowitz, Joseph, *Arrau on Music and Performance* (Mineola, New York: Dover Publications Inc., 1999).

Hoskyns, Janet, 'Music Education and a European Dimension' in Gary Spruce (ed.), *Teaching Music* (London and New York: Routledge, 1996).

Houle, George, *Meter in Music, 1600–1800* (Bloomington and Indianapolis: Indiana University Press, 2000).

Howson, Colin and Urbach, Peter, *Scientific Reasoning* (La Salle: Open Court Publishing Company, 1991).

Hsu, Madeleine, *Olivier Messiaen, the Musical Mediator* (London: Associated University Presses, Inc., 1996).

178   *Reading Musical Interpretation*

Hudson, Richard, *Stolen Time: The History of Tempo Rubato* (Oxford: Oxford University Press, 1994).

Joachim, Joseph, *Violischule* (Part III) (Berlin: N. Simrock, 1905).

Johnson, Peter, 'Performance and the Listening Experience: Bach's "Erbarme Dich"' in Nicholas Cook, Peter Johnson and Hans Zender, *Theory into Practice: Composition, Performance and the Listening Experience* (Leuven: Leuven University Press, 1999).

Johnson, Peter, 'The Legacy of Recordings' in John Rink (ed.), *Musical Performance, A Guide to Understanding* (Cambridge: Cambridge University Press, 2002).

Johnson, Peter, '"Expressive Intonation" in String Performance: Problems of Analysis and Interpretation' in Jane Davidson (ed.), *The Music Practitioner* (Aldershot: Ashgate, 2004).

Johnson, Peter, 'The Science and Psychology of Music Performance: Creative Strategies for Teaching and Learning' (book review), *Musicæ Scientiæ*, IX/1 (2005): 196–202.

Johnston, Sheila, 'Film Narrative and Structuralist Controversy' in Pam Cook (ed.), *The Cinema Book* (London: British Film Institute, 1985).

Jones, Richard, 'The Keyboard Works: Bach as Teacher and Virtuoso' in John Butt (ed.), *The Cambridge Companion to Bach* (Cambridge: Cambridge University Press, 1997).

Jørgensen, Harald, 'Strategies for Individual Practice' in Aaron Williamon (ed.), *Musical Excellence* (Oxford: Oxford University Press, 2004).

Juslin, Patrik, 'Communicating Emotion in Music Performance: A Review and Theoretical Framework' in Patrik Juslin and John Sloboda (eds), *Music and Emotion* (Oxford: Oxford University Press, 2002a).

Juslin, Patrik and Persson, Roland, 'Emotional Communication' in Richard Parncutt and Gary McPherson (eds), *The Science and Psychology of Music Performance* (Oxford: Oxford University Press, 2002b).

Juslin, Patrik; Friberg, Anders; Schoondervaldt, Erwin; and Karlsson, Jessica, 'Feedback Learning of Musical Expressivity' in Aaron Williamon (ed.), *Musical Excellence* (Oxford: Oxford University Press, 2004).

Kant, Immanuel, *Critique of Pure Reason*, English translation by Vasilis Politis (London: J.M. Dent (Everyman), 2004).

Kennedy, Michael, *The Concise Oxford Dictionary of Music* (Oxford: Oxford University Press, 1991).

Kenyon, Nicholas, 'Authenticity and Early Music: Some Issues and Questions' in Nicholas Kenyon (ed.) *Authenticity and Early Music* (Oxford and New York: Oxford University Press, 1988).

Kinderman, William, *Beethoven* (Oxford: Oxford University Press, 1997).

Kirkpatrick, Evron Maurice (ed.), *Chambers 20th Century Dictionary* (Edinburgh: W. & R. Chambers Ltd, 1983).

Bibliography

Kirnberger, Johann Philipp (1982 [1776]), *The Art of Strict Musical Composition*, English translation by David Beach and Jurgen Thym (New Haven and London: Yale University Press, 1982).

Kivy, Peter, *The Corded Shell: Reflections on Musical Expression* (Princeton: Princeton University Press, 1980).

Kivy, Peter, *Authenticities* (Cornell: Cornell University Press, 1995).

Kivy, Peter, *New Essays on Musical Understanding* (Oxford: Oxford University Press, 2001).

Klein, Michael, *Intertextuality in Western Art Music* (Bloomington and Indianapolis: Indiana University Press, 2005).

Koch, Heinrich Christoph, *Musikalisches Lexicon* (Kassel: Bärenreiter, 2001).

Kramer, Lawrence, *Musical Meaning: Toward a Critical History* (Berkeley and Los Angeles: University of California Press, 2002).

Kramer, Lawrence, 'Subjectivity Rampant!' in Martin Clayton, Trevor Herbert and Richard Middleton (eds), *The Cultural Study of Music* (New York and London: Routledge, 2003).

Kripke, Saul, *Naming and Necessity* (Oxford: Basil Blackwell, 1981).

Lamb, Andrew, 'Galop' in Stanley Sadie (ed.), *The New Grove Dictionary of Music and Musicians*, volume 7 (London: Macmillan Publishing Limited, 1980).

Lawson, Colin and Stowell, Robert, *The Historical Performance of Music* (Cambridge: Cambridge University Press, 1999).

Lee, Douglas, 'C.P.E. Bach and the Free Fantasia for Keyboard: Deutsche Staatsbibliothek Mus. Ms. Nichelman I N' in Stephen Clark (ed.), *C.P.E. Bach Studies* (Oxford: Oxford University Press, 1988).

Lester, Joel, 'Performance and Analysis: Interaction and Interpretation' in John Rink (ed.), *The Practice of Performance* (Cambridge: Cambridge University Press, 1995).

Levinson, Jerrold, 'Performative vs. Critical Interpretation' in Michael Krausz (ed.), *The Interpretation of Music* (Oxford: Oxford University Press, 1993).

Levinson, Jerrold, *Music in the Moment* (Ithaca and London: Cornell University Press, 1997).

Levy, Benjamin, *Beethoven: The Ninth Symphony* (New York: Schirmer Books, 1995).

Lieberman, Richard, *Steinway & Sons* (New Haven and London: Yale University Press, 1995).

Linge, David, 'Editor's Introduction' in David Linge (ed.), *Philosophical Hermeneutics* (Berkeley: University of California Press, 1977).

Little, Meredith and Jenne, Natalie, *Dance and the Music of J.S. Bach* (Bloomington and Indianapolis: Indiana University Press, 2001).

Littlewood, Julian, *The Variations of Johannes Brahms* (London: Plumbago Books, 2004).

MacDonald, Malcolm, *Brahms* (London: J.M. Dent & Sons Ltd, 1990).

Mach, Elyse, *Great Pianists Speak for Themselves* (London: Robson Books, 1981).

Maconie, Robin, *The Concept of Music* (Oxford: Oxford University Press, 2000).

Manildi, Donald, *Wilhelm Kempff: An Appreciation* (CD liner note) (Berkeley: Music and Arts Programs of America, Inc. CD-1071, 2000).

Martin, Robert, 'Musical Works in the Worlds of Performers and Listeners' in Martin Krausz (ed.), *The Interpretation of Music* (Oxford: Clarendon Press, 1993).

Mattheson, Johann, *Der Volkommene Capellmeister*, English translation by E.C. Harriss (Michigan: UMI Research Press, 1981).

Matthews, Denis, *Brahms's Three Phases* (Newcastle-upon-Tyne: University of Newcastle-upon-Tyne, 1972).

May, Florence, *The Life of Brahms*, second edition (London: William Reeves, 1948).

McEwen, John and Vantyn, Sydney, *The Foundations of Musical Aesthetics: Modern Pianoforte Technique* (London: The Waverley Book Company, 1917).

Messiaen, Olivier, 'Préface' in *Quatuor pour la Fin du Temps* (Paris: Editions Durand, 1942).

Messiaen, Olivier, *Technique de mon langage musical* (Paris: Alphonse Leduc, 1944).

Methuen-Campbell, James, 'Brahms/Variations and Fugue on a Theme by Handel/ Jorge Federico Osorio', *The Gramophone* (November 1988): 812–16.

Meyer, Hans, 'Der Plan in Brahms' Händel Variationen', *Neue Musikzeitung*, 49/11, 14, 16 (1928): 340–46, 437–45, 503–512.

Meyer, Leonard, *Emotion and Meaning in Music* (Chicago and London: The University of Chicago Press, 1956).

Meyer, Leonard, *Music, the Arts and Ideas* (Chicago and London: The University of Chicago Press, 1967).

Meyer, Leonard, *Style and Music* (Philadelphia: University of Pennsylvania Press, 1989).

Mill, John Stuart, *A System of Logic Ratiocinative and Inductive* (London: Longmans, 1961).

Miller, Alexander, 'Philosophy of Language' in John Shand (ed.), *Fundamentals of Philosophy* (London and New York: Routledge, 2003).

Milsom, David, 'The Violin and its Languages: Styles of Playing in Recording from 1900 to 1930', case study presented at a study day, *Music and Recording: A Century of Change*, in the British Library, 24 March 2001.

Milsom, David, *Theory and Practice in Late Nineteenth-century Violin Performance: An Examination of Style in Performance 1850–1900* (Aldershot: Ashgate, 2003).

Monelle, Raymond, *The Sense of Music* (Princeton and Oxford: Princeton University Press, 2000).

Monsaingeon, Bruno, *Sviatoslav Richter Notebooks and Conversations*, English translation by Stewart Spencer (London: Faber and Faber, 2001).

Bibliography

Moroney, Davitt, 'Couperin, Marpurg and Roeser: AGermanic Art de Toucher le Clavecin, or a French Wahre Art?' in Christopher Hogwood (ed.), *The Keyboard in Baroque Europe* (Cambridge: Cambridge University Press, 2003).

Morrison, Bryce, 'Bach/Toccatas/Angela Hewitt', *The Gramophone* (October 2002): 80.

Mozart, Leopold, *A Treatise on the Fundamental Principles of Violin Playing*, English translation by Editha Knocker (Oxford: Oxford University Press, 1951).

Musgrave, Michael, *The Music of Brahms* (Oxford: Oxford University Press, 1996).

Musgrave, Michael, *A Brahms Reader* (New Haven and London: Yale University Press, 2000).

Narmour, Eugene, 'On the Relationship of Analytical Theory to Performance and Interpretation' in Eugene Narmour and Ruth Solie (eds), *Exploration in Music, the Arts, and Ideas* (Stuyvesant: Pendragon Press, 1988).

Nattiez, Jean-Jacques, *Music and Discourse*, English translation by Carolyne Abbate (Princeton: Princeton University Press, 1990).

Nettl, Bruno, 'The Institutionalisation of Musicology' in Nicholas Cook and Mark Everist (eds), *Rethinking Music* (Oxford: Oxford University Press, 1999).

Neuhaus, Heinrich, *The Art of Piano Playing*, English translation by K.A. Leibovitch (London: Barrie & Jenkins Ltd, 1983).

Oliver, Michael, 'Messiaen/Vingt regards sur l'enfant-Jésus/Yvonne Loriod', *The Gramophone* (December 1994): 127–8.

Oliver, Michael, 'Messiaen/Vingt regards sur l'enfant-Jésus/Pierre-Laurent Aimard', *The Gramophone* (April 2000): 106.

Parncutt, Richard and McPherson, Gary (eds), *The Science and Psychology of Music Performance* (Oxford: Oxford University Press, 2002).

Parncutt, Richard and Troup, Malcolm, 'Piano' in Richard Parncutt and Gary McPherson (eds), *The Science and Psychology of Music Performance* (Oxford: Oxford University Press, 2002).

Peirce, Charles, 'What Is a Sign?' in Peirce Edition Project (ed.), *The Essential Peirce: Selected Philosophical Writings*, volume 2 (Bloomington and Indianapolis: Indiana University Press, 1998).

Philip, Robert, *Early Recordings and Musical Style: Changing Tastes in Instrumental Performance, 1900–1950* (Cambridge: Cambridge University Press, 1992).

Philip, Robert, *Performing Music in the Age of Recording* (New Haven and London: Yale University Press, 2004).

Pierce, Alexandra, *Deepening Musical Performance through Movement* (Bloomington and Indianapolis: Indiana University Press, 2007).

Pople, Anthony, 'Messiaen's Musical Language: An Introduction' in Peter Hill (ed.), *The Messiaen Companion* (London: Faber and Faber Ltd, 1995).

Quantz, Johann Joachim, *On Playing the Flute*, English translation by Edward Reilly (Boston: Northeastern University Press, 2001).

Rachmaninov, Serge, 'Essentials of Artistic Playing' in James Francis Cooke (ed.), *Great Pianists on Piano Playing* (New York: Dover Publications, Inc., 1999).

Rast, Nicholas, 'Bach/Keyboard Toccatas/Glenn Gould', *The Gramophone* (September 1994): 80.

Ratner, Leonard, *Classic Music* (New York: Schirmer Books, 1980).

Repp, Bruno, 'On Determining the Basic Tempo of an Expressive Music Performance', *Psychology of Music*, 22/2 (1994): 157–67.

Ricoeur, Paul, *The Rule of Metaphor*, English translation by Robert Czerny (Toronto, Buffalo, London: University of Toronto Press, 2000).

Ridley, Aaron, *The Philosophy of Music* (Edinburgh: Edinburgh University Press, 2004).

Rink, John, 'Musical Structure and Performance' (book review), *Music Analysis*, 9/3 (1990): 319–39.

Rink, John, 'Playing in Time: Rhythm, Metre and Tempo in Brahms's Fantasien Op. 116' in John Rink (ed.), *The Practice of Performance* (Cambridge: Cambridge University Press, 1995).

Rink, John, 'Opposition and Integration in the Piano Music' in Michael Musgrave (ed.), *Brahms* (Cambridge: Cambridge University Press, 1999a).

Rink, John, 'Translating Musical Meaning: The Nineteenth-Century Performer as Narrator' in Nicholas Cook and Mark Everist (eds), *Rethinking Music* (Oxford: Oxford University Press, 1999b).

Rink, John, 'Analysis and (or?) Performance' in John Rink (ed.), *Musical Performance, A Guide to Understanding* (Cambridge: Cambridge University Press, 2002).

Rink, John, 'The State of Play in Performance Studies' in Jane Davidson (ed.), *The Music Practitioner* (Aldershot: Ashgate, 2004).

Rorty, Richard, *Deconstructionist Theory*, http://prelectur.stanford.edu/lecturers/derrida/rorty.html (1995, accessed September 2005).

Rosen, Charles, *The Classical Style* (London: Faber and Faber Limited, 1971).

Rosen, Charles, *Critical Entertainments* (Cambridge and London: Harvard University Press, 2000).

Rosen, Charles, *Piano Notes* (London: Penguin Books, 2002).

Rosenblum, Sandra, *Performance Practices in Classic Piano Music* (Bloomington and Indianapolis: Indiana University Press, 1991).

Russell, Bertrand, *History of Western Philosophy* (London: Routledge, 2000).

Sainsbury, Mark, 'Philosophical Logic' in A.C. Grayling (ed.), *Philosophy 1* (Oxford: Oxford University Press, 2003).

Salmon, Paul and Meyer, Robert, *Notes from the Green Room* (San Fransisco: Jossey-Bass Inc., Publications, 1992).

Samson, Jim, 'Analysis in Context' in Nicholas Cook and Mark Everist (eds), *Rethinking Music* (Oxford: Oxford University Press, 1999).

Samson, Jim, *Virtuosity and the Musical Work* (Cambridge: Cambridge University Press, 2003).

Samuel, Claude, *Conversations with Olivier Messiaen*, English translation by Felix Aprahamian (London: Stainer & Bell, 1976).

Samuel, Claude, *Olivier Messiaen: Music and Colour*, English translation by Edward Thomas Glasow (Portland: Amadeus Press, 1994).

Samuels, Robert, *Mahler's Sixth Symphony: A Study in Musical Semiotics* (Cambridge: Cambridge University Press, 1995).

Sándor, György, *On Piano Playing* (New York: Schirmer Books, 1981).

Schenker, Heinrich, 'Brahms: Variationen und Fuge über ein Thema von Handel, Op. 24', *Der Tonwille*, 4/2–3 (1924): 3–48.

Schenker, Heinrich, *The Masterwork in Music*, volume 1, William Drabkin (ed.), English translation by Ian Bent, Richard Kramer, John Rothgeb and Hedi Siegel (Cambridge: Cambridge University Press, 1994).

Schenker, Heinrich, *Five Graphic Analyses*, English translation with Introduction and Glossary by Felix Salzer (New York: Dover Publications Inc., 1969).

Schenker, Heinrich, *The Art of Performance*, Heribert Esser (ed.), English translation by Irene Schreier Scott (Oxford: Oxford University Press, 2000).

Schmalfeldt, Janet, 'On the Relation of Analysis to Performance: Beethoven's Bagatelles Op. 126, Nos 2 and 5', *Journal of Music Theory*, 29/1 (1985): 1–31.

Schnabel, Artur, *My Life and Music* (New York: Dover Publications, Inc., 1988).

Schonberg, Harold, *The Great Pianists* (London: Victor Gollancz Ltd, 1969).

Schonberg, Harold, *The Great Pianists* (New York: Simon & Schuster Inc., 1987).

Schopenhauer, Arthur, *The World as Will and Idea*, David Berman (ed.), English translation by Jill Berman (London: Everyman, 2004).

Schulenberg, David, *The Keyboard Music of J.S. Bach* (London: Victor Gollancz Ltd, 1993).

Schulenberg, David, 'Versions of Bach: Performing Practices in the Keyboard Works', *Bach Perspectives*, 4 (1999): 111–35.

Scott, Marion, *Beethoven* (London: J.M. Dent & Sons Ltd, 1974).

Scruton, Roger, *The Aesthetics of Music* (Oxford: Oxford University Press, 1999).

Scruton, Roger, *Modern Philosophy* (London: Pimlico, 2004).

Seashore, Carl, *Psychology of Music* (New York: Dover Publications, Inc., 1967).

Shakespeare, William, *Hamlet* (Harmondsworth: Penguin Books, 1980).

Sheinberg, Esti, *Irony Satire, Parody and the Grotesque in the Music of Shostakovich* (Aldershot: Ashgate, 2000).

Sherlaw Johnson, Robert, *Messiaen* (London: J.M. Dent & Sons, 1975).

Sherman, Bernard, 'How Different was Brahms's Playing Style from our Own?' in Bernard Sherman and Michael Musgrave (eds), *Performing Brahms* (Cambridge: Cambridge University Press, 2003).

Shove, Patrick and Repp, Bruno, 'Musical Motion and Performance: Theoretical and Empirical Perspectives' in John Rink (ed.), *The Practice of Performance* (Cambridge: Cambridge University Press, 1995).

Sisman, Elaine, 'Variations' in Leon Botstein (ed.), *The Compleat Brahms* (New York and London: W.W. Norton & Company, 1999).

Sloboda, John, *The Musical Mind: The Cognitive Psychology of Music* (Oxford: Oxford University Press, 1985).

Small, Christopher, *Musicking* (Middletown: Wesleyan University Press, 1998).

Smith Brindle, Reginald, *The New Music* (London, New York and Toronto: Oxford University Press, 1975).

Spitzer, Michael, *Metaphor and Musical Thought* (Chicago and London: The University of Chicago Press, 2004).

Stainer, John and Barrett, W.A., *A Dictionary of Musical Terms* (London and New York: Novello, Ewer & Co., 1898).

Stauffer, George, 'Changing Issues of Performing Practice' in John Butt (ed.), *The Cambridge Companion to Bach* (Cambridge: Cambridge University Press, 1997).

Stein, Erwin, *Form and Performance* (London: Faber and Faber, 1962).

Steptoe, Andrew, 'Negative Emotions in Music Making: The Problem of Performance Anxiety' in Patrik Juslin and John Sloboda (eds), *Music and Emotion* (Oxford: Oxford University Press, 2002).

Stern, Laurent, 'Interpretation in Aesthetics' in Peter Kivy (ed.), *The Blackwell Guide to Aesthetics* (Malden, Oxford and Victoria: Blackwell Publishing, 2004).

Stockfelt, Ola, 'Adequate Modes of Listening' in David Schwarz, Anahid Kassabian and Lawrence Siegel (eds), *Keeping Score* (Charlottesville and London: University Press of Virginia, 1997).

Stojowski, Sigismund, 'What Interpretation Really Is' in James Francis Cooke (ed.), *Great Pianists on Piano Playing* (New York: Dover Publications, Inc., 1999).

Storr, Anthony, *Music and the Mind* (London: HarperCollins Publishers 1997).

Stravinsky, Igor, *Poetics of Music* (Cambridge and London: Harvard University Press, 1998).

Sumner, William Leslie, *The Pianoforte* (London: Macdonald, 1971).

Swoyer, Chris, *Relativism*, http://plato.stanford.edu/entries/relativism (2003, accessed October 2005).

Taruskin, Richard, *Text and Act* (New York: Oxford University Press, 1995).

Thom, Paul, *For an Audience* (Philadelphia: Temple University Press, 1993).

Thurmond, James Morgan, *Note Grouping: A Method for Achieving Expression and Style in Musical Performance* (Galesville: Meredith Music Publications, 1991).

Todd, Neil, 'A Model of Expressive Timing in Tonal Music', *Music Perception*, 3/1 (1985): 33–58.

Todd, Neil, 'A Computational Model of Rubato', *Contemporary Music Review*, 3/1 (1989): 69–88.

Todd, Neil, 'The Auditory "Primal Sketch"', *Journal of New Music Research*, 23/1 (1994): 25–70.

Tolhurst, William, 'On What a Text Is and How It Means', *British Journal of Aesthetics*, 19 (1979): 3–14.

Tomes, Susan, *Beyond the Notes* (Woodbridge: The Boydell Press, 2004).

Tosi, Pier Francesco, *Observations on the Florid Song*, English translation by John Ernest Galliard (London: Stainer and Bell, 1987).

Tovey, Donald, *Essays in Musical Analysis: Chamber Music* (London: Oxford University Press, 1967).

Tovey, Donald, *Essays in Musical Analysis: Supplementary Essays Glossary and Index* (London: Oxford University Press, 1969).

Trawick, Eleanor, 'Order, Progression, and Time in the Music of Messiaen', *Ex Tempore: A Journal of Compositional and Theoretical Research in Music*, 9/2 (1999): 64–76.

Troeger, Richard, *Playing Bach on the Keyboard* (Pompton Plains and Cambridge: Amadeus Press, 2003).

Türk, Daniel Gottlob, *School of Clavier Playing*, English translation by Raymond Haggh (Lincoln: University of Nebraska Press, 1982).

Valéry, Paul, 'Leçon inaugurale du cours poétique au Collège de France' in *Variétés V* (Paris: Gallimard, 1944).

Walls, Peter, *History, Imagination and the Performance of Music* (Woodbridge: The Boydell Press, 2003).

Walther, Johann Gottfried, *Musicalisches Lexicon* (Leipzig: Wolfgang Deer, 1732).

Williamon, Aaron (ed.), *Musical Excellence* (Oxford: Oxford University Press, 2004).

Windsor, Luke, 'Data Collection, Experimental Design, and Statistics' in Eric Clarke and Nicholas Cook (eds), *Empirical Musicology* (Oxford: Oxford University Press, 2004).

Wilde, Oscar, 'The Critic as Artist' in *Complete Works of Oscar Wilde* (Glasgow: HarperCollins Publishers, 1994).

Wilkinson, Anthony, *Liszt* (London and Basingstoke: Macmillan London Ltd, 1975).

Wittgenstein, Ludwig, *Philosophical Investigations*, English translation by Gertrude Anscomb (London: Blackwell, 1978).

Wittgenstein, Ludwig, *Tractatus Logico-Philosophicus*, English translation by David Pears and Brian McGuinness (London and New York: Routledge, 2004).

Wu, Jean Marie, 'Mystical Symbols of Faith: Olivier Messiaen's Charm of Impossibilities' in Siglind Bruhn (ed.), *Messiaen's Language of Mystical Love* (New York and London: Garland Publishing, Inc., 1998).

Wynn Parry, Christopher, 'Managing the Physical Demands of Musical Performance' in Aaron Williamon (ed.), *Musical Excellence* (Oxford: Oxford University Press, 2004).

Young, Rida Johnson, *Ah! Sweet Mystery of Life*, http://www.nuspel.org/ahsweetm. html (1910, accessed April 2007).

Zászkaliczky, Tamás, *Bach Toccaten* (Budapest: Könemann Music Budapest, 1998).

Zimdars, Richard Louis, *The Piano Masterclasses of Franz Liszt* (Bloomington and Indianapolis: Indiana University Press, 1996).

Discography

Bach, Toccata in D Major BWV 912, Glenn Gould, Sony Music (2002), SMK87762 (original recording: 16, 17, 31 October and 1 November 1976).

Bach, Toccata in D major BWV 912, Angela Hewitt, Hyperion (2002), CDA67310.

Bach, Toccata in D major BWV 912, Sviatoslav Richter, Live Classics (2002), LCL 402 (original recording: 10 May 1992).

Bach, Violin Concerto in A minor BWV 1041, David Oistrakh/Royal Philharmonic Orchestra/Eugene Goossens, Deutsche Grammophon (1962), 138 820.

Bach, Violin Concerto in A minor BWV 1041, Catherine Mackintosh/The King's Consort/Robert King, Hyperion (1989), CDA66380.

Beethoven, Piano Concerto No. 5 Op. 73, Wilhelm Kempff/Berlin Philharmonic Orchestra/Ferdinand Leitner, Deutsche Grammophon (1986), 419 468-2 (original recording: 1962).

Beethoven, Piano Concerto No. 5 Op. 73, Robert Levin/Orchestre Révolutionnaire et Romantique/John Eliot Gardiner, Deutsche Grammophon Archiv (1996), 447 771- 2 (recorded: January 1995).

Beethoven, Sonata in C major Op. 53, Solomon, EMI (1976), RLS 722 (original recording: June 1952).

Beethoven, Sonata in C major Op. 53, Claudio Arrau, EMI (1991), CZS 7673792 (original recording: 20 December 1956 and 19 May 1957).

Beethoven, Sonata in C major Op. 53, Wilhelm Kempff, Deutsche Grammophon (1995), 447 966-2 (original recording: 24 September 1951).

Beethoven, Sonata in F minor Op. 57, Sviatolslav Richter, RCA (1987), GD86518 (original recording: 1960).

Beethoven, Sonata in F minor Op. 57, Wilhelm Kempff, Deutsche Grammophon (1995), 447 966-2 (original recording: 22 September 1951).

Beethoven, Sonata in E major Op. 109, Denis Matthews, Pearl (2002), GEM 0162 (original recording: 1946).

Beethoven, Symphony No. 9 Op. 125, Roger Norrington/London Classical Players, EMI (1987), 7 49852 2, 1987.

Beethoven, Symphony No. 9 Op. 125, Philippe Herreweghe/Orchestre des Champs Elysées, harmonia mundi (1999), HMC901687 (recorded: October 1998).

Brahms, Intermezzo Op. 119/3, Moura Lympany, Classics for Pleasure (1974), CFP 40066.

Brahms, Intermezzo Op. 119/3, Stephen Kovacevich, Philips (1994), 442 589-2 (original recording: August 1968).

Brahms, *Variations and Fugue on a Theme by Handel* Op. 24, Claudio Arrau, Ermitage (1990), ERM 104 (original broadcast: 20 May 1963).

188   *Reading Musical Interpretation*

Brahms, *Variations and Fugue on a Theme by Handel* Op. 24, Claudio Arrau, Philips (1991), 432 302-2 (original recording: April 1978).

Brahms, *Variations and Fugue on a Theme by Handel* Op. 24, Stephen Kovacevich, Philips (1994), 442 589-2 (original recording: August 1968).

Brahms, *Variations and Fugue on a Theme by Handel* Op. 24, Jorge Federico Osorio, ASV (1995), CD QS 6161 (original recording: 1988).

Brahms, *Variations and Fugue on a Theme by Handel* Op. 24, Benno Moiseiwitsch, The Piano Library (1997), PL 265 (original recording: 1930).

Brahms, *Variations and Fugue on a Theme by Handel* Op. 24, Egon Petri, The Piano Library (1998), PL 286 (original recording: June 1938).

Grieg, *Lyric Pieces*, Leif Ove Andsnes (playing Grieg's piano), EMI Classics (2002), 7243 5 57296 2.

Lawson, Colin, *100 Years of the Simple-System Clarinet*, Colin Lawson and Francis Pott, Clarinet Classics (2005), CC0044.

Liszt, Sonata in B minor, Claudio Arrau, Philips (1991), 464 713-2 (original recording: March 1970).

Liszt, Sonata in B minor, Claudio Arrau, aura–music (1999), AUR 182-2 (original broadcast: 17 September 1971).

Messiaen, *Quatre Études de rythme*, Olivier Messiaen, FMR Records (2003), FMRCD120-L0403 (original recording: 1951).

Messiaen, *Vingt regards sur l'Enfant-Jésus*, Yvonne Loriod, Erato (2000), 8573-85666-2 (original recording: 5–9 October 1973).

Messiaen, *Vingt regards sur l'Enfant-Jésus*, Peter Hill, Regis (2000), RRC 2055 (original recording: September 1991).

Messiaen, *Vingt regards sur l'Enfant-Jésus*, Pierre-Laurent Aimard, Teldec (2000), 3984-26868-2 (recorded: July 1999).

Mozart, Sonata in A major K 331, Glenn Gould, Sony Classical (1995), 52627 (original recording: 16 December 1965 and 11 August 1970).

Rachmaninov, Piano Concerto No. 3 in D minor Op. 30, Vladimir Horowitz/ RCA Victor Symphony Orchestra/Fritz Reiner, RCA Victor (1989), GD87754 (original recording: 8 and 10 May 1951).

Rachmaninov, Piano Concerto No. 3 in D minor Op. 30, Moura Lympany/New Symphony Orchestra of London/Anthony Collins, Decca (2004) 475 6368 (original recording: 1952).

Rossini, Overtures, Royal Philharmonic Orchestra/Colin Davis, Classics for Pleasure (1962), CFP 40077.

Index

Note: Numbers in brackets preceded by *n* are footnote numbers.

accelerando 71, 72, 76–7, 80, 105
accents 93–4, 99, 100, 110–11, 125–6
   -*diminuendo* 125–6(*n*4)
   and technique 136
acciaccatura 42
acoustic trace 51–2, 58, 87, 89, 128, 159
aesthetics 6–7, 18, 22, 23, 51–2, 58,
      91(*n*2), 100, 116, 118
agogic accentuation 17, 57, 127, 128
Aimard, Pierre-Laurent 90, 95, 100, 101
   duration manipulation of 106, 107
   interpretative tower for 113
   sonic moderation of 108–10
   tempo of 102–6
alla breve 42
allegro 28, 41, 85
allotrios 36–7
American style of pianism 126
analysis trace 52, 58
analyst-performance relationship 22, 23–5
analytical framework 21–59
   Bach case study *see* Toccata in D major
   impartiality/neutrality in 53, 59
   informants in *see* informants
   interpretative tower *see* interpretative
      tower
   and knowledge 23
   method 53–8
      artists' names in 57
      evidence presentation 55–6
      evidence-gathering 55
      language used in 56–7
      models used in 58
      recordings used in 53–4
      reviews used in 56
   nine steps of 22
   philosophy in 22, 23–5
   primary/secondary interpretation 51–2

   score-performer dialogue in 27–8
   score/text in 23, 25–6
   technique in 30
   tempo measurement in 55
   visual representation in 48–51, 55–6,
      59
Andsnes, Leif Ove 12
ANS (autonomic nervous system) 54
Anthoni, Nalen 14
Appassionata Sonata (Beethoven) 13, 45
Aristotle 36–7
arpeggiando 76–7
Arrau, Claudio 10, 42, 45, 162
   in Brahms case study 121, 122,
      126–32, 145, 145–50, 157
      expression in 126–7, 146, 147
      informants for 128, 129–30, 131,
         146–50
   era (style) and 130
   interpretative tower for 131, 149
   live/studio recordings 54
articulation 55, 64, 76, 80–81, 85, 92, 108
artistic prerogatives 18, 118–19
aural tradition 8, 164
authenticity 11–14, 64, 82–3, 88, 160–61
   historical 11–12
   personal 13–14, 17
   see also HIP; *Texttreue*
authorship (score) informant 32–4, 47
   in case studies 85–6, 94–5, 142, 149
   and era (style) 71, 72, 73, 75, 76–8, 85,
      96, 161
   and experimental scores 164
   in thin works 63
   visual representation of 48–51, 55
   see also interpretative tower; *and see*
      under specific works/performers

Bach, C.P.E. 43, 63–4, 68, 70, 79
Bach, J.S. 32
    Brandenburg Concerto No. 3 BWV
        1048 42–3
    era-related writings on 63–4
    French Suite No. 5 BWV 816 79
    gigues of 79
    Goldberg Variations 35
    and HIP 63
    Italian Concerto 87
    ornaments of 75(n10)
    piano/harpsichord interpretations of 64
    and tempo 42–3
    thinness of scores 63
    Violin Concerto in A minor BWV 1041
        163
    Well-tempered Clavier 79
    see also Toccata in D major
Badura-Skoda, Paul 64, 72, 80, 85
balance 12, 17, 163
Bärenreiter Bach edition 66–7
Baroque era/style 30, 38, 63–4, 72, 84, 85,
    95, 120
    tempo of 42–3
Battel, Giovanni 29
Bazzana, Kevin 81, 83–4
Beardsley, Monroe 24, 166
Beethoven, Ludwig Van 37, 125(n4), 165,
    166
    Appassionata Sonata 13, 45
    Diabelli Variations 35, 119, 133
    Eroica Variations 35, 36(n9)
    Hammerklavier Sonata 14
    Ninth Symphony 9
    Piano Concerto No. 5 31
    Sonata in A major Op. 101 138–9
    Sonata in E major Op. 109 27
    and authorship 49–50
    Sonatas, Op.2/2/Op.2/3 43
    String Quartet in F major Op. 135
        42(n17)
    tempo headings of 41, 42, 43, 119
    variations 35–6(n9)
    Waldstein Sonata Op. 53 42
Berlin Philharmonic Orchestra 31
Berry, Wallace 6
Bischoff, Hans 75(n9)
borrowing/displacement of meaning 36–7

Botstein, Leon 119
Boulez, Pierre 89
Bowen, José 164
Brahms, Johannes 14, 30, 157
    Fourth Symphony 35
    Intermezzo Op. 118/1 6
    Intermezzo Op. 119/3, hemiolas in 40
    and Romanticism 119–20
    violin sonatas 12
    see also Variations and Fugue on a
        Theme by Handel Op. 24
Brendel, Alfred 5, 10, 35–6(n9), 38, 127
brilliante 39–40
brio 42
British style of pianism 49–50, 122
Brown, Clive 119
Browning, John 46
Busch Quartet 42(n17)
Busoni, Ferruccio 34, 124
    Bach's Chaconne arrangement 38
Butt, John 33, 75(n10), 87

Cantéyodjayâ (Messiaen) 93
characterizer 34, 40, 47
    in case studies 75, 76–8, 85, 86, 101–2,
        113–15, 128
Cherkassky, Shura 45
Chopin, Frederick 6
    espressivo in 124
    Grande Polonaise Brilliante 39–40
    interpretation of 39, 44, 45
    Mazurka Op. 17/4 15
    Nocturne in E flat 44
    Nocturne in G minor Op. 15/3 44
    Nocturnes Op. 9 124
    Prelude in E minor Op. 28/4 16, 17–18,
        125
    Scherzo No. 1 Op. 20 39
    tempo and 44
Clarke, Eric 14, 15, 16, 26(n1), 43
Classical era/style 30, 31, 35, 43, 95,
    119–20
Cognetti, Luisa 39
Collins, Anthony 163
Coltman, Rod 24, 52
composers
    and genre 35–6
    idioms/traits of 32–4

Index

intention of *see mens auctoris*
poietic urge of 51
and score *see* score/notation
concatenationism 7(*n*2)
Cone, Edward 6, 32
connotative/non-connotative names 30–31, 34
contemporary performance theory 7–10
Cook, Nicholas 6, 7–8, 15, 21, 22, 23, 40, 101, 130, 164, 167
Cooke, James 30
Cossel, Otto 133
Couperin, François 96–7, 137
Cramer, J.B. 50
crescendo 42, 71, 72, 73, 76–7, 93, 109
critical reviews 56
Culler, Johnathan 50
Cumming, Naomi 18, 23, 44, 56, 69, 111(*n*20), 165
Czerny, Karl 43, 44, 87–8, 133

Dahlhaus, Carl 112
dances 37–8, 39, 79, 84, 98
Davies, Stephen 41, 54, 63, 89
de Larocha, Alicia 46
de Pachmann, Vladimir 57
Debussy, Claude 91–2, 108
performance instructions of 92, 92–3(*n*7)
Desain, Peter 14
dhenki rhythm 97–8, 100
Diabelli Variations (Beethoven) 35, 119, 133
Dibben, Nicola 22
diminuendo 72, 93
dolce 38, 118
doloroso 39
Dummett, Michael 39
Dunsby, Jonathan 117, 156
duration manipulator informant 43–5, 48, 49
in case studies 75, 76–8, 80, 85–6, 100, 106–7, 113–15, 146
dynamics 5–6, 11, 12, 15, 17, 48, 55, 57, 82–4
instructions for 92
of recording 84(*n*17)

eighteenth-century style 11–12
fantasy genre 64, 72
Eisert, Chrisian 66
Elgar, Edward 33–4
Eliot Gardiner, John 31
emotion *see* expression
English gigue style 79
enthousiasme 100, 105
era (style) informant 30–32, 37, 39, 47, 164
in case studies 85, 86, 141
visual representation of 48–51, 55
see also interpretative tower; *and see under specific works/performers*
Eroica Variations (Beethoven) 35, 36(*n*9)
espressivo 14, 38, 121, 123–6, 133, 134, 167
and nocturnes 124
esthetic *see* aesthetics
expression 14–17
defined 14–15
descriptive language for 56–7
and grammar/syntax 15, 72
and metaphor/codes 16–17
non-structural 15–16
extempore music 8

Fanning, David 90, 99, 105, 106
Färbung 39
Flonzaley Quartet 42(*n*17)
Fontanier, Pierre 130
forte/fortissimo 45, 109
Foucault, Michel 33, 96
Fraser, Alan 15–16, 44, 110–11
free fantasy genre 64, 72
freefall technique 110
Frege, Gottlob 26, 39
French style 63(*n*1), 65, 96–7
siciliano 137, 138–9
Friberg, Anders 29
Frisch, Walter 157
fugue 36, 79, 120
counter-subject articulation 80–82, 83(*n*16)
Fulcher, Jane 96

Gabrielson, Alf 15, 41, 102, 103
Gadamer, Hans-Georg 24, 25, 32, 58, 96(*n*11), 166

galop rhythm 132, 133, 136
Geiringer, Karl 117
genre informant 34–6, 40
   in case studies 75, 76–8, 85, 86, 96–7,
     132–4, 135
   visual representation of 48–51
German Baroque 38
   North 65, 68
gigues 79, 84, 150
Godlovitch, Stan 8, 13, 154
Godowsky, Leopold 30
Goehr, Lydia 4–5, 10, 29
Goossens, Eugene 163
Gould, Glenn 27, 45, 64, 65, 73–6, 160
   and authenticity 76
   authorship (style)/era (score) in 75, 76
   duration manipulation of 80, 86
   dynamics of 83–4
   idiosyncratic style of 50, 51, 76, 80–81
   interpretative tower for 75, 76, 78,
     85–6
   ornamentation of 73–5
   sonic moderation of 80–81, 83–4, 86
   tempo of 73, 79, 85
   see also under Toccata in D major
     BWV 912
Gramophone, The 56, 65, 148
Grieg, Edvard 12
Griffiths, Paul 96–7

haletant 92, 98, 100
Hamlet (Shakespeare) 13
Hammerklavier Sonata (Beethoven) 14
Handel, George Frideric 120
Handel Variations see Variations and Fugue
   on a Theme by Handel Op. 24
Hanslick, Eduard 127–8
harpsichord 64, 83
Harrison, Max 122, 148
Hatten, Robert 36, 37, 138
Haydn, Joseph 124
   Sonata in F major HobXVI/23 38
Hellaby, Julian 65, 72–3, 91
   authorship (score)/era (style) in 73, 147
   in Brahms case study 122, 126, 128,
     129–30, 131, 134, 139–41, 142,
     145–50, 151–4
   characterizer in 101, 102, 146

colouring/dynamic of 73, 84, 100,
   140–41
duration manipulation of 80, 86, 106,
   107, 146
interpretative towers for 76–7, 85–6,
   113, 115, 129–30, 131, 142, 148–9,
   155
sonic moderation of 80, 81, 84, 86,
   108–10, 146
tempo of 72–3, 79, 102–6, 128, 134,
   139–40, 145–6
see also under Toccata in D major
Henle Verlag Bach edition 66–7
hermeneutics 18, 23–5, 37
Hernnstein Smith, Barbara 9
Herpers, Ulla 95
Hess, Myra 126
Hewitt, Angela 64, 65, 71–2, 77, 87
   colouring/dynamics of 71–2, 83
   duration manipulation by 80, 86
   era (style)/authorship (score) in 72
   interpretative towers for 72, 77, 85–6
   sonic moderation by 80, 81, 82, 83, 86
   tempo of 71, 79, 85
   topic and 72, 85
   see also under Toccata in D major
Heywood, Andrew 53
hierarchy of the bar 82–3, 85
Hill, Peter 90, 93, 96, 97, 98, 99, 101, 102,
   116
   duration manipulation of 106, 107
   dynamics of 108–9
   interpretative tower for 114
   sonic moderation of 108–11
   tempo of 102–6
HIP (historically informed performance)
   11–12, 63, 87, 160
Hogwood, Christopher 11(*n*6)
Holden, John 82–3
Honing, Henkjan 14
Horowitz, Vladimir 46, 163
horse/galop rhythm 132, 133, 136
Houle, George 82
Howson, Colin 21
Hsu, Madeleine 91
Hudson, Richard 44
hypervigilance 54

Index

impressionism 91–3
indices 116
informants 29–48, 58, 159
    categories outlined 30–46
    see also interpretative tower; *and see*
        specific informants
inheritance 34
Intentional Fallacy 24–5, 52
interpretation 3, 23–8, 39–40
    diminished in modern pianists 161–2
    and informant hierarchy 29, 47–8,
        55–6, 58–9
    primary/secondary 51–2, 58
    romantic 57
    and technique 45–6
    and *Texttreue* 160–61
    and thin works 63
    voluntary 40, 101, 130
interpretative tower 29, 46–51, 55–6, 58–9,
    63, 159–67
    authenticity issues and 160–61
    explanatory functions of 161–2
    flexibility of 159, 164
    future adaptations of 163–6, 167
    graphic representation of 48–51, 55–6,
        114–15, 117–18, 156–7, 164–5,
        167
    and hermeneutics 166
    role of 162
    and semiotics 165–6
Italian style 65
    gigue 79

jazz 8, 63, 164
Jenne, Natalie 79, 80(*n*13), 84(*n*18), 150
Joachim, Joseph 32
Johnson, Peter 16(*n*11), 42(*n*17), 57, 58,
    163
Johnston, Sheila 26
Jones, Richard 65, 69
Juslin, Patrik 14(*n*9), 15, 16–17, 56, 112,
    124, 125, 157

Kalmus Bach edition 66–7, 75
Katchen, Julius 6
Kempff, Wilhelm 31, 42, 45, 141(*n*14)
Kenyon, Nicholas 11
King, Robert 163

Kirnberger, Johann 79, 82(*n*14), 83
Kivy, Peter 13, 16, 24, 29, 116, 160
Klein, Michael 37, 50, 116, 132, 165
knowledge 23
Koch, Heinrich Christoph 36
Könemann Bach edition 66–7
Könemann Brahms edition 121, 169
Kovacevich, Stephen 14, 40
    authorship and 128–9, 130, 152
    in Brahms case study 121, 122, 126,
        127–31, 145–50, 151–4, 157
    duration manipulation of 146
    expression in 127
    informants for 128–9, 131, 145–50
Kramer, Lawrence 166
Krause, Martin 126
Kripke, Saul 26, 34

Lamb, Andrew 133
language
    and metaphor 36–7
    of scores 25–6, 28, 38–40, 165–6, 167
    syntax 39, 72
    see also text
large-scale works 7(*n*2), 163
Larghetto 138
Lawson, Colin 12, 32, 46, 82
Lee, Douglas 64
legato 45, 99, 100, 109, 124, 146
leitmotif 37
Leitner, Ferdinand 31
Leonhardt, Gustav 11
Levin, Robert 31
Levinson, Jerrald 7(*n*2), 46
Lieberman, Richard 96(*n*10)
Lindström, Erik 15, 41
Linge, David 24
listener 3–4, 21–2
    and analytic approach 6–7, 22–3, 50,
        52, 55
    and expression 14–17
    and interpretation 23–5
    and period-instrument performances
        11–12
    and refraction model 18
    two types of 22
    and *Werktreue/Texttreue* 5–6, 10
    and work/performance 10–11

Liszt, Franz 6, 39, 119, 167
  Hungarian Rhapsody No. 1 38
  Sonata in B minor 54
  written instructions of 12, 92(*n*4)
Little, Meredith 79, 80(*n*13), 84(*n*18)
Littlewood, Julian 117–18, 120, 146–7, 150, 156
live recordings 53–4
logical philosophy 18, 23
Loriod, Yvonne 90, 98, 99, 101, 102
  duration manipulation of 106–7
  interpretative tower for 114, 115
  sonic moderation of 108–11
  tempo of 102–6
loure 79, 98
Lympany, Moura 40, 163

MacDonald, Malcolm 117
Mach, Elyse 10, 46
Mackintosh, Catherine 163
maestoso 38
Mahler, Gustav 35
marcato line 93–4, 99, 108–9
march 42
Martin, Robert 7
Mattheson, Johann 68, 70, 79
Matthews, Denis 26, 36, 49–50, 122
May, Florence 14, 30, 127
Mead, Philip 96
mechanical instruments 63(*n*1)
melodic line 57
Mempell, Johann 65
mens auctoris 10–11, 23–5, 27, 94–5
Messiaen, Olivier 55, 90
  Cantéyodjayâ 93
  Catholicism of 97
  and colour 91, 93, 107–8
  and Debussy 91–3, 108
  dynamic indications of 93
  music history and 96–7
  performance instructions of 91–4, 101–2, 118–19
  performances of own pieces 101–2(*n*13)
  and performers 95
  Quatuor pour le Fin du Temps 101–2(*n*13)
  topical mode and 92

  see also 'Première communion de la Vierge'; *Vingt regards sur l'Enfant-Jésus*
metaphor 36–7
Methuen-Campbell, James 122
metronomes 17, 41(*n*16), 43, 55, 87, 92, 99, 102–6
Meyer, Hans 117
Meyer, Leonard 16, 32, 33, 38, 80(*n*12), 124
Meyer, Robert 54
Mill, John Stuart 30(*n*4), 34
Miller, Alexander 26
Moiseiwitsch, Benno 57, 121, 157, 162
  duration manipulation of 140
  sonic moderation of 134–5, 140–41
  tempo of 134, 139–40
Monelle, Raymond 36, 37, 133
Monsaingeon, Bruno 5, 69
Morrison, Bryce 65, 72
Mozart 124, 167
  Sonata in A major K331 27, 138–9
    Gould's interpretation 50, 51, 160
  Sonata in F major K332 34
  tempo headings of 41
musette 38
Musgrave, Michael 117, 119, 133, 140
musical eras/styles 30–32
musical work 4–5
  analytic approach to 6–7
  and performance-as-work 7–10, 21
  and *Werktreue* 4–6, 10
  see also score/notation
musicological listener 22–3

Narmour, Eugene 6
Nattiez, Jean-Jacques 51
Neuhaus, Heinrich 65
New Queen's Hall Orchestra 12
'Nimrod' (Elgar) 33–4
nineteenth century music 132–3, 165
North German style 65, 68
note values 101–2

Oistrakh, David 163
Oliver, Michael 90, 112(*n*21)
opera 44(*n*18), 164
Orchestre Révolutionnaire et Romantique 31

ornamentation 64, 73–4, 120
Osorio, Jorge Federico 121, 122, 139
  duration manipulation of 134, 140
  interpretative tower for 142–3
  sonic moderation of 135, 140–41
  tempo of 134

Paderewski, Ignacy Jan 44, 57
pastoral topic 137, 138–9
pedalling 45, 55, 92–3, 109, 145
Peirce, Charles 26, 69, 116, 165
performance
  -as-work 7–10, 154–6
  diminishing diversity of 161–2
  as listening experience 21–2
  and musical work 4–11, 58
  mystery of 3, 21, 159, 167
  recordings of 53–4
  and text 38–40
performance directions (in a score) 38–46,
    91–4, 101–2, 118–19
  lack of, and interpretation 39, 42–3
  sonic directions 45–6
  for tempo 41–5
  and topical mode 38–40
performance studies
  diverse approaches to 3
  gaps in 4, 18
  see also analytic framework
performer 4
  and analytical approach 6–7
  and authenticity 11–14, 17
  and composer's intention *see mens
    auctoris*
  and refraction model 17–18
period-instrument performance *see* HIP
personal authenticity 13–14, 17
Persson, Roland 157
Peters Bach edition 66–7, 75(n9)
Petri, Egon 121–2, 155
  interpretative tower for 153–4
  sonic moderation of 152–3
  tempo of 151
Philip, Robert 12(n7), 31–2, 33–4, 45, 54,
    64, 161–2
phrasing 5–6, 17, 57
piano/pianissimo 45, 108
piano/pianists 18–19, 23, 44–6

and harpsichord 64, 83
nineteenth century 132–3
sonority and 95–6
Pierce, Alexandra 6–7
pitch variability 163
poietic/esthesic process 51–2, 100, 159
polonaise 39
Pople, Anthony 91
Praxistreue 11
Préludes (Debussy) 92
'Première communion de la Vierge' (Mes-
    siaen) 59, 89–116, 161, 163
  accents in 99, 100, 110–11
  Aimard's interpretation 98, 99, 100, 101
  analytical strategy for 94
  articulation in 93–4, 99, 108
  artistic freedom in 89, 101, 106, 109,
    114
  bars 47–70 101–2
  cadenza-like passage (bars 34–35)
    104–5
  Catholicism in 97
  climactic passage (bars 37–61) 109–11
  contemplation in 91, 97, 100
  dynamics/colour in 93, 99, 108–11
  Hellaby's interpretation 100, 101
  Hill's interpretation 97, 98, 99, 100,
    101
  interpretative tower for 94–116
    authorship (score) 94–5, 112, 116
    characterizer 101–2
    data summarized 112–16
    duration manipulator 100, 106–7
    era (style) 95–6
    genre 96–7
    sonic moderator 100, 107–11
    tempo 102–6, 112–13
    topic 97–100
    topical mode 100–101, 105
  Loriod's interpretation 98, 99, 100, 101
  Magnificat passage 112–13
  metronome marks in 92, 99, 102–6
  note values in 101–2
  pedalling instructions in 92–3
  performance instructions for 91–4, 116
  recording quality of 105(n16), 108
  reviews of recorded performances
    90–91

rhythm in 97–9, 100, 102
Thème de Dieu 108
thickness of 89, 94, 95, 100, 116
top-layer informants in 92–3, 101
and *Vingt regards* cycle 94
projection, Wittgenstein's law of 8–9, 14, 15, 52, 160

Quantz, Johann Joachim 43, 82–3
quasi Recitativo 38
quasi Tromboni 38
Quatuor pour le Fin du Temps (Messiaen) 101–2(*n*13)

Rachmaninov, Serge 30, 35
    Piano Concerto No. 3 163
    Variations on a Theme by Corelli 35
rallentando 43
Rast, Nicholas 65
Ratner, Leonard 36, 37
recordings 51–4
    by mechanical instruments 63(*n*1)
    as documents for analysis 53–4, 59
    edited 54
    live 53–4
    sound properties 32, 163
Reiner, Fritz 163
Rellstab, Ludwig 133, 136
Repp, Bruno 14
rhythm 48
    cross- 34, 40
    dhenkî 97–8, 100
    galop 132, 133, 136
    hierarchy of the bar 82–3, 85
    see also timing
rhythmograms 15
Richter, Sviatoslav 5, 45, 64
    authorship (score) and 71
    colouring/dynamics of 70, 83
    duration manipulation of 80, 86
    interpretative towers for 71, 77, 78, 85–6
    literalist approach of 69, 70–71
    sonic moderation of 80, 81, 83, 86
    tempo of 69–70, 80, 85
    topic and 85
    see also under Toccata in D major
Ricoeur, Paul 36–7, 130

Ridley, Aaron 8, 10, 15
Rink, John 3, 6, 30, 33, 117, 118, 156
    refraction model 17–18, 21
ritardando 40, 43
ritenuto 55, 73, 76–7, 80, 100, 107, 126–7, 140, 146
Romantic era/style 35, 57, 88, 95, 119, 128
    and *espressivo* 124
    grotesque in 119, 141
romantic playing 57, 124, 128
Rorty, Richard 26
Rosen, Charles 31, 45, 119, 120
Rossini, Gioacchino 133, 136
rubato 12, 15, 17, 32, 44, 55, 80, 85, 105, 126, 127, 146
    and romantic playing 57
Rubinstein, Anton 13
Rubinstein, Artur 45

Salmon, Paul 54, 80(*n*12)
Samson, Jim 111, 119
Samuel, Claude 97, 108
Samuels, Robert 36
Sándor, György 104(*n*15)
sarabande 38
Schenker, Heinrich 5, 28, 117, 165
Schmalfeldt, Janet 14
Schnabel, Artur 138
Schonberg, Harold 44, 50, 57, 126, 141
Schopenhauer, Arthur 40
Schubert, Franz 125(*n*4), 133
    E flat Trio 54
    Piano Sonata in C minor D 958 132, 165
Schulenberg, David 64, 68, 76, 76(*n*10)
Schumann, Robert 166
score/notation 8–10, 32–4, 51–2
    -performance analysis 27–8
    authority of 9
    experimental 164
    interpretation of 23–6
    interpretive categories of 29–30
    language of 25–6, 28, 38–40, 165–6, 167
    Schenkerian analysis of 28
    text of *see* text
    thick/thin works 63, 89, 164
    traditional analysis and 21, 23

Index

197

work-as- 10, 23, 25
Scruton, Roger 8, 37(*n*12), 40
Seashore, Carl 14, 105
semiotics 15, 18, 23–4, 25–6, 37, 116
serialism 93
Sheinberg, Esti 36
Sherlaw Johnson, Robert 108
Sherman, Bernard 157
Shostakovich, Dmitri 36, 165
Siciliano 38, 98, 137, 138–9, 151
Simeone, Nigel 93
simple-system English clarinet 12
Sisman, Elaine 133, 144
Sloboda, John 23
Small, Christopher 4, 7, 8, 156
Solomon 42
sonata 35
sonic moderator informant 45–6, 48, 49
    in case studies 75, 76–8, 80–84, 85–6,
       107–11, 113–15, 146–7
spiritual/metaphysical dimension 5
staccato 45, 80–81, 84, 93, 100, 134, 136,
    152
Stauffer, George 88
Stein, Erwin 6
Steptoe, Andrew 54, 102
Stern, Laurent 24
Stockhausen, Karlheinz 164
Storr, Anthony 15, 39, 56
Stowell, Robert 12, 32, 46, 82
Stravinsky, Igor 5, 9, 34
Structures (Boulez) 89
style
    and authenticity 11–13
    as informant *see* era (style) informant
subject-position 26(*n*1)
Sumner, William Leslie 95
symphony 8, 35

Taruskin, Richard 5, 88, 112
teaching/teachers 16–17
technique 30, 45–6, 110–11, 136
tempo 5–6, 9(*n*4), 11, 28, 41–5, 55, 87–8
    in case studies 76–8, 79–80, 85–6, 92,
       102–6, 113–15
    expressively modified 43–5, 124,
       126–7
    guides to 42, 44

as informant character 31, 41–3, 48
stealing/restoring 44
see also interpretative tower; met-
    ronomes; *and see under specific*
    works/performers
tendre 100
Text *see* performance directions
Texttreue 5–6, 27, 49, 58, 69, 106, 122,
    160–61
thick/thin works 63, 89, 94, 95
Thom, Paul 46
time signature 42, 79
timing 55, 105
    and heart rate 104(*n*15)
tocatta 68
Toccata in D major BWV 912 (Bach)
    58–9, 63–88
    composition date 65
    con discrezione passage (bars 111–26)
       66, 68–79, 161
       authorship (score)/era (style) bal-
          ance in 71, 72, 73, 75
       colouring/dynamics in 70, 71–2,
          73, 75
       Gould's interpretation 73–6, 78
       graphic representation of 78
       Hellaby's interpretation 72–3, 76–7
       Hewitt's interpretation 71–2, 77
       interpretative towers for 71, 75,
          76–8
       reviews of recorded performances
          65
       rhythmic freedom in 68–9, 76
       Richter's interpretation 69–71,
          77, 78
       tempo changes in 69–70, 71, 72–4
    gigue/fugue 68, 79–86
       counter-subject articulation 80–82,
          83(*n*16), 84
       duration manipulator in 80
       dynamics in 82–4
       interpretative towers for 85–6
       sonic moderator in 80–84
       tempo in 79–80, 85
       topic and 84–5
    Gould's interpretation 64, 65, 73–6, 78
       authorship (style)/era (score) in 75
       interpretative tower for 75

ornamentation in 73–4
tempo in 73
Hellaby's interpretation 65, 72–3, 76–7
authorship (score)/era (style) in 73
colouring/dynamic in 73
interpretative tower for 76–7
tempo in 72–3
Hewitt's interpretation 64, 65, 71–2
colouring/dynamics in 71–2
era (style)/authorship (score) in 72
interpretative tower for 72, 77
tempo in 71
and HIP 63, 87
Richter's interpretation 64, 65, 69–71,
77, 78
authorship (score) and 71
colouring/dynamics in 70
interpretative tower for 71, 77, 78
literalist approach of 69, 70–71
tempo in 69–70
sources for 65–8, 87–8
variations in 66–7, 75
strict contrapuntal/fugal passages
80–85
sonic moderator 80–84
tempo 79–80
and topic 84–5
Todd, Neil 14, 15
Tolhurst, William 25
Tomes, Susan 54
tone 45–6, 57
topic/topical mode 36–40, 47, 165–6
in case studies 75, 76–8, 84–5, 86,
97–100, 113–15, 141
visual representation of 48–51
see also interpretative tower; *and see
under specific works/performers*
Tosi, Pier Francesco 44
Tovey, Donald 35, 117
trace, acoustic 51–2, 58, 87, 89, 128, 159
Troeger, Richard 64, 68, 83
Tureck, Rosalyn 64
Türk, Daniel Gottlob 37–8, 42–3, 44
twentieth century music 36, 161–2

Urbach, Peter 21
Urtext 29, 31(*n*7), 38, 87, 160

Valéry, Paul 51(*n*19)
variations 35–6
*Variations and Fugue on a Theme by Han-
del* Op. 24 (Brahms) 35, 36, 39, 59,
117–57, 161
ambiguity in 119–21
dynamic markings in 117–18
editions of 121, 140–41(*n*12)
historical aspects 121
interpretative tower for 120–21, 154–7
topical mode 126, 166
keys in 123
and performer dependency 155–6
performance duality in 157
reviews of recorded performances
121–2
source for 120
structure/performance issues 117–19,
139, 145, 150
artistic prerogatives 118–19
Texttreue model 120, 154–6
thinness of 119
Variation 5 123–32
authorship in 128–9
dynamic markings/phrasing in
125–6
dynamics of 126–7
interpretative towers for 129–30,
131
minor key of 123, 128
and nocturne 124, 128
performances compared 126–32
tempo of 127–8
Texttrreue model 123, 130–32
topical mode/*espressivo* in 123–6,
127, 128
Variation 7 132–7
dynamics/articulation of 132,
134–5, 137
genre in 133
interpretative towers for 135–6
performances compared 134–7
rhythm of 133
tempo of 132, 134, 135
Texttreue model 132, 134, 137
topic/genre in 132–4, 135
Variation 19 137–44
dynamics of 140–41

interpretative towers for 141–3
pastoral (siciliano) topic of 137–9, 142, 151
performances compared 139–44
tempo of 137, 139–40
Texttreue model 137, 142–3
Variation 20 125, 144–50
dynamics/phrasing in 145, 146–7
interpretative towers for 147–9
performances compared 145–50
tempo of 145
Texttreue model 144–5, 150
Variation 23 150–54
gigue topic of 150
informatative towers for 153–4
performances compared 151–4
staccato in 152–3
tempo of 151–2
Texttreue model 150–51
vibrato 11
Vingt regards sur l'Enfant-Jésus (Messiaen) 90
articulative markings in 92, 93
Catholicism in 97
dynamic instructions in 92, 93
historical aspect of 96–7
performance instructions for 91–4
rhythm of 97–8
topical mode and 92
see also 'Première communion de la Vierge'

virtuosity 111
vivace 138, 139, 141, 152
vivace ma non troppo 41
voluntary interpretation 40, 101, 130

Wagner, Richard 133
leitmotif 37
Waldstein Sonata (Beethoven) 42
Walls, Peter 11(*n*5), 64
Walther, Johann Gottfried 85
Well-tempered Clavier (Bach) 79
Werktreue 4–6, 10, 11, 88
and listener 5–6
Wiener Urtext Bach edition 66–7
Wilde, Oscar 13
William Tell (Rossini) 133, 136
Wimsatt, William 24, 166
Windsor, Luke 24
Wittgenstein, Ludwig 8, 26, 28, 35, 52, 58, 160, 167
Woodhouse, Violet Gordon 32
work-as-performance 7–10, 154–6
work-as-score 10
works *see* score/notation
Wu, Jean Marie 97
Wynn Parry, Christopher 45

Young, Rida Johnson 3

Zászkaliczky, Tamás 65